THE
BARON
& THE
BEAR

THE

Rupp's Runts,
Haskins's Miners,
and the Season
That Changed
Basketball Forever

BARON

DAVID KINGSLEY SNELL

& THE

Foreword by Nolan Richardson

BEAR

University of Nebraska Press · Lincoln and London

Library of Congress
Control Number: 2016951590

Set in Lyon Text by Rachel Gould.

For Mary Lou

In memory of the point guards:

Bobby Joe Hill

Tommy Kron

CONTENTS

Foreword   ix

Prologue   1

1. A Drop of Water   5

2. "No Good, Even If It Goes!"   9

3. A New Direction   13

4. Brothers against the Bastard   18

5. The True Religion   23

6. The Big Change   28

7. A Synchronized Leap   38

8. Finding His Team   44

9. He Didn't Recruit; He Chose   51

10. Never Gave It a Thought   61

11. Intensity, Thy Name Is Adolph   67

12. The Haskins Way   78

13. "Quite Improbable"   87

14. The Games Were the Break   97

15. Seeing Things I Really Like   102

16. Things That I Can't   107

17. Give Iowa a Try   114

18. Neutral-Court Advantage   117

19. The Break from Hell   122

20. "The Secret of Basketball"   125

21. Togo Time   130

22. Clyde and the Commodores   132

23. They Could Be Very Good   134

24. The Naked Truth   137

25. Working Hard and Hardly Working   143

26. Tennessee Two-Step   146

27. Seattle Surprise   154

28. The Mountain Man and Cazzie   159

29. Time and Overtime   173

30. Larry Conley's Ass   180

31. The Runnin' Utes   187

32. The Real Championship Game   192

33. The Smart Money   198

34. And Then There Was David   207

35. An Unreal Thing   220

36. A Matter of Pride   228

37. He Changed Basketball   232

     Epilogue   237

     Where Are They Now?   253

     Acknowledgments   259

     Appendix: 1965–66 Team Rosters
and Season Results   263

     Index   267

FOREWORD

I can never think about the 1966 NCAA Championship without remembering that Kentucky star Pat Riley later called the game "the Emancipation Proclamation of college basketball." That victory shook the game to its very foundation. And that's what I think *The Baron and the Bear* does, too. Author David Kingsley Snell challenges conventional wisdom about Coaches Don Haskins and Adolph Rupp. And the book puts the reader back into the climate of a racially divided 1960s America. This story is a timely reminder of past prejudices and captures the feel and flavor of two historically significant teams and their Hall of Fame coaches.

In the fifty years since mighty Kentucky, with its all-white team, was beaten by upstart Texas Western's all–African American lineup, both coaches have undergone radical makeovers in the media. First, in the immediate aftermath of the game, Haskins received bundles of crude hate mail from racists who believed his all-black lineup had somehow tainted college sports.

In 1968 *Sports Illustrated* accused the University of Texas at El Paso (which by then had changed its name from Texas Western) of abusing their minority students, particularly their athletes, who were, according to the article, discarded once their eligibility was over. The accusation wasn't true—only two of the twelve players on that year's team failed to graduate, and both of them went on to highly successful careers.

By then Haskins was already getting mail from African American ministers and community leaders, charging him with exploitation. Rival coaches used the *Sports Illustrated* article to muck up the recruiting advantage Haskins should have reaped from his NCAA Championship.

As the anniversary of that championship season passed—twenty,

twenty-five, thirty years—what was considered true about the 1966 game and Coaches Haskins and Rupp shifted, took on other perspectives. For a while it was a straightforward story of David and Goliath. Rupp would be reviled as a racist, Haskins seen as the hero of racial progress.

In 2005 Dan Wetzel teamed up with Coach Haskins to write his autobiography, *Glory Road*, a book that captured the gruff coach's voice, giving him the important space to tell his life story. But there was a Hollywood movie of the same name that came out that year, and the film overshadowed the book. The problem was that the film got so many important points wrong, and once again history got rewritten. For one thing, Haskins won the championship in his fifth year, not his first. For another, there were already two black players on the Texas Western team before Haskins set foot on campus. One of them even averaged twenty points a game before Haskins turned him into a defensive stopper. Within two years Haskins had cut this lefty's scoring average in half. The former high-point man was me.

I hated Haskins at first. He demanded that I stop shooting so much and start playing the defense I was capable of. He had me so frustrated mentally that even my free-throw percentage dipped. Over the years, as I began my own coaching career, I came to understand Don Haskins in a deeper way. I appreciated how stubborn and demanding he had been with us. By the time I was coaching at the University of Arkansas, I found myself being just as hard on my Razorbacks as he had been on his Miners. Like Haskins, I never apologized for being so strict.

While my first coaching job at an El Paso high school gave me a ringside seat for the Miners' championship seasons, much of what I know about Coach Rupp is second or thirdhand and until now remained a mystery. In following Rupp's undersize team through the season, *The Baron and the Bear* gives us a behind-the-scenes picture of the man who was, at that time, the winningest coach in the history of college basketball.

Over the years so many people got the story wrong. As *The Baron and the Bear* makes clear, Haskins was an accidental hero, which to me is a more interesting story. He didn't set out to make a statement; he was trying to recruit—and then play—the best players he could find. He indirectly challenged all college coaches to play the best players available, regardless of race. And slowly, that's what began to happen. Once, when I congratulated him for his role in changing the game of basketball, he responded, "I'm glad everybody feels that way, but I'm just an old country boy who wanted to coach, and it just so happened that things worked out for all of us."

Basketball fans will find the similarities between the Rupp and Haskins coaching styles detailed in this book fascinating. Yet their differences are equally striking: Whereas Haskins's emphasis was on defense taught through mind-numbing repetition, Rupp concentrated on offense, going over and over the same play. Haskins, just thirty-six, still liked recruiting; Rupp did not.

While many of us assumed that Adolph Rupp staunchly defended the segregationist policies of the Southeastern Conference, Snell paints a very different picture of a coach who was aloof from the recruiting process and tried ineptly to recruit a player of transcendent ability to be his Jackie Robinson, to break the SEC color barrier.

You might not agree with all of David Snell's conclusions in this captivating book. To be perfectly frank, when my own biography, *Forty Minutes of Hell*, came out in 2010, hell, I didn't like everything in that book, either. But we need to disrupt the status quo and challenge all of our assumptions. Like our full-court press at Arkansas, this book will rattle you, make you sweat, and always keep your attention.

I've come to understand that the world is a complicated place, and I'm suspicious anytime all of the media agree on some hot-button issue. I've felt that way when our country has gone to war, and I felt that way when I got fired from the University of Arkansas in 2002. Now? More than a decade has passed, and I've come to think of even that incident differently. For one thing, I think that history is on my side, and I hope that my legacy as a pioneering African American coach will stand the test of time. Yet like many people, I continue to think about the debt that I owe to that 1966 game.

Of course, there wasn't a single black coach at a major American college at the time my career began in the 1960s. Haskins was my only role model, one of the few college coaches I knew personally, although I had heard about stymied legends such as Clarence "Big House" Gaines and John McClendon. The fact that there are now a number of African American coaches in college basketball is another Don Haskins legacy. The openings he helped create for the black players slowly impacted the coaching profession. History demanded that John Thompson, John Chaney, and I become groundbreaking pioneers of racial progress, to open the door for the next generation of coaches of color.

I've heard people say that history is written by the winners, and that is often true. But the losers often have an interesting tale to tell. And the fact that one of the nation's best basketball programs of all time might be best known for a loss some fifty years ago? That's a fascinating start right there. What really unfolded in Lexington in the mid-1960s? Was Adolph Rupp as complex as Don Haskins? How were they different? How were they alike? How has history changed the way we should view Rupp and his Wildcats? That's got to be a great story.

I was raised by my grandmother, whom everyone called "Ol' Mama." She used to say if you wanted to change the world, you had to wait for a door to open a crack—and then kick that door down. That's the way I think about *The Baron and the Bear*. It's a good, strong kick to a door that needed kicking.

NOLAN RICHARDSON

THE

BARON

& THE

BEAR

Prologue

It happens every year. Two college basketball teams catch lightning in a bottle. Sometimes they seem to have perfect chemistry from the beginning. Sometimes there is a slow build as a team gradually comes together at just the right moment. Either way, there are always two teams that end up winning game after game down the stretch to reach the Big Dance, the Final Four, and the game for the NCAA Championship.

This is the story of two very different basketball teams. Each entered the season with low expectations and caught the lightning from opening tip-off. It is the story of Adolph Rupp (the Baron of the Bluegrass) and Don Haskins (the Bear), two intensely passionate coaches who used remarkably similar techniques to lead their teams through the ups and downs of a college basketball season. And, finally, it is the story of a history-bending game that has come to be recognized as a milestone in America's civil rights movement.

In the 1966 NCAA Championship game, an all-white University of Kentucky team was beaten by a team from Texas Western College (now UTEP) that played only African Americans. It had never happened before. It would never happen again. By beating mighty Kentucky, tiny Texas Western helped to destroy invidious stereotypes about black athletes and open the door to their greater participation in colleges and universities across the country. It also sounded the death knell for whites-only athletics, long considered essential to maintaining the southern way of life.

Looking back through the hazy gauze of history, it is easy to think of the story in stereotypic terms. There is the villain, Kentucky coach Adolph Rupp, standing astride college basketball, determined to protect the integrity of the White Man's Game, yelling *Stop!* There is the

1

hero, Coach Don Haskins, marching through the pages of history arm in arm with Rosa Parks, Thurgood Marshall, and Martin Luther King Jr., determined to right the wrongs visited upon African Americans since the first slave ships arrived in the New World. The reality of the season is very different, the truth about Rupp and Haskins more nuanced than has ever been told. With race in the news more than at anytime since the 1960s, the story is a timely reminder of past prejudices and what some have called "the Emancipation Proclamation of college basketball."

To fully appreciate the importance of the 1965–66 college season and the championship game that followed, it is important to understand the context. The game was played in the middle of a decade when long-dormant seeds of racial unrest were finally coming to the surface. There were the lunch-counter sit-in at a Woolworth's store in Greensboro, North Carolina (1960); the vicious attacks on the Freedom Riders in Anniston, Alabama (1961); the bombing that killed four young girls at Birmingham's Sixteenth Street Baptist Church (1963); the murder of three civil rights workers in Philadelphia, Mississippi (1964); and Bloody Sunday in Selma, Alabama (1965).

The 1966 NCAA Championship game was played in Cole Field House on the campus of the University of Maryland, barely seventeen miles from the Lincoln Memorial, where Martin Luther King Jr. delivered his "I Have a Dream" speech just three years earlier. But despite passage of the Civil Rights Act of 1964 and the Voting Rights Act of '65, there was a psychic distance yet to be traveled before college athletics would be ready to sit down at Dr. King's "table of brotherhood."

The laws had changed, but college basketball teams in the North still limited their recruitment of black players and adhered to an unwritten rule limiting their participation: *two at home, three on the road, and four when you're behind*. The laws had changed, but on southern campuses (including the University of Kentucky) athletics continued to be a whites-only activity. The laws had changed, but there was still a gentlemen's agreement that northern schools were expected to leave black players behind when they journeyed into the Deep South. The laws had changed, but many still believed that permitting African Americans to participate as equals in athletic competition would lead inexorably to a sense of equality in their daily lives and irrevocably destroy a *precious southern heritage*.

Dr. King's "fierce urgency of now" was still being met with determined resistance. The Ku Klux Klan was morphing into White Citizens' Councils, but states from Louisiana to Mississippi to Alabama and Georgia, the backbone of Kentucky's Southeastern Conference, were still electing segregationist governors. There was "Stand Tall for Paul" Johnson, who admonished his supporters to vote against those who would change Mississippi's "way of life." There was Lester Maddox, whose refusal to serve black customers in his Atlanta restaurant acted as a springboard to the Georgia governor's mansion. There was George Wallace, elected governor of Alabama on the slogan "Segregation now, segregation tomorrow, and segregation forever."

While Kentucky's governor Edward "Ned" Breathitt Jr. had managed to pass the first civil rights law in any state south of Ohio, the basketball team of the state's flagship university remained all white. Adolph Rupp had tried, ineptly at times, to recruit his Jackie Robinson. He was seeking a player of transcendent ability to break the SEC color barrier, as Robinson had in Major League Baseball. To that end Rupp sought the advice of Branch Rickey, the general manager who brought Robinson to the Brooklyn Dodgers in 1947.

Although Rupp was widely recognized as the number-one coach in the history of college basketball, the last of his four national championships was eight years earlier, and even his most ardent supporters were starting to wonder if the game had passed him by. Over the years the preeminence of the Kentucky basketball program allowed Rupp to choose from the top high school players in the country rather than actively recruit. Now he had four returning starters but no dominant big man. In a game trending to behemoths, his tallest starter was only six feet five, earning his team the nickname Rupp's Runts.

Texas Western College already had African Americans on its basketball team when Coach Don Haskins took over the program in 1961. With a minuscule budget compared to Kentucky's, he didn't set out to make a statement or take a stand. He recruited the best players he could find, black or white, who could help him win basketball games. By the championship season seven of the twelve players on the team were African Americans. Most of them had been ignored by other schools.

Although their approach to the game was remarkably similar, the life experiences of the two coaches had been totally different. While Rupp was racking up the last of his national championships in 1958, Haskins was coaching both boys' and girls' teams in a small Texas high school and driving a school bus to make ends meet.

At season's end it was a classic David and Goliath story with a biblical outcome. Nolan Richardson, who played for Haskins two years before the championship season and went on to a Hall of Fame coaching career, said, "If ever there was a turning point in basketball, this was it." Conventional wisdom that black players lacked the discipline to win without a white player to lead them fell away. Northern schools began to abandon unwritten quotas limiting the number of African Americans on the floor at one time. And southern schools, where athletics had always been a whites-only activity, began a gradual move toward integration.

Before all that there were two improbable teams and two driven coaches determined to beat the odds and their opponents. Rupp was sixty-four, in the twilight of his Hall of Fame career. Haskins was thirty-six, with little reason to believe that he, too, would one day share that honor. Despite their difference in age and pedigree, the two men were similar in many ways. Both coached with almost fanatical intensity. Both insisted on absolute silence in their practices. And, because of the way the season ended, both coaches and their teams are forever linked in popular memory. This, then, is their story.

1

A Drop of Water

Adolph Rupp looked down at the handsome watch he'd just been given and shook his head. He didn't need another watch. What he needed almost more than life itself was a fifth national championship. An hour ago that still seemed possible. That was before the Texas Western Miners pulled off what came to be known as the biggest upset in the history of college basketball. Now, as the team bus made its way through the flickering lights of late-night traffic from Cole Field House on the campus of the University of Maryland to their hotel in Silver Spring, Rupp and his team were in a daze.

Later, Adolph would say in an interview, "They beat us fair and square." What he said now, in the quiet of the bus, was "Harry, this looks like a nice watch, but I'm not going to wear the damn thing because every time I'd wear it, I'd be thinking about this fucking game."

Everyone on the bus that night—players, coaches, and one student manager—had been given identical watches as mementos of their Final Four experience. Gold, waterproof, shock-resistant Bulova watches, each with the inscription *NCAA Basketball Finalist 1966*. While the watch represented failure to Rupp, for his team it was a reminder of the Rupp's Runts season and that day in late November when the prospects of a successful season seemed bleak.

"MANAGER!"

Coach Rupp was standing in a low crouch, staring at the center circle.

"GET ME A GODDAMN TOWEL," he growled, in a voice that was part southern and part Kansas twang.

"THERE'S A GODDAMN DROP OF WATER ON THE FLOOR."

A student manager dropped to his knees and toweled up the offending drop.

"Must be a leak in the goddamn ceiling," Rupp said, looking skyward. "'Cause none of these sonsabitches are playing hard enough to work up any kind of a sweat."

Practice had been lethargic. The White Shirt Team, supposedly Rupp's best five, was moving up and down the floor in a funk, like zombies in a slow-motion movie. It was as if they were already drowsy from tomorrow's turkey dinner. The Blue Team—substitutes in Rupp's limited rotation—wasn't much better. Everybody was looking forward to the traditional Thanksgiving break. It didn't happen.

On the sideline Coach Rupp was fuming the way he always did when practices were sluggish. With his freshly starched khaki shirt and pants and black high-top Converse All-Star basketball shoes, balding with a hook nose and a potbelly spread that strained his belt and blood pressure, he could have passed for one of the janitors anywhere else. This wasn't anywhere else. This was Memorial Coliseum, on the campus of the University of Kentucky. *Here* he was the Man, the indefatigable, infallible pope of the state's true religion. Idealized in Kentucky, Adolph Frederick Rupp was known wherever the game was played as the winningest coach since James Naismith hung a peach basket in that Massachusetts YMCA.

"All right, hold it!" he called out, bringing things to a halt.

That started a routine his players knew very well. Coach walked across the floor—his belly bouncing along, a scowl on his face—to check the stats, the way he always did. The players lined up to shoot free throws, the way they always did. The student managers scrambled to make sure everyone had a ball, the way they always did. That was when the normal routine of the closely choreographed Rupp practice veered into a different dimension. Digging deep into his formidable arsenal of scatological invective, Coach Rupp called that single drop of water every name in the book. "A goddamn drop of water. Shit, damn sonofabitchin' water. Where the hell did it come from? Jesus H. Christ, a fucking drop of water right here in the middle of the coliseum. Goddamn it all to hell."

Words used on the water were reused with added venom on this team of miscreants who'd been weighed in Adolph's inestimable balance and found wanting, worthy of condemnation by God, country, and, most especially, the Big Blue Nation, Kentucky's fan base that was the biggest and most loyal in the country.

For the past several years there had been talk that Adolph Rupp was losing his touch. The headline in one Kentucky paper put it bluntly: "One SEC Title in Past Seven Years! A Clue to Cage Decline at Kentucky." Rupp, they wrote, was a "basketball anachronism" and suggested that he confine his animal interest to livestock (he bred prize Hereford cattle) rather than Wildcats. Since this was essentially the same team that struggled through the previous season with a mediocre 15-10 record, there was cause for concern.

All across the SEC, teams like Georgia, Tennessee, and Vanderbilt had twin-tower forwards and sky-scraping centers. Rupp had Thad Jaracz (rhymes with "Harris"), a six-foot-five sophomore about to get his first varsity playing time as the team's center. Larry Conley and Pat Riley were six feet three, Tommy Kron six feet five, Louie Dampier six feet even. It was beginning to seem possible this could be the first losing team since Rupp arrived at the University of Kentucky from Illinois's Freeport High School in 1930. Coach Rupp didn't think so. "You're going to read a lot of stories about how you're not going to be very good," he told the team in an uncharacteristic courtside homily on the first day of practice. "Don't believe that. You're going to be very good. I'm going to get things out of you that you don't know you have in you."

From the start Rupp upped the ante with first-ever double practices on Tuesdays and Thursdays. They were practicing seven days a week, but, somehow, it just wasn't working. Since October 15 good practices following bad ones must have had Rupp feeling like Sisyphus, condemned to spend eternity pushing a boulder up the mountain only to have it fall back of its own weight.

Now he looked at the stat sheet. "You sonsabitches ever play this game before? Dampier: turnover. Kron: turnover. Goddamn it, Jaracz, think you could go get a rebound? Just one? Hell, my grandma can block out better than that." Ripping the damning evidence into tiny pieces, he threw it over his shoulder and stomped back across the floor, giving the now dry spot in the center circle another glare and a few more expletives. "All right, let's go."

Over his thirty-six years as Kentucky's coach there had been countless times when a Rupp Rant worked its magic. Not this time. This time the scrimmage was getting uglier by the minute. Rupp's face was flushed, and his hands were balled up into tight fists, red on the outside, white in his blood-starved palms.

On the floor the White Team was stuck in the mud, while the Blue Team, rising to the occasion, looked like All-Americans on a romp. Their defense was stifling, their offense whirring along like a finely tuned instrument. It went on that way for five, ten, fifteen minutes, with the coach becoming increasingly agitated. Suddenly, there was a loud crash, and everybody turned toward the sound. Coach Rupp had picked up the front row of seats—three folding chairs with padded seats and backs— and hurled them into the stands.

"None of you sonsabitches are getting any goddamn turkey tomorrow." He paused for the reaction he knew wouldn't come. In a Rupp practice players didn't talk. Ever. "Thanksgiving be damned, you're staying right here on campus, running your asses off until you learn to play this fucking game."

While Rupp was being hyperbolic, on some level everybody in the gym that day understood that he was dramatizing an essential truth: his players weren't fully committed to the level of effort required for them to become the team he envisioned. Rupp had his virtuosos. He had Louis Dampier and Pat Riley, who were big scorers. He had Tommy Kron, whose height made him a matchup nightmare for opposing guards. He had Thad Jaracz, who was proving himself capable of running the court and pounding the boards. And he had Larry Conley, one of the best passers of his era. There was the potential for beautiful music, but heading into that Thanksgiving weekend it was, to quote the biblical definition of *faith*, "the substance of things hoped for, the evidence of things unseen."

2

"No Good, Even If It Goes!"

"Coach, I've been invited to have dinner with one of the local families," said an anxious freshman the Monday before Thanksgiving 1961, Haskins's first year as coach of the Texas Western Miners. "When will we be practicing on Thanksgiving?" "Nine, one, and six," growled the Bear, a nickname he earned because of his hulking size and often grizzly disposition.

That was how it was for Texas Western roundballers. As long as Haskins was coach, his teams enjoyed (endured) three-a-day Thanksgivings, without complaint. "I was too tired to eat anybody's turkey," said Nevil Shed, a six-eight forward on the championship team. And if anybody thought to complain (and nobody ever did), the Bear had a ready response. He was actually going easy on his players. During what he referred to as "four years of hell" playing for "Mr. Iba," as he called Oklahoma A&M coach Henry "Hank" Iba, Thanksgiving was always celebrated with four practices. Otherwise, Haskins's practices were perfect replicas of the ones he'd suffered under Iba in the early 1950s. Defense, defense, defense, with no water breaks.

Where Adolph Rupp had his team running and rerunning offensive drills, Haskins concentrated on defense. Two, three, up to four hours each practice, his teams worked on his meticulous defensive strategy: a helping man-to-man. You denied your opponent the baseline and the sideline and turned everyone into the middle of the court. "The defense was like a zone," said David Lattin, the six-foot-six center on the championship team, "but it wasn't a zone because you followed your man through." *Follow* is too soft a word. A Haskins player learned to fight through screens. You didn't switch. You didn't go behind. You fought your way through. "He had rigid, specific rules," said Steve Tredennick, a point guard who graduated a year before the big game. "You followed them or you sat."

The Haskins defense sounds simple enough. Making it work was a matter of repetition; tedious, mind-numbing repetition. It was the same thing over and over and over again. The physical demands were one thing; young guys were used to running. The mental fatigue was worse. It was boring, monotonous, demanding.

"No, no, no!" Haskins would shout two steps into the drill. "Do it again." The drills were designed to program minds and muscle memory. When the ball went to one side or the other, players away from the ball—on the weak side—had to adjust. "Your reaction had to be without thought," said Tredennick. "It had to just happen. If you had to stop and think, you were too late." Little by little, with repetition after repetition, "and somebody constantly yelling at you, all of a sudden, it just becomes part of your deal." When Haskins stopped one drill and switched to another, his players knew the Bear was finally satisfied.

And if your man beat you, there was always someone there to help. If an opponent drove into the middle, he was driving into a gauntlet. There was going to be a foul, and it was going to be the kind of foul that would make him think long and hard about whether he really wanted to go in there a second time.

Looking back, Haskins's players talk of "the joy" of watching the flow of a helping man-to-man much as ballet impresario George Balanchine might have referred to a perfectly executed *Nutcracker* or *Swan Lake*. It was a beautiful thing to watch. An opponent would drive into the middle, and the helping defense would close in, meaning there had to be somebody open. There had to be . . . somebody . . . but . . . he couldn't find him.

"I think Coach Haskins loved practices more than games," said Fred Schwake, a student trainer on the team who would go on to a career as a trainer in the National Football League. "In games he had to mess with officials, he had to worry about time-outs, he had to worry about fouls and substitutions. In scrimmages he coached both teams, made all the substitutions he wanted to, and didn't have to worry about fouls or officials. He controlled the whole thing."

With Haskins offense seemed almost an afterthought, which came as something of a surprise for the New Yorkers on the team. Nevil Shed recalls the moment when he and six-foot-five Willie Cager arrived in El Paso, meeting Coach Haskins for the first time. "The heat and wind said whoosh!" as they stepped down from the plane. "Coming through the dust toward us was this hulking bear of a man [Haskins] and [assistant coach] Moe Iba." It was like a scene from a spaghetti western. "Grab your luggage," said Haskins. "Let's go down to the gym and see what you can do."

Unaware at the time of NCAA rules regarding practice time, the Bear was holding a full-scale August workout. "I got the ball off the backboard and took off dribbling," Shed recalls, only to be brought up short. "He was yelling at me—'Ah, Shed. We don't sprint down the floor like a wild man. We pass the ball.' I thought the guy was crazy."

It was a new kind of basketball for Shed, Cager, and another kid from the Bronx who would join the team the following year, Willie Worsley. In New York you ran, ran, ran. In El Paso, if you wanted to play for the Bear, your offensive pace needed to be slow and deliberate. "Pass the ball fifteen times before you shoot," said Cager, exaggerating the Haskins approach only slightly. "That wasn't for me." The way Lattin tells it, "We were like a Porsche, but we had to go fifty-five miles an hour." Or slower, more like a Model A with a governor to retard its speed.

Haskins loved the dunk, and Shed, Cager, and the five-foot-six Worsley could all "flush it." Otherwise, the Haskins offense was simplicity itself. Shoot an ill-advised shot, and you'd hear him yell, "That's no good, even if it goes!" Whether it went in or not, you'd get a lecture: "You had no damn business shooting that shot."

There were very few drills in a Haskins practice, but he ran them again and again. Post-and-pick drills, three-man weaves. It was the kind of thing you might have taught to a junior high team, said one player. "Nothing complicated about what we did. Nothing strange."

One Haskins rule *was* a bit strange. He wanted two-handed passes and only two-handed passes. No bounce passes. "If you can't hit the man with a two-handed chest pass," Haskins said, "you don't need to be passing to him." If the fast break isn't your game (and it wasn't his), one basket at a time makes the passing game absolutely essential. The Texas Western Miners were a pass-and-move, screen-and-roll team. Period.

Bobby Joe Hill was the exception. After two years of chewing on him about his Fancy Dan behind-the-back dribbling and passing, Coach Haskins gave in. A five-foot-ten point guard who'd led his Highland Park, Michigan, high school team to the state championship his junior year, Hill became a better passer under Haskins's guidance, but his style of play was uniquely his own, and finally allowed. A left-hander, B.J. had the kind of quickness that made even the quickest cat seem somewhat lethargic. When B.J.'s defender forced him to the right, he obliged with a few quick right-handed dribbles, then crossed over to his left hand, leaving his hapless defender pawing air. With a minute and a half to play in a game and a lead of only a few points, Haskins would sometimes say, "Okay, Bobby, put it on ice. Dribble it out."

That was offense. Where Bobby Joe Hill really shined was defense, defense and acting. "Nobody could limp like B.J.," said Lou Baudoin, a six-foot-seven forward his teammates called Flip. "He'd come up on somebody, and they were convinced this guy was going to die right there in front of them, nailed to the floor. All of a sudden they wouldn't have the ball anymore, and he'd be shooting a lay-up," usually with a satisfied little grin on his face.

3

A New Direction

Thanksgiving weekend in Lexington went by in a blur, with two practices on Thursday, two on Friday, two on Saturday. It was eat, sleep, and practice basketball. The only break in the routine came after Sunday-morning practice because Coach Rupp had an afternoon television program.

On Thanksgiving Day—the first he'd spent away from family in his twenty-one years—student manager Mike Harreld called home, looking for a little sympathy. Instead of Sympathy Central he'd reached the Owensboro chapter of the Big Blue Nation, where the university fight song was a sacred hymn and Go Big Blue the daily liturgy. His mother asked a few perfunctory questions about his well-being—how was he feeling (okay), if he'd had a turkey dinner (he hadn't)—but the rest of the household, as basketball crazy as big brother, had larger concerns. "What about it, Mike," his dad asked, "the team going to be any good this year, or what?" On that particular Thanksgiving night in 1965, he honestly didn't know. On that particular night he would have given better odds on TV's talking horse, Mr. Ed, winning the Kentucky Derby than this team making it to the Final Four.

Practices that day had been like a root canal. Coach Rupp had calmed down about 90 percent overnight, but his level of agitation would have driven most sentient mortals to the emergency room or at least a tranquilizing sedative. Conditioning wasn't a factor (the team had spent preseason doing wind sprints), but patience was. Rupp had the team run the same play over and over and over. When he spotted a problem, he'd yell, "No, goddamn it, you're supposed to plant your foot here and turn like this!" In demonstration mode Rupp moved with all the grace of an elephant trying to toe dance. "You've got to execute to make it work."

Looks were exchanged, but nobody laughed. In an Adolph Rupp practice, nobody ever laughed.

In the second Thanksgiving Day practice, he was working on a different play but with the same mind-numbing repetition. Again and again Louie Dampier came off a Larry Conley pick at the top of the key and shot a nineteen-foot jumper. Twenty times he shot; fifteen times it was nothing but net (the man could shoot the basketball). Adolph went into one of his teaching demos, something about Conley's feet not being in the right place. "All right," he said, stomping back to the sideline. "Run it again, only this time let's put it in the basket."

In the next day's scrimmage the Blue Team was beating the White Team again, as it had in the Blue-White game a week ago. On that night, with a near-capacity crowd looking on, the second team put on the kind of show that added fuel to the fire and cemented what people were already saying: Last year was bad, and this year won't be better. Rupp had read the papers and was not happy.

Sometimes when Blue beat White he would rail at the student manager wielding the whistle. "Come on, Slim [his name for Mike], for God's sake. Watch the goddamn game." But this time Tommy Kron was in the spotlight. When his pass to Pat Riley ended up in the hands of a Blue Team forward, Rupp yelled, "Jesus, Kron, you're wearing a white shirt, remember? A bounce pass and we had an easy basket." Two plays later Kron had the ball at the top of the key when Thad Jaracz came off a Riley pick and cut for the basket. It was a perfect pass if Thad had been a seven-footer or the comic-book superhero Plastic Man, who could stretch his arms to any length necessary. When it sailed over Thad's head, the coach exploded. "Oh, shit, Kron, a whole wagonload of it." Again, no laughter, but Tommy Kron had a new nickname. From that point on his teammates called him Wagon.

Practices that weekend, like all Rupp practices, were almost eerily quiet, as if the team had taken a Benedictine vow of silence. Ralph Beard, star of Rupp's Fabulous Five in the late 1940s, said, "It was like you were in a vacuum." Rupp's longtime assistant Harry Lancaster told the story of a player whistling in practice. "Coach Rupp came up like a dog on point and said, 'Harry, who the hell is doing the whistling? By God, if he wants to sing, we'll send him over to Guignol [the fine arts theater], but here we play basketball.'" When a reporter asked if players were allowed to talk in practice, Rupp responded, "Yes, if they think they can improve on silence." They almost never could.

Aside from the coach the only sounds were the soft squeak of rubber-soled shoes on hardwood and the bouncing basketball. And when the system was really working, the sound of the ball was mostly eliminated. "Rupp teams did not dribble," wrote Lancaster in his book *Adolph Rupp as I Knew Him*. "The ball moved. The players moved. They did not dribble." Rupp's son, Herky, who played on his dad's 1958 championship team, recalls one practice that year when a player dribbled too much for his dad's taste. "Here, take this ball back to the dorm, and see if you can get yourself dribbled out before practice tomorrow." Harry recalled Rupp halting a preseason scrimmage with, "Gentlemen . . . let me introduce Willie Rouse, the goddamnedest dribbler in the world." Rouse got the message. This team didn't. Not yet.

Frustrated that this year's team wasn't coming together as he'd envisioned, Coach Rupp upped the decibel level of his sideline critiques. As his rants got louder, their impact diminished. Over the years the Rupp approach had turned good players into great players and greats into All-Americans. Along the way there were good (even gifted) players who were ground down by the Rupp intensity and insistence on total dedication and were dropped from the team or simply quit. Some went on to play for other colleges, and some just walked away, blending into campus life as if they had never dreamed of Wildcat glory. This time, away from the pounding pressure at the coliseum, individual angst and frustration threatened to metastasize into open rebellion. Some talked about quitting. Others wanted to go to the university president and complain about Rupp's abusive behavior.

"Nope," said Larry Conley at an impromptu team meeting after everyone else had their say. "That's not going to happen." Calmly, like a counselor talking defiant campers down from a sugar high, Larry said, "We're going to do what the old man says. We're going to work hard. We're going to do our best." There were nods of agreement, but also heads down in frowning defiance. "Here's what's going to happen," said cocaptain

Tommy Kron. "We're going out of here, and we're going to lay it on the line. You got that?"

The holdouts were coming back when Pat Riley, who'd been silent until then, got to his feet. The best athlete on the team, Pat had the broad shoulders of an enforcer and a presence that gave added impact to his words. "Larry and Tommy are right," he said quietly. "We're going to go to classes, and we're going to work our butts off in practice." Defiance turned to resignation. "Another thing," said Riley, making eye contact with a few targeted players. "It's okay to have a girlfriend, but if I catch you with one of these tarts that are always hanging around, I'm going to bust your chops."

It was never clear if Rupp learned about the meeting or if he simply accepted the next day's transformation as the natural result of his coaching genius, but overnight things changed. There were still mistakes that brought standard Rupp responses—"No, goddamnit, it's pick-and-roll. Pick first, then roll, all right?"—but the endless repetition of plays that had seemed clunky started clicking into the flow of play like carefully calibrated parts in a finely tuned machine. Intangibles that never make the stat sheet—passes, block-outs, and picks—were executed with grace and style, less like a whirring machine than a finely crafted ballet.

Later that season a photographer with one of those constant-click cameras would capture a sequence where Jaracz cleared the defensive board and hit Kron at midcourt, who passed to a streaking Dampier for a lay-up, all in 1 second on the clock. Probably it was 1.9 seconds, but when the same thing happened in that Thanksgiving weekend scrimmage, Slim almost blew his whistle in celebration.

What was happening was the kind of unselfish teamwork coaches strive for but seldom achieve, something that had been missing on last year's team. "We were all moving in different directions [last year]," said Larry Conley. "There was never this coming together." Now there was. Some of that was senior leadership, provided by Conley and Kron. Some of it was the fact that Pat Riley and Louie Dampier, good the year before, had upped their games. All of it contributed to what Conley called "a difference in chemistry."

"And throwing in that weird six-five guy in the middle [Thad Jaracz] just made it so different," said Conley. John Adams, who played center a year earlier, wasn't an accomplished player. "His approach to playing center and Thad's approach was like daylight and dark, totally different. So that combination at that position . . . and the improvement of Dampier and Pat had a lot to do with it."

Conley and Kron weren't concerned about who scored the points as long as Kentucky got the W. "They left their egos at the door," said Jaracz. "They wanted everybody to be special." It was infectious. When you're open, you get the ball. When you're double-teamed, you hit the guy left open. If there'd been a column on the stat sheet that day for dribbles, it would have been nearly empty.

When things started to click that Thanksgiving weekend, it was so sudden and so unexpected it was like old Archimedes running naked into the street after solving a vexing scientific problem shouting, "Eureka, I have found it!" By Sunday Mike (Slim) had an answer to his dad's question. The 1965–66 Kentucky Wildcats had endured seven of the most grueling practices ever. They came out on the other end of that weekend a different team. Nobody had called them that so far, but Rupp's Runts had arrived.

4

Brothers against the Bastard

When official—NCAA-approved—practices began on October 15, it was two-a-days of three to four hours each for the Texas Western Miners. Seven to eight hours of tough, unrelieved practice where the basketball sometimes seemed irrelevant. Half of each practice was defensive drills, with the other half devoted to conditioning so you'd be ready to play defense. Sometimes it was Run the Bleachers, up and down, up and down, until your legs felt like you were carrying fifty-pound sacks of flour up Endless Mountain. However, mostly it was Run the Lines, a form of wind sprints not so affectionately referred to as "Suicides."

Nobody knows the identity of the coach who first said, "Run the lines," but anybody who runs them more than a few times has him pegged as sadistic, diabolical, or worse. You line up on the end line, run to the free-throw line, touch it, run back, touch the end line, run to half court, touch it, back to the baseline, and on and on and on. Memorial Gymnasium in El Paso had five distinct lines to be touched. "I mean, after a while, every time you reached down to touch a line it would cut your breath off," said Harry Flournoy, a six-foot-five forward his teammates called Cricket because of his powerful thighs and his ability to jump out of the gym. "Lines were hard, and we did them every day." Again and again and again.

The only way you could play Haskins's kind of basketball was to not get tired, not be fatigued at the end of the game. Like Rupp at Kentucky, Coach Haskins believed if he could get any team on his schedule within three points in the last two minutes, he'd win the game because his players were in better condition.

If Haskins's practices were drudgery for his players, they could sometimes be entertaining to fans in a kind of Roman Colosseum sort of way. On Wednesdays—Lab Day at the college—practices were held in the evening and open to the public. Businessmen, donors, and students taking a break from studies would show up to watch the Christians get eaten by the lions, or in this case the Bear. While those practices were open, the rule was the same one so rigidly enforced by Adolph Rupp in Lexington: absolute silence. The only permitted sounds were the squeaking of shoes on hardwood and the coach's voice (like Rupp, he never used a whistle). During one Wednesday practice the year before the championship season, Haskins became exasperated. "Damn it, Shed, you're like a Mother Goose waking up to a new world every day."

The line brought a ripple of laughter from a tight little group of spectators, halfway up the stands at midcourt. Haskins froze. Then, deliberately, he lumbered up nine rows of pullout bleachers, his face reddening with every row and his anger climbing accordingly. Gripping the handrail in front of the permanent section of the stands, he scowled. "You think this looks easy?" Ashen faces flushed a deep pink with a combination of shock and surprise that the invisible wall between actor and audience had suddenly been breached. "Why don't you come down here and show us how?" When a portly fiftysomething man nearest Haskins visibly recoiled, the coach gave him the full force of his rage. "When you're in my gym, at my practice, you keep your damn mouth shut." Portly nodded, contritely. "GOT IT?" Portly's head was now bobbing up and down like a bobblehead doll. "Shut up or get out."

Turning abruptly, with a slight nod to Nevil Shed, Haskins was back on the floor, back to teaching. Sometimes, if he was mad enough at some failure of execution, he'd stop whatever drill he was running and say, "Hit the lines!" Other times he would say, "Fellas, we're not running lines to punish anybody here, but it looks like you may be a bit out of shape, a bit heavy-legged, so I think a few lines might be just what you need."

Either way the psychology was the same. You lined up according to your presumed quickness, guards with guards, forwards with forwards, centers with centers. If somebody dogged it, everybody had to run it again. That was the part the players hated. Nobody wanted to go back to the locker room as the one who made the other guys run a couple more times.

They didn't know it at the time, but the tedious and repetitive drills not only got them in condition but also created a bond. It was them against Haskins. In his book *Glory Road* (written with Dan Wetzel), Haskins said his practices were like boot camp. "You make it so hard on them—you make them hate you so much—that they don't have the time or energy to turn on each other—sort of a band of brothers against the bastard."

Like their counterparts in Lexington, the Texas Western Miners often thought they were playing for a crazy man. "I hated Haskins," says Willie Worsley. "I think we all did." "He was a horse's ass," said Willie Cager. "It was his way or no way." "I was afraid of him and I hated him at the same time," says Harry Flournoy. "You see him coming and something inside of you would freeze up." But while hate and fear were universal emotions back then, time brings perspective. "Well, that's the last time I'll have that SOB yell at me," thought Steve Tredennick as he boarded the plane to leave El Paso after graduation the spring before the championship season. "As the years passed, you grow up and realize you were lucky to be part of it. You grow up and look back and realize the guy was special."

At the start of each season some players would arrive in tip-top shape, most were about 75 percent, and then there was Bobby Joe. Bobby Joe Hill loved to eat. On his first campus visit he went into the cafeteria for a pregame meal, ate his steak, ate half of another player's steak, and then ate another one. Every August when he arrived back at school it was the same. Teammates who loved him (and everybody loved Bobby Joe) say he always looked like "a Butterball," the "Pillsbury Doughboy," or "a pig ready to be butchered."

Running the lines was hard on everyone. If you were out of shape, as Bobby Joe was every fall, it was excruciating. For him, and for others who showed up less than ready, there was always a student manager standing by with towels to wipe up yesterday's tacos and enchiladas. Even players who kept in shape over the summer went back to the dorm after practice totally exhausted. Many told the story of not being able to sleep at night because they were so tired. *I couldn't sleep. I couldn't eat. It was hard, really hard.*

Aside from his uncanny quickness, the thing that set Bobby Joe Hill apart was his competitive drive. "Everybody talks about Michael Jordan," said Harry Flournoy. "M.J. had nothing on B.J. He didn't want to lose. I don't care what it was. You could be throwing grains of sand into a gale-force wind. He'd want to win." It was his competitiveness that drove him to push through the pain and suffering required to regain his playing weight. It was his competitiveness that made him the floor leader Coach Haskins needed for the season ahead.

Despite his different emphasis—defense to Rupp's offense—and a twenty-eight-year difference in age (Don was born the year Adolph started coaching at Kentucky), the similarities between Haskins and Rupp are striking. Both were hard-nosed, no-nonsense, my-way-or-the-highway coaches. Both ran rigorous, mind-numbing practices. Both emphasized conditioning. Both hated to lose, and both displayed a stern, menacing countenance. "I didn't realize [Haskins] had a sense of humor until after I quit playing for him," said Flournoy. "Cuz, oh God, every day he'd come out there. People can say they weren't, but everybody had some fear of him. All of us did, but that was part of his style. I don't think his style was much different than Coach Rupp's style as far as getting his players ready."

There were two major differences this season. In his first four years Haskins's pregame meal was pretty much like Rupp's: steak, baked potato, two pads of butter, peas, and honey with two slices of peach for dessert. Early in the championship season Bobby Joe Hill and Willie Worsley approached the coach. "Steak is fine and all, but we'd rather have fried chicken." *Fried chicken?* The very thought would have sent Adolph into cardiac arrest. Don was a stickler about some things. Ever since Coach Iba caught him eating ketchup on french fries back at Oklahoma A&M, it had been an article of faith that ketchup cuts your wind. That didn't need scientific verification; it was *Revealed Truth*. The steak-and-potatoes pregame fare was also *Revealed Truth* until he put the matter to team trainer Ross Moore. Moore assured him that fried chicken was okay. If it was okay with Moore, it was okay with Haskins. From then on the pregame meal du jour for Hill and Worsley (and others so inclined) was fried chicken.

The second major difference between Rupp and Haskins had to do with motivation. While Adolph was telling the Runts they were going to be a lot better than sportswriters were saying, Don told his team just the opposite. With four outstanding players—David Lattin, Willie Worsley, Willie Cager, and David Palacio, a scrappy Hispanic guard—up from last year's freshman team more than compensating for players lost to graduation, the Miners were looking good, maybe as good as his '64 team that was just a game away from the Final Four. From all reports Haskins thought so too, but what he said was "You guys are the worst-looking bunch of athletes I ever saw, just a pitiful bunch. I doubt if we'll win even half our games."

5

The True Religion

Most people in Kentucky are Baptist. There are a few Methodists and a sprinkling of Presbyterians and Catholics to round out the mix. But while there are theological differences, one thing is certain: the true religion that unites everybody is basketball. For years that meant University of Kentucky basketball. On nights when the Kentucky Wildcats were playing basketball, everybody stayed home. The reason the streets were nearly empty was because most cars in the late 1940s and early '50s didn't have radios. So as game time approached, streets across the state emptied of traffic and living room radios were tuned to Clear Channel 840 WHAS Louisville with Cawood Ledford or the Kentucky Network with Claude Sullivan.

Wherever the University of Kentucky Wildcats played, it was thrilling, but nowhere compared to the heart-stopping excitement of a game at "Magnificent Memorial Coliseum," where it was so loud players talked about feeling the sound waves on the hair of their arms. For those home games people in front of their radios across the state knew they would hear the band playing the University of Kentucky fight song—"On, on, U of K, we are right for the fight today." When it was a home game the fight song would end with a deafening roar from a jam-packed crowd of diehard Kentucky fans, and listeners knew Coach Adolph Rupp— "the winningest coach in all of basketball"—was walking onto the floor.

To really appreciate how popular Rupp was in those days, you have to understand his importance to the state. Kentucky was rural and poor back in the 1940s, '50s, and '60s. While other states bounced back from the Depression and war, Kentucky was lagging behind. There wasn't much to be proud of in those days, said one wag, except bourbon, horses, and pretty women. In the middle of all that were Adolph Rupp and University of Kentucky basketball. Year after year he kept putting together these incredible teams—mostly with homegrown Kentucky boys—that made the state proud. It was Kentucky that kicked big-city butt and won all those national championships. It was *our* Wildcats who were America's team in the 1948 Olympics, going off to London, bringing home the gold. All across the state, from Ashland to Corbin, from Dawson Springs to Guthrie to Ludlow and Morgan's Gap, from Shively to Lexington, there was a feeling of pride, a coming together. More than a mere basketball coach, Adolph Rupp became an icon whose unrelenting pursuit of excellence was a source of pride for everyone.

Growing up in Owensboro seven-year-old Mike Harreld knew all about Coach Rupp and how he'd led the Kentucky Wildcats to two national championships. Before he knew what the words meant, Mike was saying, "Goo Bee Boo," to the delight of his parents. But this year was special. *His* Kentucky Wildcats were playing the Kansas State Wildcats for the 1951 NCAA Championship, and he was front-row center, in the family living room, sitting cross-legged in front of the Philco upright radio. The game would forever be locked in his memory because his daddy's Foo Foo dust made the difference. "Every time a Kansas Stater went to the free-throw line, Daddy would say, 'Foo Foo dust,' like he was blowing some dust in the player's face." It worked. Kansas State made only twelve of twenty from what the announcer called "the charity stripe." With his Wildcats up ten points in the final minute, Mike started jumping up and down. "We did it! We did it! We did it!" he shouted, dancing around the room, giving his mother hugs. Someday, he knew with a seven-year-old's confidence, he would be a Kentucky All-American himself.

The excitement inside his house was reverberating throughout the neighborhood and in towns and villages across the state. Like New Year's Eve at the stroke of midnight, there were car horns and even church bells. Kentucky was still in something of a post-Depression funk, but not tonight. Tonight they were national champions. NATIONAL CHAMPIONS!

NCAA Championship games were played on Saturday nights in those days, and in church that Sunday morning you would have thought Adolph Rupp was right up there with Peter, James, John, and other saints of the church. The Reverend Herndon at the Buena Vista Baptist Church thanked God for Coach Rupp and his team with a special mention of "our Owensboro boys," Cliff Hagan and Bobby Watson. Seven-foot center Bill Spivey was the game's most valuable player, but everyone in the congregation that morning knew that without Hagan's ten points, it would have been a tie game. Without Watson's eight points, Kentucky would have lost.

A year later elation turned to despair when three players from the 1948–49 team were found guilty of point-shaving in the National Invitational Tournament. Kentucky knew all about gambling on horses. A lot of people made a bundle when a fifteen-to-one shot named Count Turf won the 1951 Kentucky Derby, but point-shaving? That was a New York kind of thing, not something Kentucky boys would be involved in. The judge said otherwise, adding that Coach Rupp had "created an atmosphere for the violations to occur." Collectively, the state believed Rupp when he said he knew nothing about it. But none of that mattered until the NCAA's ruling. Years later they would call it the "death penalty." Then it didn't have a name, but it carried the same devastating effect: no Kentucky basketball for a whole year. How could the state survive?

Five years later Rupp was making good on his promise that he "won't retire until the man who said Kentucky can't play in the NCAA hands me the national championship trophy." That didn't seem very likely back when NCAA officials scheduled the 1958 Mideast Regional in Lexington and the championship game in Louisville. Kentucky just wasn't winning enough games to be a tournament contender. Rupp told reporters his Wildcats were pretty good country fiddlers but had a Carnegie Hall schedule. "I'll tell you, it will take violinists to play that competition. What we've got is a bunch of fiddlers."

The Fiddlin' Five lost six games that season, three of them by a single point. It was more games than a championship team had ever lost. Having won the regional against Miami of Ohio and Notre Dame on their home court as well as a squeaker against Temple in the semifinal game, Kentucky was back to fiddlin' midway through the first half of the championship game, despite their second home-court advantage of the tournament (the game was played at Louisville's Freedom Hall). With

All-American Elgin Baylor leading the way, the Chieftains ran up an eleven-point lead in the first half and seemed invincible. In the second half, when Seattle went to a zone defense to protect Baylor, who was in foul trouble, Vern Hatton and Johnny Cox started hitting from the outside for Kentucky, ending with thirty and twenty-four points (to Baylor's twenty-five). The Wildcats pulled back even with six minutes to go.

"The bunch regarded as fiddlers," wrote Larry Boeck in the next day's *Louisville Courier-Journal*, "ended the season blissfully and sounding like Heifetz playing Brahms on a Stradivarius." Final score: 84–72, no Foo Foo dust needed.

Talk about excitement. "The entire state was busting with pride, and Rupp was the reason," wrote assistant coach Billy Wireman in his book, *Lessons from the Big Guys*. "The famous bluegrass in central Kentucky was said to stand at appreciative attention. In your mind's eye you could see the thoroughbred racehorses at famous Calumet Farm outside Lexington as they pawed at the floor in their immaculately clean white stalls, rearing their heads with lusty 'I-told-you-so' snorts."

Mike, now fourteen years old, was just as excited as he was when his Wildcats won it all back in '51, but now he knew a few things about himself he didn't know before. With his voice he wasn't going to be the next Elvis Presley. With his eyesight he would never be an astronaut, and with his limited athleticism he wasn't likely to taste basketball glory, let alone win a place in the pantheon of Kentucky All-Americans. That's when he first met Coach Bobby Watson, the very same Bobby Watson who helped the '51 Wildcats to the national championship. Watson was the basketball coach at Owensboro High School, and he needed a student manager. Mike decided then and there, if he couldn't play the game, he would be a world-class student manager. Four years later, with Watson's recommendation, he became student manager for Coach Rupp and his Kentucky Wildcats.

Another teenager who watched the 1958 championship game with his parents had his own dreams. A year younger than Mike, he was already blossoming into an excellent athlete in Schenectady, New York. On that night he decided he would one day play for Coach Rupp's Kentucky Wildcats. His name was Pat Riley.

Back then there were stories of Kentucky fans in Florida who drove to the highest spot they could find to listen to games bouncing off the ether from WHAS radio in Louisville. A thank-you note from a Kentucky couple would be one sentence about a wedding present and paragraphs of speculation about the prospects for yet another NCAA Championship. Only in Kentucky.

One fellow brought his fiancée home to Lexington from North Carolina to meet his parents but had forgotten to explain the nature of true virtue, Kentucky style. On Saturday night, as the family settled down in front of the television to watch a UK game, the fiancée thought it would be a good time for a little get-acquainted visit. As the game got under way she said something to her future mother-in-law, who reached over and patted her gently, but firmly, on the wrist. "Honey," she said, "we don't talk during the basketball game."

Other basketball-crazy states like Indiana and North Carolina have professional teams to root for, wrote Darrell Bird in *Cats' Pause* magazine. "Kentucky has basketball. We own it. We adore it. We obsess over it." Statistical proof that the magnificent obsession Adolph Rupp started back in the 1940s, '50s, and '60s continues unabated comes from the Nielsen Company, the television rating firm: 67 percent of people in Kentucky "watch, attend or listen to UK basketball games."

Any last lingering doubts about the transcendence of UK basketball vanished in an Owensboro traffic court toward the end of the Rupp's Runts season. Slim was there on a Monday morning because Sunday evening he'd been ticketed for failing to come to a complete stop before turning onto the highway. "I thought you had practice this afternoon," said Mr. Griffin, the Daviess County prosecutor. Mike nodded contritely. After moving Mike's case to the head of the docket, Mr. Griffin introduced him to the judge. "Mr. Harreld is the student manager of the number-one basketball team in the country, Your Honor. He needs to get moving because practice this afternoon is in Lexington, three and a half hours away."

"That's good enough for me," said His Honor. "Case dismissed."

6

The Big Change

Grandpa Richardson called him Sam because his given name seemed too sedate for such a rambunctious boy. His other grandchildren seemed completely normal: mostly happy, sometimes sad, predictably unpredictable. Not Sam. From the time he was a toddler, Sam was even-tempered no matter what happened. Because they lived in a Hispanic neighborhood Sam got translated into "Samuel" among his friends, but he was the same on the playground as he was under his grandpa's watchful eye, always going full out, never bothered by anything. Sam was ten years old before he discovered his real name was Nolan.

Over the next few years Nolan Richardson became known as an athlete who was equally good at any sport he tried. At El Paso's largely Hispanic Bowie High School he was a hard-hitting first baseman and pitcher on the baseball team, an outstanding wide receiver in football, and the city's Mr. Basketball two years running. By the time he graduated he'd been named to all-state teams in all three sports. As a senior he set a school record, racking up forty-nine points in a single game. After a year of junior college he moved back to El Paso to play for Texas Western, the only school in the state's university system where the color of his skin wouldn't bar him from participation. In his sophomore year he led the team in scoring; sportswriters around the country were calling him a player to watch. There seemed no limit to his potential until Don Haskins arrived on campus.

"I hear you're the leading scorer on the basketball team," said Haskins in his flat Oklahoma accent after Sam helped to move the coach, his wife, Mary, and their four sons, between the ages of one and nine, into a three-room apartment on the ground floor of Miners' Hall, the athletic dorm where room and board would supplement the coach's $6,500 starting salary.

"Yes, sir," said Sam.

"Averaging twenty-one points a game."

"Yes, sir," said Sam, pleased that this new coach knew about his scoring prowess and envisioning bigger things to come.

Haskins nodded, took a beat, and continued. "Well, I also hear you can't guard a telegraph poll."

Sam didn't know how to respond. Haskins seemed friendly enough while they were unloading the U-Haul, but the conversation had taken an ominous turn. Defense? There had been times last season when Coach Davis chewed him out for passing up open shots, but with his ability to score the basket nobody had ever questioned his defense. It got worse.

"I understand you're a pretty good football player and you turned down a baseball contract."

Sam waited, not knowing where this was going.

"If you can't guard anybody, maybe you ought to pick one of those other sports to play."

Sam swallowed hard. Quit basketball? He liked playing football and baseball, but basketball had always been his true love. As long as he could remember he had loved the games and loved to practice. When there was nobody around to play against, he would shoot by the hour. On dirt, cement, or the hardwood, all he needed was a ball and a basket and he was content. He'd pick a spot twenty to thirty feet from the basket and shoot again and again and again. He had a cross-the-center-line-and-let-it-fly kind of range. Because most outdoor baskets had frayed nets or none at all, the ball would sometimes hit the post holding the backboard and bounce back. When it didn't, or when he missed, Sam followed the shot, grabbed the rebound, and banked it in with either hand, which was part of the reason he'd led the Miners in stick-backs. Until this very moment he'd thought he just might be good enough to play at the next level. And now here was this high school coach, this bear of a man who had never seen him play a single game, telling him he should give it up altogether. Because of defense. Defense?

"I don't think I'm going to play basketball this year," he told his wife that evening. From the look on her face he knew his matter-of-fact statement seemed as bizarre to her as it did to him. She knew Sam was excited about the players outgoing coach Harold Davis had recruited, including three talented African Americans. And now he was talking about quitting? She wouldn't have been more surprised if he'd announced plans to walk across the Rio Grande on the railing of Smelter Bridge blindfolded.

The decision to quit basketball lasted about as long as it took him to say the words. He wasn't about to be driven away from the game he loved. Despite what Haskins said, he'd always been a pretty fair defensive player, and down deep he believed his offensive skills would win Haskins over, just as they had every coach he'd ever played for. During shootaround on the first day of practice, one of the new players passed the ball back to him after he hit one of his long-range jumpers. He made the next one and the next and the next. In rhythm Sam could make six, eight, ten shots in a row. One player watching his shooting exhibition muttered in awe, "Man oh man, what a shooter."

No more.

"Your elbow," said Haskins one day when Sam was in the middle of one of his shooting streaks. "It's getting too far out there." In games, even when the shot went in, there would be Coach Haskins shouting, "Watch your elbow!" Coming off a season where he took eighteen to twenty shots a game, Richardson was lucky to get six or seven. Before Haskins he never worried about missing a couple of shots. Now he thought they might get him taken out of the game. Over time fewer shots and Haskins's elbow obsession worked together to zap his confidence. It was one of the negative lessons Richardson learned from playing for Haskins. "You don't fix nothing in the damn game. Coach would fix you, it didn't matter when, where or what."

It didn't take many practices for Sam to get the message: the only way he was going to play significant minutes was by being one of the best defensive players on the team. It was a mind-bending adjustment but one he had to make. As his offensive output dropped from twenty-one points a game to fourteen as a junior and ten as a senior, two things happened. He became something of a defensive specialist, and the Miners started winning. Winning, it turned out, was even more fun than being the leading scorer. What wasn't fun was practice.

Always before, practices were the highlight of any day. Now he hated practices and hated Haskins. So did most Haskins players, until later. "That tells the story," said Richardson. "You didn't love him while he is working your butt off, but you appreciated what he'd done for you when it was over. We hated him together and we loved him together." After Richardson became a coach himself, Haskins explained his coaching philosophy. "'Sam, does your team like you?' he asked. [Richardson] said, 'Well I don't know. I think they do.' 'Let me tell you something,' [said Haskins]. 'If your team likes you you ain't going to be worth a shit. You don't want them to like you, you want them to respect you.'"

The year before Haskins arrived on campus the intensity level on the basketball team was somewhere in that peaceful netherworld between serene and tranquil. Outgoing coach Harold "Happy" Davis liked to win games as much as the next guy until the next guy turned out to be Don Haskins. Harold Davis wasn't about discipline. Don Haskins was. The team's 12-12 record for the 1960–61 season was okay by Harold. Not by Don. Like the Man in the Brown Suit up in Lexington, Don Haskins wanted to win and dedicated himself to the preparation necessary to make that happen. Players expecting to ease back into shape in the forty-five days between the October 15 start of official practice and the team's first game found themselves in August two-a-days that were nothing like what they had experienced before. Instead of Happy Harold, they were confronted by the Bear. It was the very definition of culture shock.

While Happy Harold's demeanor was upbeat positive, Don's could become border-line grizzly if he wasn't getting the kind of effort he demanded. Once when he was chewing out a player for failing to fight through a screen, Haskins shouted, "You look at me when I'm talking to you!" A few minutes later the player stopped dead in his tracks and fixed the coach with a hard stare as Haskins berated him. "Damn it," said Haskins, "don't look at me that way when I'm talking to you!" As one player would remark years later, "You never knew whether to stare him down like a man or look away." Practices were always a physical challenge, but the bigger question—for everyone every day—was could they take the mental part?

Some, like Nolan Richardson, Paul Hines, Danny Vaughn, and Bobby Lesley, responded by digging in and working harder. Some decided the new regimen just didn't fit their idea of how things ought to be. It took only two days of Haskins-inflicted practice for six-foot-eight center-forward Phil Sargeant to reach that conclusion. Already intimidated by this new, unwanted presence in his life, he packed his suitcase and waited. When all was quiet in Miners' Hall late that night, he tiptoed past the Haskins ground-floor apartment—suitcases in hand—and out into the muggy-dry heat of an El Paso August evening, never to be seen again. Midnight (and sometimes midday) defections were to become a regular part of Haskins's coaching history.

An example of the Haskins intensity happened one afternoon when, because of injuries, he was one player short for the five-on-five defensive drill he was planning to run. Enter Lance. A five-foot-eight assistant trainer who hadn't played a lick of basketball since grade school, Lance was dutifully going through the motions of setting a pick when Haskins spotted a flaw in his execution. "Damn it, Lance, if you're going to be out there, do it right." As an isolated incident it was merely funny, but it illustrated an important tenant of the Haskins coaching philosophy. When even the guy beyond the last man on the bench is upbraided for insufficient effort, it creates a psychological us-versus-him dynamic: hate your enemy; love each other.

Respect would come later, but practices were now. "I knew we're going to run and run and run," said Richardson. "It was nothing to have three-and-a-half- or four-hour workouts." Sometimes, when they hadn't played up to their coach's expectations in an away game, there would be an after-midnight practice when they got back home. "We didn't like losing. He drove us to that. We'd do whatever it took to be a winner. If that meant workouts at midnight, we'd do it. He kind of hammered that down to us; that you do whatever it takes to be a winner. Your feet could be bleeding. It didn't matter. Tape them up and let's go. Man, it was brutal." Brutal, but ultimately rewarding. Until Haskins defense was always a secondary consideration. Now it was central. Practices were no longer fun, but the competitive drive Grandpa Richardson had noticed some twenty years ago kicked in, and his grandson came to pride himself on being Haskins's go-to guy on defense.

"You might be scoring on those other guys," he'd announce to the opposing team's star player, "but I'm going to shut off your water." Usually, he made good on his promise. And while dreams of a professional playing career were no longer realistic, he was already thinking ahead to a coaching career that would take him to the University of Arkansas, a national championship, and, ultimately, a place alongside Haskins in the Basketball Hall of Fame.

"[Coach Haskins] made his team play the game as he saw it. We played through his eyes, we didn't play through ours. If you had to pass it ten times before you took a shot, or if you had to get it inside before you took a shot outside, that was just part of the game and if you didn't do it you weren't going to play. He made us play through his eyes."

At first, playing through Haskins's eyes made Sam feel like a "puppet on a string," with the coach "moving whatever cord he wanted to." By his senior year something unexpected began to happen. "You could see the old wheels were coming off and the new wheels were coming on and we were buying into his philosophy, the way he wanted us to play. That's coaching."

Another part of successful coaching is finding the player who can be the team leader, a proverbial coach on the floor (and in the locker room) who can get through to the players when the coach can't. It didn't take Haskins long to figure out Sam was his man. The only returning letterman, Richardson had the maturity to understand the frustrations of his new coach. For two years he was Haskins's back-channel solution. "We got to get after him, Sam, 'cause I'm going to ride his ass." Sam would take the player aside for straight talk, combining we're-in-this-together commiseration with a primer on how to avoid the coach's wrath.

"Coach is rough, and coach is on our ass, but we've got to pull together," he'd say before launching into a little tutorial. "When you're busting it do you hear him saying anything? Here's your problem, man, you don't bust it enough. You go at it pretty good for a few minutes, then you sort of disappear. Want to get him off your back? Don't take any plays off, okay?" Usually, the player would rise to the challenge, but there was always the kicker. "You better get your ass in gear or I'm going to be all over you, too. We've got to get it done, Hoss. We got a game coming up."

In his senior year Nolan Richardson played another role little noted at the time but one that was the first step in the early evolution leading to the black-versus-white championship game against Kentucky that vaulted Haskins into the national spotlight. With more and better African American players, Haskins was starting three and sometimes four blacks—three or four, but never five. Richardson didn't know it at the time, but Haskins was under a lot of pressure about the racial makeup of his team. One day he called Richardson into his office. Their relationship had grown far closer in their time together, but now Haskins seemed tentative, almost nervous.

"Look, Sam, I've got to say something and I don't know how you're going to feel about it." Richardson sat there staring at Haskins, as confused as he'd been in their first conversation nearly two years before. "You're a senior. You live in El Paso. Everybody knows you." Okay, where is this going? "And since you're a senior, if you wouldn't mind, I'm not going to start you tonight."

If I wouldn't mind? I'm cocaptain of the team, a starter for three seasons. Richardson waited.

"I can't do it with the other guys," said Haskins, looking Richardson in the eye for the first time. "But I figure you're mature enough to handle it." Haskins paused, as if waiting for Richardson's approval before adding, "Within a minute I'll have you in the game."

"Sure coach, whatever."

"It's all about how many I need to start."

"How many you need to start?" Richardson was confused.

"I'm getting flak about how many blacks I play here in El Paso." Some of the flak came in the form of hate mail, some from school president Joseph Ray by way of athletic director George McCarty, who were getting pressure from some of the school's most influential donors. Ray's instruction: *No more than three black boys at a time.*

"That's fine with me, coach. The bottom line is playing time."

That night, right before the game, Haskins called Richardson over to where he was standing by the team bench. "I don't give a damn about that kind of crap, Sam. You're starting tonight." Nobody beyond the El Paso city limits was paying much attention to Texas Western in those days, but two years before their championship season Don Haskins had made a decision few coaches in the country were prepared to make. Ignoring an unwritten rule—two blacks at home, three on the road, four if you're behind—he was starting his best five players. Five athletes who just happened to be black.

The following year Haskins's best five at any given time tended to include a white player, either Steve Tredennick or Bobby Dibler. When Steve was in the game as point guard he was pared with Orsten Artis in the shooting-guard slot. When Bobby Joe Hill played point, Bobby Dibler, like Artis a lights-out shooter, played the two spot. The pairings had to do with tempo, not color. Steve and Orsten tended to play at a more conservative pace, while Hill and Dibler were more up-tempo.

Playing against Air Force in a game the Miners dominated, Dibler had a typically good shooting night, making five out of six field-goal attempts but missing his only free throw. "Dibler, I want to see your ass on the free-throw line," growled Haskins at practice the next afternoon. "How the hell are we gonna win basketball games if you can't make a damn free throw?" Chastened, Dibler went to the foul line, while his coach mumbled and grumbled as if the miss cost Texas Western the game. It was Haskins the psychologist making sure his guard didn't get too cocky about an excellent shooting night.

As the start of a new season approached, Haskins was always anxious to assess his team's competitive capability by seeing them play against another college team that wasn't on their schedule. One fall he hatched a plan with his friend Gene Gibson, coach of the Texas Tech Red Raiders. The two teams met for a daylong scrimmage in the little town of Hobbs, New Mexico, easy driving distance from El Paso and Lubbock. All day long the two teams battled each other, giving both coaches the opportunity to try various combinations of players up and down their benches. Late in the afternoon Gibson said, *How about it, Coach? Have we had enough?* Exhausted players on both teams awaited Haskins's verdict.

Give me the key and I'll lock up, he said. *I think we need a little more work.* By Haskins's reckoning his team always needed more work.

A year later, November 22, 1963, Haskins had scheduled another scrimmage with Texas Tech in Hobbs. Then, at 12:30 p.m. local time, Walter Cronkite made the announcement on El Paso's CBS affiliate, KDBC. President John F. Kennedy had been shot to death while riding in a motorcade in Dallas. As word of the assassination spread across the country, businesses, schools, and government offices closed their doors. Concerts and sporting events were canceled. Radio and television stations abandoned their regularly scheduled programming to report exclusively on the tragedy. Everything shut down, with the exception of Texas Western Miners basketball.

With just ten days before their first game, mourning could wait. The Miners needed work. As three cars caravanned north on the two-hundred-mile trip, radios were tuned to the continuing coverage from Dallas. "There was all this speculation about who killed the president," recalls Fred Schwake, a student trainer on the team. Some thought it might be a communist, possibly an agent of Cuban president Fidel Castro. Haskins, who was driving one of the cars, shook his head sadly. "Coach said, 'I just hope it wasn't a black man.' I've never forgotten that."

The players who made the Hobbs trip have never forgotten the day's grueling scrimmage: three twenty-minute halves and then, at Haskins's request, another. While players on both teams were leaning over, grasping their knees in exhaustion, Haskins lobbied for one more half, explaining, "I think we need the work." In the silence that followed, Tech All-American guard Dub Malaise looked up at his Texas Western counterpart and mumbled, "How the hell can you play for that sonofabitch?" "I had no energy to reply," recalls Steve Tredennick. "If I had, I wouldn't have known what to say."

Nolan Richardson had endured the first Hobbs trip but was nearly three months into his postgraduate job as an assistant coach at El Paso's Bowie High School on that November day. Since he was right there in town, and now an adult, his relationship with Coach Haskins moved to a different level. He was there to witness the coach's roiling frustration with Bobby Joe Hill. Along with Hill's quickness came a through-the-legs, behind-the-back flair that had to be harnessed. And all attempts to tame the little guard were like trying to teach debutante manners to a cheetah.

"I'm going to have to run him off, Sam," said Haskins one day. "All that hot-dog crap . . . I can't take it."

"That's his game, Coach," said Richardson, shaking his head. As a player he had explained the coach to his teammates; now it was city ball to a country boy. "That's the way Detroit and New York City kids play." The hot-dogging was in his DNA.

Haskins remained dubious, but little by little he came around, and the show was on. Haskins adjusted to B.J., not the other way around. Years later he would say letting Bobby Joe be Bobby Joe was the best decision he ever made.

7

A Synchronized Leap

After Kentucky's Thanksgiving weekend, it was pretty obvious things had changed, but it was hard to know whether this was a final coming together or something ephemeral that would dissolve as quickly as it appeared. Later, after Kentucky had run off sixteen straight victories, Louie Dampier used the *D* word in describing the previous (1964–65) season. "There was dissention on the team last year," Louie told *Sports Illustrated*. "We were always bickering, and by the end of the season we knew we were holding onto the ball instead of passing it." There wasn't much bickering as official practice got under way at the start of the 1965–66 season, but the ball seemed to be sticking a fraction too long for real teamwork. Now, despite Coach Rupp's prediction that this team could be special, it was more of the same.

One day during a particularly boring practice when Rupp had run the same play multiple times with only minor adjustments, assistant coach Joe B. Hall heard one of the players mutter, "Fuck you, old man." After practice Hall asked Adolph and the managers to leave. "You've got the greatest coach in the history of the game," he told the team. "The next time I hear somebody cuss Coach, I'm stopping practice and you're going to repeat that face-to-face with Coach Rupp."

"We used to say that about him every day," said Larry Conley. "There wasn't anything [Hall] could say that would make us change our minds. We all respected Coach Rupp. We didn't like him. Don't ever believe that I ever liked the man, okay. I respected him. I totally respected everything he did, and I would have done anything for him. But would I get angry? Oh hell yes."

The negative thoughts were still there the next day, but practice was the same as always. Players arrived on the floor—taped, dressed, and ready to go—by 3:15. Punctuality was so ingrained that, fifty years later, former Rupp players still have nightmares. *Oh, my God! Three o'clock. Got to run. Legs too heavy. Flag down a passing car. Drive up to the coliseum door. Still might make it. Doors locked. Pounding, pounding, pounding. Nobody answers.*

For the next thirty minutes everybody is in Adolph Rupp's vacuum. No conversation. Not a word. The only sound is basketballs hitting the floor, hitting the backboards, hitting the rims, hitting the nets of six different baskets, two on each side of the court and one at each end, that and the squeaking of rubber soles on hardwood. For thirty minutes it is shoot, run, and get the ball, shoot again, fourteen players in constant motion, simulating moves they would make under game conditions. Nobody walked. Nobody stopped, not ever.

"I tell people that story today, and they look at me like I've lost my mind," said Conley. "Are you serious?" Deadly serious. Adolph and his assistant coach Harry Lancaster sat at midcourt watching as each player worked with a quiet intensity on his moves and shots. Every now and then, if Harry thought someone had lost focus, he would break the silence by saying a name. Because everyone knew what they were supposed to be doing, that, and a look, was all that was necessary.

Like most of the players, Conley had a routine he worked through. At least twenty times he would take the ball to midcourt, dribble hard to the free-throw line, stop, and shoot a jump shot. It was a shot he often got in a game. Louie Dampier's routine was to simulate specific plays, driving to a spot on the floor at the top of the key, as if he was coming off a Kron screen, and shoot his jumper. "Nobody was just dribbling around," said Conley. They were working. "Really hard. Really hard."

With two or three players on each of the six baskets, if a ball bounced toward another player he would grab it and throw it back. Not Riley. Pat was total concentration. He always shot on a side basket by himself and wouldn't even look at a ball coming into *his space.* "Damn it, Riley, kick it back to me," said Bob Tallent, a sophomore guard who led last year's freshman team in scoring. "Son, this is my basket," said Riley, as the ball bounced by him toward the end line. "You get the hell out of here."

It was another example of Riley's competitive nature. "You had to kill him to beat him," said Brad Bounds, a junior forward from Bluffton, Indiana, who often guarded Riley in scrimmages and had the scars to prove it. "He's just that competitive." Riley was the master of what Bounds calls the "short elbow." He would get the inside position under the basket, make contact with his defender, and hit him with a series of four-inch jabs, "boom, boom, boom." Another Riley trick was to grab the defender's jersey just long enough to guide him to where he wanted him to go. "He knew every trick in the book," said Bounds with admiration. "He [was] one mean sonofabitch."

While the rest of the team worked individually, Thad Jaracz, Cliff Berger, and Larry Lentz played one-on-one over on a side basket under the watchful eye of Coach Rupp, Thad against Berger, Lentz against Thad, and then Berger against Lentz. It didn't take an expert on low-post play to spot the difference. Berger and Lentz, a six-foot-eight senior from Lakeview, Ohio, were taller, but Thad was quicker, a lot quicker. Even though they knew he was going to the left, they just couldn't keep up. He'd catch the pass from Rupp in the high post near the free-throw line, put the ball on the floor, break to the basket, and shoot a running left-handed hook, usually off his left foot instead of his right. Even before it became obvious the strength of the Runts would be speed and that he was by far the fastest runner, Thad was winning the starting job in those one-on-one drills on the side basket.

At 3:45, still without a word having been said, the old man materialized at midcourt. The players hadn't been watching, but suddenly, as if his foot touched a hidden switch on the center line, basketballs joined the silence. No dribbles. No shots. Nothing. Everybody, players and managers, ran to center court and stood there as if the next words out of Rupp's mouth would provide the key to their very survival. He'd make whatever point he had to make and, three minutes later, the drills: setting picks, blocking out, rebounding.

With four returning starters from the previous year—Louie Dampier and Tommy Kron at guard, Pat Riley and Larry Conley at forward—there was only one position on the 1965–66 team up for grabs. Because Cliff Berger had played center to Thad Jaracz's forward on the previous year's freshman team that *Basketball* Magazine rated top five in the country, he seemed the logical choice. At six feet eight, Cliff was about the same size as John Adams, who'd graduated the previous spring, and he was a better shot—better than Adams, better than Jaracz. It would be a Battle of the Titans. On a Rupp team there was no such thing as rotation. There were starters and there were practice players, and practice players didn't get in the game unless the man in front of them was in foul trouble or injured. Period.

Thad Jaracz had been something of an afterthought in the recruiting process. The other four starters on the previous year's freshman team came with big-time credentials: Berger and Bob Tallent were high school All-Americans; the other two were first-team all-staters. And then there was Thad. He was like a pup without a pedigree, an okay practice player but not really much of a prospect. In one scrimmage against the varsity his freshman year, Thad was flying up the right side of the court on a fast break when Tallent threw him a long pass he wasn't expecting. The ball hit him on the head, bounced up, and hit him again. Of course, Rupp stopped practice, smiling and shaking his head in disbelief. "Thad, son, just go in and get a bath. You're nothing but a Shetland pony in a stud-horse parade."

Berger played with the starters on the White Team in early scrimmages, with Jaracz playing with the Blues. It didn't last. "The team was so fast," said Tallent, "[that] by the time Cliff got down to the offensive end, they were heading back on defense."

Adolph had virtually invented fast-break basketball, and Thad, it turned out, was the better runner. "What we discovered was that Cliff was probably the better shooter," Thad recalled over lunch in a Louisville restaurant nearly fifty years later, "but he wasn't as fast getting up and down the floor. It looked like that might be the identity we could get our hands around." Larry Conley had another concern. "How can I say this in a kind way? [Berger] had terrible hands. Couldn't catch the ball. I like Cliff really well, [but] you have to trust the person you're throwing the ball to is going to catch it. A couple of times he fumbled or lost the ball. He couldn't hold onto it. That's it for me, buddy. I like you, but it ain't coming in there anymore."

While other teams had centers five to seven inches taller than Thad, most big men of that era were no match for his athleticism. "They had to worry about chasing me down the floor," says Thad. "Because if we were going to run and I was going to fill the lane, Larry's going to throw [me] the ball. I felt the pressure of trying to find myself a position on this team, but I didn't feel the pressure of thinking this can really be special."

"Special" hadn't kicked in yet, and it was far from certain it ever would. When the fast break worked, there was a kind of magic. When it didn't, a smoothly running machine became a clunker. The wide-open fast break was the only exception to an ironclad Rupp Rule: you never shoot unless there is someone under the basket to rebound—never. The corollary to the fast-break rule: you always use the backboard to maximize chances of success. That meant looking for an angle to the basket. Rupp teams didn't dunk, and laying it over the front rim in a finger roll, pretty as that might be, brought a Rupp eruption. He played the percentages. Always. Another Rupp Rule, taught by Harry to his freshman team as if it had come down from Mount Sinai, was that "to win you need at least two shots every time you come into the front court." By the time they were playing for the latter-day Moses—the Man in the Brown Suit—it had been written on their minds and in their hearts.

Because Rupp assistant Harry Lancaster had been around from the start, everybody pretty much took the fact that he and Rupp worked in tandem as a given. The closeness of their relationship was most graphically on display in an earlier season. The game was all but over. Kentucky was up by sixteen points with less than a minute to go. The Vanderbilt center rebounded the ball under Kentucky's basket and passed it—baseball style—to a guard at half court on the right side. With only two refs in those days—one leading the play, the other running up the left side—they didn't see what was obvious from Rupp's vantage point on the bench under Kentucky's basket: the Vandy guard caught the ball with his foot on the sideline. As he streaked in for a lay-up at the other end of the floor, Adolph and Harry came off the bench in a synchronized leap, faster than any basketball move of the night, as if they'd been poked in the rear by an enormous two-pronged branding iron.

Together, they charged out on the floor, halfway to the foul line, screaming at the top of their lungs, both of them pointing at an Egregious Violation, a Tragedy of Total Injustice. Then came the realization: nobody but the people on Kentucky's bench saw what they saw; nobody cared. "Coach, Coach, they're killing us!" screamed Harry. "Harry, I know it, I know it!" yelled Adolph, grabbing Harry in a big bear hug. It was the perfect illustration of what Larry Conley says: "When Adolph exhaled, Harry inhaled."

The Wildcat lead was so big there wasn't the slightest chance they would lose, yet these two lunatics acted like they were eyewitnessing Armageddon, with Vanderbilt in the role of the Antichrist. By any normal standards, both of them were certifiably crazy. Coach Rupp was more volatile than Harry, but both were hair-on-fire focused and intense. Others might say, "You win some, you lose some"; for Adolph and Harry, each point was a matter of life and death.

Finding His Team

It was a sunny day in the spring of 1962, and Harry Flournoy was hungry. An eighteen-year-old, six feet five, he was nearly always hungry. Others might bring their lunches or eat in the high school cafeteria, but not Harry. He lived more than a mile from school, but most days, even though he had to run some of the way to make it home and back on time, it was well worth the trip. On this day he was thinking about his mother's apple pie. Amy Flournoy made the best apple pie in seven counties, and Harry knew there was one piece left, waiting just for him. Then, suddenly, his reverie was interrupted by a white car. The car pulled up beside him. It was a Ford with two white men inside.

Even though Gary, Indiana, is a northern city, there were times in the early sixties when it seemed to have been plucked from Mississippi or Alabama and plopped down on the south shore of Lake Michigan, with its southern ways stubbornly, rigidly, in place. There had been a lot of racial tension that spring, and a young black man, even one as big and strong as Harry, couldn't be too careful. With the car now moving along beside him, he kept walking. His eyes were fixed on the sidewalk with a concentration he usually reserved for basketball.

"Hey, my name is Coach Don Haskins," said the man in the passenger seat, leaning out the window. "I'm head basketball coach at Texas Western College in El Paso, Texas."

Harry had heard of El Paso, but not of a college named Texas Western.

"Get in," said Haskins. "I'll take you home."

"No, that's okay."

Haskins was persistent, but so was Harry. *I'm not getting in a white car with two white guys over by the school. They'll never hear from me again.*

When he got home the white car was parked in his driveway. "I walked in the house, and they're at the kitchen table," Harry recalls, "and Haskins is eating *my* pie. I hated him."

Whatever Harry's feelings, Amy Flournoy was in the process of being sold. Away from basketball Don Haskins could be a charmer. He sat there at the kitchen table, eating Harry's pie, and telling Harry's mother the kinds of things a mother wants to hear. If her son had basketball issues, Haskins would take care of them. If he had academic issues, he'd take care of them, *and* he would let her know.

"I hated him," said Harry, "and she was saying, 'Yes, I think you would do very well at that school.'"

"I don't want to go to Texas. Why would I want to go to Texas?"

"I think you're going to Texas."

Haskins, who'd never seen Harry play, was going on the recommendation of a high school coach from Gary who had been a senior playing for Coach Iba when Haskins was a freshman. Sight unseen, Haskins was offering a four-year scholarship. It turned out other schools had expressed interest, too, but Harry didn't find out about them until he came back from his campus visitation. By then he was as sold on Texas Western as his mother. "When I got to El Paso I met some of the nicest people I'd ever met in my life."

Unlike Adolph Rupp at Kentucky, Don Haskins had a minuscule recruiting budget. Unlike Rupp, he lacked a storied program to serve as a magnet for star players. What Haskins had that Adolph lacked was an easy manner and the ability to feel comfortable in the homes of black athletes. "When I go recruiting as a college basketball coach," Haskins wrote in his book *Glory Road*, "we'd go into some of the most depressed neighborhoods in America—real tough, troubled spots—but I was always comfortable." He was comfortable on the basketball court, too.

Haskins wrote about spending his entire recruiting budget during his first year at Texas Western—five thousand dollars—driving back and forth between El Paso and Lawton, Oklahoma, trying to recruit Jim Barnes, who was playing for Cameron Junior College. A gifted athlete and prolific scorer, the six-foot-eight Barnes was being heavily recruited by big-name schools across the country but was having trouble deciding where he wanted to go. Haskins was out of money and out of options. "So I bet Barnes that I could beat him in a free-throw shooting contest. He laughed and figured this thirty-something dude would be easy to take."

He wasn't.

"The stakes of the bet were simple," wrote Haskins. "We'd each shoot twenty-five free throws. If he hit more than I did, then I would go back to El Paso and never bother him again. If I hit more, then he would sign with Texas Western right then and there."

Barnes made seventeen of twenty-five. Haskins made eighteen in a row and got the player he needed so badly to solidify his program. In his first year at the school Barnes averaged nineteen points and seventeen rebounds a game, leading Texas Western to the NCAA Tournament, the first in school history. In his senior year he upped those averages to twenty-nine and nineteen, again leading the team to the NCAA. "More importantly," Haskins wrote, "[Barnes] showed kids around the country that Texas Western was a place where great players played. . . . Nothing attracts great recruits like great players."

Bad News Barnes, as sports information director Eddie Mullens dubbed him because he was bad news for Texas Western opponents, gave Haskins's program a certain prestige. His recruiting budget might still have been an insurmountable problem in those early seasons except for one thing: he had friends who alerted him to gifted athletes who would otherwise have gone unnoticed.

The same Gary, Indiana, coach who told Haskins about Harry gave him a heads-up on Orsten Artis. A six-foot-one guard with a silky-smooth shooting stroke, Artis played his high school ball at Gary's Froebel High School. In addition to his ability to score the basketball, Artis had speed and college-potential ball-handling skill. And even more important to Haskins, he was a strong defensive player. Haskins couldn't have known it at the time, but two of his championship-game starters were now in place.

Three other players who figured prominently in that game Haskins recruited by remote control from New York City. Nevil Shed played for Morris High School in the Bronx. Willie Cager, a high school dropout, was spotted playing city-league ball, moved to El Paso on his own, and graduated from El Paso Technical High School, becoming, at twenty-three, a Texas Western freshman. Willie Worsley, who led DeWitt Clinton High School to the New York City championship in 1963 (becoming the game's MVP), arrived in El Paso the following fall.

The other two who played in the championship game—David Lattin and Bobby Joe Hill—were the only ones Haskins actually saw play before signing them to scholarships. And both of them took circuitous routes to El Paso.

Haskins scouted Lattin at Houston's Worthing High School, where he was averaging twenty-nine points a game, leading his team to the state championship. Lattin is a classic story of a clumsy six-footer cut from his eighth grade team by a coach who told him that to improve his strength and leaping ability, he should run the bleachers at Rice University stadium. All summer long he did just that, running up and down the top hundred steps, wearing a fifty-pound weight belt. The conditioning and the fact he grew six inches over the summer turned his world around. The game got a lot easier, and a six-foot-six ninth grader who could dunk was impossible to ignore.

While most of Haskins's early recruits flew under the radar, Lattin was a *Parade* High School All-American (along with a fellow from Schenectady, New York, by the name of Pat Riley) and was recruited by college coaches across the country. There seemed little chance of convincing Lattin his future was with the little-known Miners. Still, Haskins kept asking, and Lattin finally agreed to come to El Paso for a visit. It didn't take. Although he was intrigued by the challenge of breaking Jim Barnes's multiple scoring and rebounding records, he decided to attend Tennessee A&I, a traditional all-black school in Nashville that agreed to give scholarships to him and his four high school teammates, something Haskins declined to do.

Lattin spent only one semester at A&I, but it was long enough to make a lasting impression on a Nashville high schooler named Perry Wallace. Wallace, who would become the first African American to integrate the rigidly segregationist Southeastern Conference, thought he could dunk until he saw Lattin. "Big, strong, menacing" was the way Wallace described him to his biographer. "He'd be flying through the air and everybody under the basket went, 'Oooooooh shit, time to leave, time

to go, don't even mess with this.'" Wallace, who was paying close attention to a pair of professional dunk masters, Wilt Chamberlain and Bill
Russell, thought Lattin was "in another league." Long before the end
of his first semester, Lattin thought so, too. The Nashville school didn't
have the kind of challenging competition he was looking for. Dropping
out, he returned to Houston, finally calling Haskins, who was quick to
offer a scholarship.

Bobby Joe Hill presented a different challenge. Haskins and assistant
Moe Iba saw him play for Burlington Junior College in the JC National
Championship. They were impressed. Bobby Joe was the quickest defen-
sive player they'd ever seen. And with the ball in his hands he was a
veritable magician, dribbling his way through defenders as if they were
so many frozen statues. The following season, Iba recalls, "Don said,
'What do you think about finding out about that little guard we saw?'"
It turned out Bobby Joe had dropped out of Burlington after the Univer-
sity of New Mexico recruited his friend and teammate six-foot-eight
Mel Daniels but didn't want him. He had never heard of Texas Western
College, but when Haskins offered a scholarship he agreed to come to
El Paso for a visit.

"He's not on the plane," said Iba, calling Haskins from the airport.
After he got off the phone Iba looked around again. *Could that be him?*
The little guard wasn't quite so little anymore. Instead of the lithe, quicksilver player they expected, Bobby Joe Hill appeared in a plus-size version, weighing more than two hundred pounds, up fifty from his junior
college playing days.

When Iba arrived at the gym with Bobby Joe, Haskins interrupted practice. In street clothes pulled tight around his expansive middle, Bobby
Joe Hill was not exactly the image of the superquick athlete he was, but
Haskins had an idea. "Togo, you and Jimmy take him two-on-one. Keep
him from getting to half court." Ball in hand, with a toothpick in his
mouth, Bobby Joe gave his would-be defenders a little grin. Togo Railey
was thinking, *This chump can't beat us.* But then Bobby Joe ducked his
shoulder a little bit, did a crossover and a little jab step, and cut between
them, grinning all the time. Beat them on the outside, maybe, but cutting between them? It was the one thing a pair of ball-hawking guards

should never allow. *A fluke*, thought Togo. "Let's go two out of three."
Now knowing Bobby Joe was a lefty, his would-be defenders forced him
to go right. A behind-the-back dribble, a quick head fake, another crossover, same result. "Greased lightning," said Togo. "We never did stop
him. He gained my respect in a hurry."

"Don was a great basketball coach and a great person," said Moe Iba,
son of the legendary Hall of Fame coach Hank Iba and Haskins's first
assistant. "Don was the type of guy who didn't see black and white. He
didn't coach a black player any different than he would a white player."
That was part of the reason for his success. The other part was his ability
to recruit complementary players who were willing to bust their butts
in practice and wait on the bench until their services might be required.
One player in that mold was Jerry Armstrong.

Armstrong, a six-foot-four forward from Eagleville, Missouri, was
another Haskins recruit he never saw play. This time the recommendation came from a former Miner who played for Haskins's predecessor.
Jerry was excited about making the trip to El Paso but unprepared for
what he found when he stepped off the plane. In Eagleville there were
only twenty-eight students in his high school graduating class. In Eagleville you could go for months and never see a black person, let alone
a Hispanic. It was as if he'd walked off the farm into a teaming cauldron
of cultural diversity. On the other hand, he liked the campus, liked the
coaches, and decided Texas Western was the place for him. "I wanted
to go to a small [Division I] school where I could play a lot of basketball," said Jerry with a chuckle. "I didn't realize we'd have the kind of
athletes we did."

When he got home from the trip, he had an offer to fly out to the University of Maryland for a visit. Jerry wanted to go but ran into resistance.
"Dad was old-fashioned. He said, 'Son, didn't you give your word?' I
said, 'I did, but that's not really binding.' He said, 'Oh, but it is. That's
your word.'" Three years later Jerry Armstrong finally made the trip he'd
wanted to make his senior year in high school. The 1966 NCAA Final Four
was in Cole Field House on the campus of the University of Maryland.

Because most Haskins's recruits arrived in El Paso sight unseen, first
exposure to their new coach was nearly always the same. "Let's get you

some equipment and see what you can do," said Haskins when Lou Baudoin stopped in with his parents to meet the coach for the first time. For the next two hours, in the stifling ninety-degree heat of a gymnasium where the only air-conditioning was provided by panting players, it was wall-to-wall basketball while his parents sat in the bleachers watching. Haskins, wearing plain gray shorts and a white T-shirt that barely covered his ample stomach, stood on the sidelines, watching the action and shouting commands like a frustrated drill sergeant. It was the kind of practice Lou would become accustomed to, full-out, with no water breaks. By the time he hit the shower, he felt completely dehydrated and hungry enough to eat one of the armadillos that roam the desert in Southwest Texas.

By the championship season, in nominal compliance with NCAA rules, Coach Haskins watched pre–October 15 practices from the ball closet, a small equipment room just off the playing floor. He knew the rule but was constitutionally incapable of completely absenting himself from the gym while his team was practicing. So, with door ajar, he sat in that tiny room by the hour, watching and shouting his running critique.

Once official practices began Haskins was up close and personal, often very personal. More than a few players heard, "Damn it, you couldn't cover your mother" or were told to "go put on a tutu" when their defensive effort failed to measure up. One of Haskins's most pointed criticisms came when a player screwed up on the practice floor. "You wonder why?" he'd say derisively, as in, "You wonder why you're not playing more?"

9

He Didn't Recruit; He Chose

Adolph Rupp had an ego that bordered on arrogance. In fact, much of the time it was as far beyond the border as Lexington is from El Paso. On the other hand, he understood one of the most important principles of leadership: to be successful you need to surround yourself with people who have skills that are complementary to yours, people who are good at what you're not. That was Harry Lancaster. Like Adolph, he loved the Wildcats. Like Adolph, he hated to lose. Like Adolph, he was an excellent judge of basketball talent. Unlike Adolph, he seemed to enjoy the recruiting that was absolutely essential to the success of Kentucky basketball.

The best description of Adolph's attitude toward recruiting, according to Harry, was "aloof." He felt players should want to come to Kentucky. He didn't recruit; he chose. Russell Rice, sports reporter turned Rupp biographer, described it this way: "[Rupp] thought that when a Kentucky baby boy was born, the mother had two wishes for him: to grow up to be like another native son, Abraham Lincoln, and to play basketball for Adolph Rupp." When it came to players from Kentucky (and their mothers), that was usually what it amounted to. It was up to Harry to recommend whom to choose.

That's what happened with Larry Conley. A standout at Ashland High School, Larry led his team to the state championship his junior year and all the way to the championship game as a senior when he was the only returning starter. Like most Kentucky boys, he'd grown up dreaming of playing for the Wildcats, so once Harry offered the scholarship, Larry never thought of going anywhere else.

Kron was a little different. Tommy played his high school ball in Tell

City, Indiana, where he made all-state. His family moved to Owensboro right after his senior year in high school, and Harry signed him up.

A year later Indiana all-stater Louie Dampier got a lot of attention. "My scouts told me about this little shit guard up in Indiana who could shoot the ball," said Rupp. "And I said, okay, fellas, let's go take a look. So I go up and we're watching the game, and in the first half he leads the fast break down the floor twelve times. Each time he pops from the top of the key and he hits ten of them, and I turned to my scouts and said, 'By God, that's good enough for me. Sign him up. I'm going home.'" The scout in the story was Harry.

After an outstanding year on the freshman team, Louie was about to start his UK varsity career, and friends and family—twenty in all—were making the two-hundred-mile trek down the interstate from Indianapolis to watch it happen. As a newly minted varsity player, he was entitled to only four free tickets, so Harry and Adolph had to make up the difference. When the game got under way, Adolph was still grousing. "Harry, goddamn it, that little shit, getting his whole family to show up like that. We don't have time to get those tickets. We're going to have to straighten his little ass out." The words were no sooner out of his mouth than Louie pulled up for one of his signature jump shots from twenty-five feet. Swish. Nothing but net. Harry said, "Coach, if he keeps that up, I'll find the tickets."

Pat Riley was something of a self-recruit. He was watching television with his parents that night back in 1958 when Adolph Rupp led his Wildcats to their fourth national championship. Pat was only thirteen at the time, but from that day on he dreamed of one day playing basketball for Kentucky. After Riley earned All-American honors in both football and basketball at Schenectady's Linton High School, Rupp began to share that dream. Pat was widely recruited by others, including former Kentucky football coach Bear Bryant, who wanted him to quarterback his Crimson Tide at the University of Alabama. But Riley, true to his dream, signed with Adolph Rupp, who, just to make sure, flew to Schenectady to watch it happen.

Harry's recruitment of Thad Jaracz came with a twist. Thad had been playing right under Rupp's nose at Lexington's Lafayette High School, but, in the end, it was a case of the Mountain coming to Muhammad. As a team Lafayette wasn't very impressive Thad's senior year, but the district tournament was in Memorial Coliseum, and Rupp was in the stands. Thad had a couple of his best games, and Adolph was impressed. The rest was inevitable. "I had gone to University of Kentucky games since I was seven," said Thad, whose parents had season tickets. There were offers from all the SEC schools, including Auburn, which wanted him for baseball and basketball, but "if you got a chance to play for the University of Kentucky, you were going to play there. That was just the way it was."

When a player wasn't from Kentucky or wasn't succumbing to Harry's blandishments, Adolph could be a good closer. In his book Harry described Rupp's approach. After ticking off his twenty-seven SEC Championships and his four NCAA titles, Coach Rupp would say, "If you come to Kentucky you're going to play for the best basketball team in the country." Usually, it worked.

Once a player arrived on campus, his primary preseason interaction was with Harry. According to NCAA rules, there couldn't be any supervised practice before October 15. Before that players worked on their shooting and played in pickup games, half court, full court, going at it. During those unofficial practices, you could always find Harry in a little room at the top of Memorial Coliseum. He would sit there with the door open just a crack and watch by the hour. They were "unsupervised practices," but later he would have his one-on-one input with players, most of whom he had personally recruited. *Here's what I'm seeing. Here's what you need to be working on.*

There were two major changes in the practice routine that fall, and both were because of assistant coach Joe B. Hall, both examples of Rupp's open style of leadership. From the first day of classes until the official beginning of practice on October 15, Hall had the team doing conditioning drills: isometric weight training and running wind sprints over and over and over again. Both were revolutionary for the time. Everyone *knew* that weights would mess with a basketball player's touch, but Hall, who'd spent summers swinging a scythe, bailing hay, and shoveling manure on his uncle's farm, knew conventional wisdom was wrong. Because he always started the season in far better shape and with better touch than his teammates, who spent their summers bagging grocer-ies or ushering at the local movie house, he instituted rigorous training regimens with teams he coached. Said Hall, "If I coached table tennis, the players would be running and lifting."

Convincing Adolph turned out to be easier than expected. Nearly five decades later Hall recalled the conversation vividly. "I said, 'You won't have pulled muscles; you won't have burning feet. And players will be willing to go full out the first day. [Coach Rupp] said, 'Well, if it does that, I'm all for it.' So that's what we did."

Two players at a time would line up on the track and run 220-yard dashes. On the first day Hall had them running four 220s, adding one a day until they were doing ten without wilting. It was run, walk back, run again. You could take time out to vomit, something Larry Conley did seven days in a row, according to Hall. "I left my green beans on the turn," Larry remembers. "And then I started learning to eat my lunch earlier and not eat as much because I knew I would throw it up." After that first week, if you took more than thirty-two seconds (world-class sprinters run it in twenty), you ran it again.

For Thad Jaracz, whom Hall described as a "big, old, fat doughboy," it was an almost impossible task in the beginning. The others could do it but were not happy. "They threw up, they complained, they threat-ened to quit," said Hall. "So Coach called me in, and he said: 'Joe, the boys say you're killing them.' And I said, 'You come out and observe.'"

The next day Coaches Hall and Rupp sat in the judge's stand near the finish line and watched as the players ran their heats. As Hall recalls, after about the fourth 220, Riley came back in front of them and col-lapsed. "He's lying there face-down in the dirt, quivering. Coach Rupp turned to me, his eyes popping out—this is his All-American—and he said, 'Joe, what are you going to do?' And I said, 'I'm going to give him an Academy Award, kick him in the ass, and put him back over there in the [starting] blocks.' I said, 'Riley, get your butt up and get back across that field and get ready to run.' He was staggering a bit when he got up, but he ran the rest of the heats."

Coach Hall tells the story of a time when Pat Riley was excused from running to take an accounting test. "The next day Louie comes up and said, 'I've got an accounting test.'" Dampier wasn't taking accounting, and Hall told him he was acting like a prima donna. Louie said, "Are you calling me a prima donna?" Coach Hall: "If you're not one, you're giving a great imitation of one." It would not be the last Hall-Dampier confrontation.

Kentucky had never had a conditioning program before, and it really made a difference. Knowing they would have those 220s to run with isometric weight training on alternate days, players got to bed earlier and, to a large extent, lost their interest in beer. After the second week there was no more upchucking, and everybody was breaking the thirty-two-second barrier. Because of all those days of running, the team started official practice in the best shape ever.

The other Hall innovation that fall was defense. Both Adolph and Harry Lancaster were offensive coaches who seemed to think of defense as what you did until you got the ball back. "[Coach Rupp's] answer to defense was, 'Guard somebody,'" said Hall. "If your man scored, he'd let you know that you broke down." Hall, who had coached at a pair of no-name colleges (Regis and Central Missouri State), persuaded Rupp to take time out of the practice routine he'd developed over thirty-six years at Kentucky to let Hall conduct training on the finer points of defense. His approach was a combination of show-and-tell.

To demonstrate how to guard a man in the low post close to the basket, Hall put Cliff Berger with his back to the basket. "Down low, you play him high on the ball side," said Hall, taking the defensive position himself. "You read where he is in relation to the ball and the basket and take away his passing lane [from the man with the ball]." Jaracz and then Berger did a walk-through, changing off again as Hall demonstrated defending the high post. "If he's above that line you play him low side, and he doesn't have a lane to the basket. And then you want to constantly change your position. Either go back side-to-side or roll over the top side-to-side."

For basketball players who had always defended more or less instinctively, practicing defense had always been drudgery. "I hated it," said Conley. "Oh, God, just awful. Nobody wants to play defense. Especially practice defense." But Coach Hall was bringing a new subtlety to the art, and the players found his tutorial riveting.

One by one players walked through defensive stances while Hall explained in detail what was happening and how small changes could result in better outcomes: Anticipating the movements of the dribbler by watching his midsection because *he can't go anywhere without it*. Filling the passing lanes. Coordinated rotation to help a teammate when his man beat him on the perimeter. It was big-*D* defense, and it showed. All of it was precisely what Haskins was teaching his charges in El Paso, not really surprising since both coaches had learned their defensive approach from the master of the art, Hank Iba.

When the Runts had the ball in the half court, the outside shooting of Dampier and Riley combined with the passing of Kron and Conley gave Kentucky the advantage, but it was the "law of easy baskets" that made the Wildcats dominant. Game after game the Runts ran opponents into the ground with a combination of defense, rebounding, precision passing, and raw stamina. Those preseason wind sprints paid off for everyone; for Jaracz, they were transformative. "It helped me immensely," said Thad. "I came out of high school thinking I was in shape. A lot of guys that I played against in the SEC—the big centers—they were good, but they weren't as athletic as centers and forwards have now become. Early in the contest they'd be with you. And then, by the time you got to the second half, they wouldn't be with you anymore." As a Vanderbilt assistant coach would tell *The Sporting News*, "Man he looks like a big freight train coming down the floor on a fast break."

Free from the necessity of devoting precious practice time to conditioning, Coach Rupp calculated exactly how much time he wanted to devote to each activity. Like the guy in the movie musical *Pajama Game*, it was an article of faith: "For a time-study man, to waste time is a crime."

There were no crimes during Adolph Rupp scrimmages, but occasionally Slim, in the role of referee, was charged with a misdemeanor. One day the Whites were busting their butts on defense and racking up three times the number of fouls as the Blues. In Rupp's view, since he'd selected his best five players for the White Team, they should always win. Adolph called a halt and walked across to look at the stat sheet. There in black and white was confirmation: the Whites had fifteen fouls, the Blues only four. "Goddamn it, Slim, you're cheating for the Blue Team."

Cheating for the Blues? Rationally, he had to know that was something that would never happen. But when things weren't going just the way he'd planned, Adolph and rationality had a strained—make that estranged— relationship. Slim had gone over to the enemy. For the rest of that practice a player on the White Team would have had to bludgeon a Blue for him to blow his whistle. After that he kept the foul count in his head, especially when the Whites were having a bad day.

While Slim plied his referee's whistle during Blue-White scrimmages, other student managers stood by on each sideline with spare basketballs. When a ball went out-of-bounds, they put a new one in play and the scrimmage continued, saving perhaps fifteen seconds. If that happened eight times in twenty minutes, two precious minutes had been saved.

Once when the freshman team was scrimmaging the varsity, one of the freshmen became the object of Rupp's special ire. Coming up court he stopped to tie his shoe before dribbling into the front court. Adolph was fuming. When the other shoe needed tying on the next possession, Rupp exploded. "Harry, by God, I think we need a shoe-tying lesson before the next practice."

At game time Harry's input came in many ways, most of which were unnoticed by Kentucky fans. During a time-out, while Rupp was berating his charges for some failure of execution, Harry would remind Dampier to force his man to go left or take Kron aside and say, "I think if we run Seven and Go Backdoor, we're going to be okay." Coming out of the break they would run Seven and Go Backdoor—instead of setting the pick the defense is expecting, Kron would roll to the basket for a lay-up—and people would say, "God, Adolph is a great coach." They were right about that. Not only was he a great coach in his own right, but as a leader he was smart enough to know what Harry added to the mix.

Harry had a brilliant basketball mind and was an excellent tactician of the game. "He had a great recognition of problems that occurred on the court and how to correct them," said Conley. "He was excellent at being able to break things down. When we had these one-minute time-outs, when we were trying to get something adjusted, we would listen to Couch Rupp cuss for thirty seconds. Then the final thirty seconds Harry would make the changes and tell us exactly what we needed to do."

Harry was also a strong taskmaster who took on a leadership role when it came to discipline. "He was a guy who would get on you if things weren't exactly the way they should be," said Thad. "He would get in your face and get mad. [He'd] berate you and talk about your performance. Mean and cutting about it. Not a bit ashamed to do that sort of thing." He was as verbally abusive as Rupp, but there was a difference. "I don't think Coach Rupp ever made it personal," said Conley. "I always had the sense he was trying to make you better. Harry made it personal."

Although Harry was often bombastic, he could also be low-key and motivational. Several seasons before, after Coach Rupp gave his standard-brand pregame talk, he said, "What you got, Harry?"

"Coach, we have what people are saying is the most talented sophomore in the Southeastern Conference," Harry said, with a look at forward Don Rolfes. "This is the start of SEC play, and I think it's time to show them that they're right." No bombast, just a straightforward statement. Up to then Rolfes, a six-foot-seven former high school All-American from Harrison, Ohio, had played pretty well in some games, not so well in others. But that night he went off, scoring nineteen points against Vanderbilt while dominating his man on defense. There's a pretty good chance that little exchange was prearranged, but often Harry's input came in pressure situations and made the difference between wins and losses.

Later that season the Wildcats were driving teams crazy with Rupp's patented one-three-one pressing zone. Once they were within thirty feet of the basket, they double-teamed the ball while the other three players positioned themselves in the passing lanes. With Tommy Kron hawking the ball with aggressiveness and the wingspan of a condor, every pass was made under duress, often leading to steals and fast-break lay-ups. Enter Mississippi State University. Before the game Coach Babe McCarthy came over and said, "It's going to be quite a game tonight, Adolph. We've got the answer to your one-three-one." McCarthy was always trying to get in Rupp's head, but on that night he was right.

The Wildcats started out with the one-three-one that Rupp, refusing to admit he ever played zone, called a "stratified transitional, hyperbolic, parabolic man-to-man." The one-three-one worked its magic when the other team tried to penetrate. Mississippi State didn't. Instead, they countered with four guys nicknamed "Stretch." There wasn't an athlete among them, but they were tall as Mississippi's iconic loblolly pines, and they enjoyed playing catch with one another. Every time State came into the front court, these goons would station themselves at the four corners—two along the baseline and two about twenty feet out—and lob the ball back and forth for minutes at a time (there was no shot clock in those days). Meanwhile, this one little guard, who could flat-out shoot the basketball, darted in and out like a peripatetic hummingbird until he worked himself open for a jumper. It wasn't much of a game unless you were into keep-away, which Babe McCarthy obviously was. At halftime the score was twelve to eight. Kentucky was the eight.

Rupp went crazy. While his players stared at the locker-room floor, the coach paced the floor in a rant that made previous eruptions seem like goody-goody Sunday-school lessons. Adolph stomped around like a penned-up bull that can see the cows he wants to get at just over the fence and out of reach. Finally, in exasperation, he stopped in midsentence. "Harry, what you got?"

"Well, Coach, our one-three-one just isn't working," said Harry, stating the obvious. "I think we should go get them with the man-to-man."

"You do?!" said Rupp, managing both a question and exclamation mark with one inflection. "All right, by God, that's what we'll do. Go get 'em, fellas."

If the first half was keep-away, the second was run-and-gun Kentucky basketball; from a septuagenarian's shuffle they moved to warp speed, blowing Mississippi State out of the gym.

While Harry appeared to play a mostly passive role during games, the intensity he shared with Adolph sometimes boiled over. With benches in the end zone under the basket, the referee was about five feet away when teams were lining up for foul shots. If the call went against Kentucky, Harry would say things like, "You goddamn stupid sonofabitch, couldn't you see that guy fouled Riley? Why the fuck don't you call the game?" Today's refs would T him up in a heartbeat and probably send him packing. Back then the ref would say, "Go fuck yourself, Harry. Sit down and shut up."

Adolph would often rage over an errant call, but his face-to-face approach to the zebras was usually more subdued. Larry Conley's dad, George, told the story of a time he was refereeing a Kentucky game when Larry was a teenager. There was a lot of physical contact that erupted into a hockey-style fistfight. Both benches cleared, and before the refs could stop it one Kentucky player got coldcocked and was lying there on the floor. The referees had a job of sorting things out and calming the ruckus. Conley looked up to see Rupp standing over him. "Ge-oorge," said Adolph, in his Kansas twang, "what is going on?" "Well, Coach, he's out of the game," he said, pointing at the guy who threw the punch. "And he's out of the game [another player involved in the scuffle]." George paused, looking around, and pointed at the Kentucky player out cold on the floor. "And he's out of the game." "Ge-oorge," said Adolph, "he's not only out. He may be dead, by God."

10

Never Gave It a Thought

Looking back, a lot of attention is paid to the racial makeup of the 1965–66 Texas Western Miners. There were seven African Americans who played in the championship game, four Caucasians and one Hispanic who didn't. Long before that game all of them had suffered the slings and arrows of Haskins's grueling practices *together*. That helped create a bond, but in the beginning the Miners were like Rupp's Runts, individuals with their own backgrounds, egos, and expectations to overcome. And at Texas Western, there was the added factor of race.

Looking back, all the players say what Jerry Armstrong says when friends ask how he got along with *the blacks*. "Well, I never gave it a thought, you know. They were my teammates. They were great people." But while there was no apparent race-based friction, in the beginning there was racial separation. Away from the basketball court, blacks hung out with blacks, whites with whites. For black players used to de facto segregation and white players with no previous interracial experience, blending together was a gradual process that seems to have started with six-foot-two Togo Railey.

It was a typical hot and humid evening in early fall of 1962 when Albert T. "Togo" Railey, a Caucasian, an El Paso native, and the only one on the freshman team who had a car, came by the dorm to show a couple of his white teammates a night on the town. Jerry Armstrong and Lou Baudoin were in the lounge watching television along with two black players. "You guys want to come along with us?" Togo asked. Orsten Artis and Harry Flournoy, newly arrived from Gary, Indiana, shrugged. *Why not?*

With Togo as guide the five teammates checked out the scenery at Loretto Academy, an all-girl Roman Catholic school on the other side of town, then took in a movie at the State Theater, sneaking in after the ticket office closed, reaching across the counter to scoop up bags of popcorn on the way. It was an evening of discovery. Both Orsten and Harry had attended all-black high schools and never socialized with whites. Jerry and Lou had attended all-white schools and never socialized with blacks. To their amazement it turned out black and white college freshmen were surprisingly compatible. For Togo, race had never been an issue. "You're just a person down here," he says. "If you can't get along with anybody in El Paso, you can't get along with anybody."

Over the next few weeks the freshmen five made other visits to the State and to the rundown Crawford Theater, which featured westerns starring singing cowboys Gene Autry and Roy Rogers. There was no sneaking in at the Crawford (admission fifty cents), your feet stuck to the floor, and you had to sit on the back of the seat with your feet on the cushion if you didn't want the rats to bite, but they were hanging out, enjoying each other's company. They discovered their one area of incompatibility at Pancho's, where a dollar bought a cheap and tasty Mexican buffet, emphasis on the cheap. Harry and Orsten turned up their noses at Togo's favorites, tacos and enchiladas, but the restaurant also featured chicken livers and gizzards, which suited them just fine.

When the season got under way, the freshman team made the two-hundred-mile trip to Roswell, New Mexico, to play the New Mexico Military Institute. After the game Flip, Togo, Jerry, Harry, and a white teammate from Mississippi named Jay Christopher stopped in at the nearest restaurant for a hamburger. "We don't serve Negroes here," said the waiter. When Harry got up to leave, so did the others, except Christopher. "Why can't we eat and bring him something back?" he asked. "What would be the harm in that?"

"You can stay and eat by your damn self," said Lou, a New Mexico native who was obviously embarrassed by the incident. At another restaurant down the street, Lou asked the question: "Can all my friends eat here?"

"That's what cemented it for me," said Harry, who has bitter memories of a teacher's reaction when he complained about being spit on by a white student on his first day as a second grader. *It's your parents' fault,* she said. *Emerson is supposed to be an all-white school.* "He didn't say 'teammates'; he said 'friends,'" Harry recalls. "So that kind of bonded me with them."

Now, increasingly, Haskins's team was together in the gym, together in the classroom (whenever they could arrange to be in the same sections of their classes), together playing cards and attending movies. Whether it was a matter of school policy or not, the one place they were not together was in campus housing. Until the championship season all black basketball players were assigned to basement rooms in the newly constructed Burgess Hall, where they could come and go without attracting the attention of the dorm counselor, a nosy old biddy who prowled the upper floors at closing time. There was a door at the opposite end of the basement, and if that was locked, ground-level windows made it easy to slip into the rooms unobserved.

The year before, when all of the roundballers were still in Miners' Hall, the athletic dorm, Harry was a case study in Freshman-Freedom Syndrome. Without Amy Flournoy to monitor his comings and goings, basketball practice was his only mooring. Night after night he was out on the town, sometimes with teammates, often with a football-player friend who was enjoying his own first taste of freedom from parental control. There were movies and clubs in El Paso, more clubs across the Rio Grande in Juárez. Classes were mandatory; studying was not, until the end of the first grading period.

"You've got yourself a problem," said Haskins, when Harry sat down in his office. The coach often used half sentences, moving on to the next thought without finishing the last, leaving listeners to search for meaning. Not this time. "I look at your high school transcript, and I look at this," he said, emphasizing each word as if he were giving dictation to a slow-witted secretary. He held up a paper with Harry's grades printed on it, shaking his head in disgust. "Are you really this lazy?" Harry swallowed hard. "You do know about classes, right? It's pretty simple, really. If you don't pass, you don't play. Got it?"

The next day Harry was called into Haskins's office again. This time as he walked through the door, he froze. There, seated across the desk from the coach, was Harry's mom. True to his word, Haskins had called to inform her of Harry's academic deficiency. True to her nature, Amy Flournoy dropped everything and made her way to Chicago's O'Hare Airport, where she boarded a plane for the 1,500-mile flight through Dallas and on to El Paso. She was not happy.

Oh, my God! Suddenly, Harry couldn't bend his knees. His mother was sitting there staring at him with that disappointed look of hers. The look alone was enough to make him feel like he was being split in half by a Samurai sword. There was more. Unlike the actress who portrayed her in the movie *Glory Road*, Amy Flournoy was a slim woman, but she was no less foreboding.

Coach Haskins didn't say a word as she flailed her son up one side and down the other. "Harry Flournoy Jr., you should be ashamed of yourself. We didn't send you fifteen hundred miles to come here and goof off." She didn't raise her voice, but it had the same steely quality that used to warn him a spanking was coming. Now, instead of his father's brown belt, her weapon was words. "You're the first one in the family to graduate from high school. You've got a chance to be the first one graduated from college. And now you're going to flunk out? Now you're going to prove those folks who say we're only fit for menial work that they're right?"

Still standing, Harry had long since abandoned eye contact for a close examination of his feet.

"You could have stayed home and saved the coach his trouble, stayed home and saved me spending money we don't have coming down here because you're not doing what's right." Her eyes were tearing up. "I'm disappointed, Junior. I'm very disappointed."

For the next week when Harry was done with practice, he reported to his mother's motel room for long evenings of study. Together they went through every class he'd had that day. It was like a Haskins defensive drill. Again and again, they went over and over the same material until she was satisfied and moved on.

In *Glory Road* she accompanied him to classes, raising her hand every time a professor asked a question, saying, "My son knows the answer." That was Hollywood being Hollywood. What really happened kept him in line long after she'd returned to Gary. Now during practices where humor had been in short supply, Harry was the butt of a never-ending joke. On the scorer's table at courtside was a phone that bore a neatly lettered sign: *Harry's Mom.*

In a way the sign was part of the bonding process. It was also a reminder that, yes, the classroom and basketball were inextricably connected. Academics were never a problem for Bobby Joe Hill when he arrived from junior college the year before the championship season. Teammates remember his photographic memory and an IQ through the roof. His ability to acclimate to Don Haskins's defensive system was a different matter. Ironically, the very thing he is most remembered for in the Kentucky game is what kept him out of the starting lineup in early games the previous season. When it came to defense, Bobby Joe loved to freelance.

Even with his excess summer poundage, B.J. could leave his man, snatch the ball, and make a lay-up at the other end of the floor before the unwary ball handler knew his pocket was picked. His steals never failed to bring the crowd to its feet. Sometimes, even then, Haskins would yank him out of a game. "Damn it, Hill, you left your man again," he would say in frustration. "We're playing team defense, here. Showboating left your man wide open."

Harnessing his explosive speed and quickness created what teammates describe as a love-hate relationship between Haskins and his point guard. "He could try the patience of Job," one of them said. "Coach, he loved him, and Bobby Joe was too bright not to get it." And once he did, his leadership became the team's biggest asset. "He was the steering wheel to our Mack truck," said Nevil Shed. "With him, we win. Without him, we probably wouldn't have."

Teammates remember an upbeat personality and a favorite saying of the transplanted northerner: "The sun will always rise in El Paso." Bobby Joe also had the reputation as the kind of guy you wouldn't want to mess with. "He was like my protector," said Jerry Armstrong, a six-foot-four white teammate who, like a number of players on the championship team, felt a special relationship with the little guard. "He said, 'If you've got any problems, I'll take care of them." On the basketball court he was the kind of player who would lead by taking a charge, but, said Armstrong, "if things weren't going right, he would get in your face in a heartbeat."

In the dorm room he shared with David Lattin, things weren't going right when it came to music. Bobby Joe brought his love of Motown—Marvin Gaye, Smokey Robinson, the Temptations—with him from the Motor City. David loved jazz, everything from Miles Davis to Ella Fitzgerald. Teammates tell the story of the day Lattin came into the room while Bobby Joe was playing something by the Supremes on the record player. When Lattin went to replace it with one of his jazz records, five-foot-ten Bobby Joe grabbed his six-foot-six roommate and threw him over his shoulder onto the floor. Never happened, says Lattin. "We didn't fuss about it. He was listening to rock, and I was listening to jazz. . . . We had to part ways as roommates."

While most Texas Western students preferred Bobby Joe's Motown, rock, or country, Lattin marched to a different drummer, hosting a jazz program on the campus radio station every night when the team wasn't practicing or playing. *This is the Big Daddy D Jazz Session on KVO FM, 88.5 megacycles on your FM radio dial*, he crooned, leaning into the microphone with his dulcet, honey-coated baritone. For the next hour, keeping his patter to a minimum with a tinkling piano in the background, Lattin served up a jazz lover's confection featuring Miles, Ella, Duke Ellington, Count Basie, and Dave Brubeck. "People caught on to his charisma," said Shed, a New Yorker who dug the sounds.

Nevil Shed was a couple of inches taller than Lattin, but, from the start, Big Daddy D was clearly the Big Man on Campus. Part of that was charisma, part presentation. Lattin tooled around the campus in a bright-red late-model Buick Riviera (a gift from a Houston girlfriend), sported a Fu Manchu mustache, and on road trips, when teammates wore gray slacks, blue blazers with a little TW emblem on the pocket, and school-color orange-and-navy-striped ties, David always showed up in sharkskin suits (a lightweight, wrinkle-free worsted with a muted two-tone look) and Italian-cut alligator loafers. "Some people know how to dress," he would say five decades later. "Back then it was a big deal."

Over time, despite their conflicting musical tastes, Bobby Joe and David became friends, bonding over endless games of hearts and Haskins's grueling practices. "Practice, eat, study together," said Lattin. "When you start winning, that makes it even better. I don't think anybody could be at odds with Bobby Joe Hill."

11

Intensity, Thy Name Is Adolph

Although Sir Laurence Olivier is widely regarded as the finest actor of the twentieth century—playing parts ranging from Romeo to Hamlet to King Lear over a fifty-year career—he always threw up before going onstage. While Coach Rupp never threw up, his game-day nerves were fueled by an obsession with winning that bordered on psychosis. To Rupp the old maxim—"It's not whether you win or lose but how you play the game"—wasn't just wrong; it was abhorrent. His response— "I'll believe that when they take down the scoreboard"—was more than Rupp wit; it was his credo. And because winning was his obsession, his entire coaching life—from his first game as Kentucky coach in 1930 (a 67–19 win over Georgetown College) to his last some forty-two years later (a 54–73 loss to Florida State)—was dedicated to one single cause, winning basketball games.

To stay in Rupp's good graces, players had to demonstrate a level of dedication that stretched well beyond basketball to . . . girlfriends. In Rupp's world girlfriends were a capital *D* distraction. Tommy Kron understood. When he and Dianne Berger went looking for an engagement ring toward the end of the Rupp's Runts season, Tommy arranged with Fuller's Jewelry Store in downtown Lexington to visit under cover of darkness. "We knew we could not go shopping for a ring in the daytime," says Dianne Kron, looking back. "It was just not acceptable, period. Your interest was in playing basketball and being a student. It was not in planning for your future and going to look for an engagement ring."

In the year before the Rupp's Runts season, Dianne and two sorority sisters, who were also dating basketball players, always arrived for home games two hours early so they could grab front-row seats. Pam Smith was there for John Adams, Marty Hibner for Louie Dampier, Dianne for Tommy. Adolph had to see them when he came out to watch the junior varsity game in the nearly empty coliseum, but his focus was on the freshman players who represented the future of Kentucky basketball, not on three studious coeds who spent most of each JV game doing homework. While the Alpha Delta Pi girls flew under Rupp's radar in Memorial Coliseum, they were totally conspicuous at Blue Grass Field when the team came home from road games.

When Kentucky won happiness reigned, and Rupp was too busy basking in the glow of adoring fans to trouble himself with ancillary concerns. When the Wildcats lost, a too frequent occurrence in the 1964–65 season, Rupp would often decree: *No Girlfriends at the Airport*. So, when the team was on the road, *the Girlfriends* gathered around the radio at the AD Pi House, listening to Cawood Ledford's play-by-play, cheering every Kentucky basket, suffering every miss, and wondering whether Rupp's decree would come tonight. If it was a bad loss, says Dianne, "You just knew from the get-go you should stay out of the way."

With only one regular-season loss in the Rupp's Runts season, the *No Girlfriends* rule was never invoked, but everything else about Rupp's approach to winning basketball was firmly in place. Over his coaching career Rupp settled into a game-day routine that was almost ritualistic. The team met for a lunch of T-bone steak, baked potato, peas, and a salad at noon. Adolph and Harry would arrive with scowls on their faces. This is serious business, certainly not a time for conversation. "If you acted like you were enjoying the food, if you had any kind of a smile on your face, they didn't like that," Thad recalled. "You weren't serious. You weren't ready to play."

There was a complete lack of conversation that always seemed profoundly odd. Here were fifteen guys and two coaches sitting around a table eating a delicious meal in total silence. Minds were supposed to be on the game, but most were concentrated on speed eating. Rupp had this saying: *The fastest eaters are the best players*. "So I'd make sure I finished my food before anybody else," said Bob Tallent. "I'd rattle my silverware on the plate so he would know that I was finished."

Then it was back to the rooms for rest and concentration on the task ahead. Some studied, but that was not recommended. Rupp had his priorities and thought his players should share them. "Damn it, Red, what did you come down here for, son, to play ball or to go to school?" Rupp asked Bob Tallent one day. "Well, Coach, I thought a little bit of both," Bobby responded. Rupp shook his head. "Wrong! You came down here to play basketball."

The team came back together again at five o'clock for a pregame meal of a small piece of steak, well done to the brink of burned, and tea. The steak was served with two pieces of toast so dry they might have been imported from the Sahara Desert, and honey. Because there was nothing to be passed, a Benedictine silence was in effect with one exception. Invariably, Thad would whisper under his breath, "Are you going to eat yours?" Tallent, whose stomach "would go crazy before games," never did, so Thad doubled up. "Thad could outeat anybody," Tallent recalled. "He'd eat mine and his. It never bothered him."

One of Slim's duties as a student manager helped him understand that Rupp's intensity extended well beyond basketball. After the lunch meal it was his job to pick up all the steak bones for Taffy, the Rupp family's cocker spaniel. Taffy, it seems, needed a little motivation, too. "Harry," said Adolph one day, "Taffy has been acting up and giving me some grief lately, so I'm not going to give him these bones until he shapes up." Motivation for the family dog? Of course.

Somewhere along in the pregame process, Slim would wander out into the nearly empty coliseum and look around. "Alonzo? Where are you?" Suddenly, a twelve-year-old with scraggly brown hair, faded blue jeans, and a ratty old sweater would materialize from out of nowhere like the Phantom of the Opera. Alonzo was ubiquitous. Nobody seemed to remember when he started showing up; he was just *there*, always smiling, always ready to run an errand. At practices he would go for towels, water, or a mop, whatever. He was so much a part of coliseum life that the student newspaper did a little feature about this kid who lived on the street behind Memorial Coliseum and just loved Kentucky basketball. The story didn't include what its writer didn't know.

Every player on the team got four tickets to each home game (student managers got two). On game day they'd walk over to the ticket office and pick up their tickets. On the day of the Vanderbilt game, one of the scalpers who was always hanging around said, "Hey, Bob, I'll give you two hundred dollars for those four." Tallent was tempted until he phoned his father. "Don't even think about it," he said. "You leave them in my name."

Pat Riley's parents lived in faraway Schenectady and never made the cross-country trip for Kentucky home games. Pat sold his season tickets to a local businessman, but every game there would be ten or twelve tickets to pass along to Alonzo. Because he knew ways in and out of the coliseum known only to God, he'd be out and back within ten minutes with a wad of money from the scalpers, as much as one hundred dollars per ticket. Memorial Coliseum was sold out for each of ten home games that season, so Slim ended up pocketing close to two thousand dollars, a nice supplement to the fifty per month he got from Reserve Officers' Training Corps. For his role in the process Alonzo got twenty dollars per game.

It was strictly against NCAA rules, of course, but all across the country the rule was mostly honored in the breach. At the start of the season Coach Rupp had lectured all of his team and especially his student manager. "Slim, I don't want you helping the boys sell their tickets." It was the only Rupp order he disobeyed. It was simply too much money to ignore. Besides, he trusted Alonzo. He was quick, knew his way around the coliseum, and was such a familiar sight that nobody would ever think to stop him or question what he was doing.

While the players were suiting up, Coach Rupp sat in the mostly empty coliseum watching the freshman game. At halftime, as the crowd started arriving for the varsity game, he returned to the locker room to escape the well-wishers who would otherwise interfere with his concentration. That created a logistical problem because he wanted to continue to follow the action. Every few minutes a manager would make the fifty-yard trip from courtside to the locker room up under the stands to update him on the score. When the crowd roared another manager double-timed another trip to tell him what happened. Then as the freshman game was winding down, Rupp gave his pregame talk.

Pregames were always fairly simple. There would be reminders of the offensive game plan, as if countless repetitions hadn't imprinted it on brains and muscle memory. Then there were specific defensive assignments. "Riley, remember your man is a lefty," or "Dampier, you need to be aggressive if Kron sets their point guard up for a trap."

In those days the team benches were behind the end lines, and because Adolph wanted the advantage of being able to call out plays near the end of a close game, the visiting team always took pregame warm-up right in front of him. Coach Rupp would sit there watching. Actually, the word *watching* is too passive to capture Rupp's intensity. He didn't just watch; he agonized.

"Oh, shit," he groaned as some sharpshooter bombed away from the corner. He clenched and unclenched his fists, rocking back with his feet coming off the floor when one of their forwards made a dunk. "Oh, my God! Did you see that, Slim?" What he'd seen was a freckle-faced kid smiling at what might have been his first dunk ever. "The guy's a fucking monster."

No matter how routine the opponent's warm-up or how dismal their record, Adolph always managed to work himself into a frenzy. By the time he got back to the locker room, he was convinced his team was in for a bloodbath.

"Fellas, these guys are fantastic," he'd say, shaking his head. "They're going to run us right out of the gym if you don't get back on defense." He looked around the locker room, wiping sweat from his forehead. "We've got to take care of the ball like never before or, by God, they'll kill us. I'll tell you, fellas, they've got the quickest hands I've ever seen." Then would come Rupp's little motivational message, that night's version of his "Fellas, I can't tell you how much this game means to the university and the city of Lexington."

Every game it was the same. By now he'd used it so many times, you'd think it couldn't possibly work. Yet somehow it did. This was the number-one coach in the country with a gazillion wins and four national championships to his credit. If he thought they were in trouble, they probably were.

While the players went through their final warm-ups, Adolph and Harry would stay back under the stands. From there he could look out at the crowd. Unless the opponent was the Little Sisters of the Poor or it was finals week, the twelve-thousand-seat coliseum would be filled to overflowing. One time when it wasn't, Rupp nearly blew a gasket. "Harry, goddamn it, I told you," he said, spotting four empty seats on the top row. "If you don't get those fucking students' asses in those seats, I'm taking them away and selling them to somebody."

Everything was carefully orchestrated. When the Wildcat pep band finished playing the fight song, Coach Rupp walked out onto the floor to a deafening roar. Everybody on their feet, watching as the Man in the Brown Suit made his grand entrance. The coliseum suddenly went black, except for a single spotlight on the American flag. While the band played the national anthem, the flag rippled in the breeze of an electric fan hidden behind the scoreboard. With the final note of the song, the game clock hit double zero, and the spotlight swept down from the flag to the bench for the introduction of the starting lineup. When the house-lights came on again, it was as if an invisible banner appeared with the words *Adolph is about to kick your ass*. Usually, that's exactly what happened. During one stretch Rupp coached his team to 129 consecutive home-court victories.

Although opposing coaches did everything they could to upset the Rupp Routine, most of them failed. The two who were most persistent were Babe McCarthy of Mississippi State and Whack Hyder of Georgia Tech. McCarthy would try to get in Rupp's head by announcing something like, "I hope you're ready for our full-court press, 'cause we're coming at you." Hyder's approach was more problematic. In Kentucky's final game with Tech, before it left the SEC to join the Atlantic Coast Conference, Hyder came walking across the floor. "We've got trouble," he said, looking as if the plague was about to sweep through the building. "We're not going to be able to play the game tonight." Coach Rupp looked like someone who just learned of the sudden death of a close friend. "The rule book says the backboards have to be clean," Hyder continued, shaking his head sadly. "These backboards are filthy." Before Rupp could work up a sputter, Slim came to the rescue. "It's okay, Coach. I'll take care of it." When the teams left the floor he got a ladder, a sponge, and a bucket of water and, to the mock applause of twelve thousand fans, washed and dried the backboards.

Sometimes Rupp's rational mind would desert him during games. One night, down the stretch of a too-close-for-comfort home game the year before the Rupp's Runts season, Kentucky had the lead, and the other team was trying everything possible to manage the clock. Intense and anxious, Adolph leaped to his feet. "Start the goddamn clock!" he screamed, pointing toward the timekeeper, a local banker and die-hard Kentucky fan. "You're giving the game away!" After the game, after the players had showered and left the building, the timekeeper came into the locker room. Rupp shook his hand cordially, probably expecting to be congratulated on a hard-fought victory. The timekeeper had a different message. "Other than you," he said, "nobody wants Kentucky to win more than me." Rupp nodded. "I appreciate that." "Please understand that when you're yelling and pointing at me, you have just precluded my helping you in any way."

While Rupp's routine usually ran smoothly enough at home, road games posed a special challenge. That players had to adjust to the other team's gym was a given, but what was less predictable was the surrounding environment. One downside of Rupp's winning ways was the fact that his teams always and forever had a target on their backs. For most teams Kentucky was the biggest game of the year. Their players were up, and so were their fans. Five decades later attendance in the SEC still increases by an average of 37 percent when the Wildcats come to town. That was especially true at Mississippi State.

It wasn't much of a surprise that there were no four-star motels in the town of Starkville, but even if there had been Hiltons, Marriotts, and Ritz-Carltons lined up side by side like Park Place and Boardwalk on a Monopoly board, there would have been no room in the inn for Kentucky basketballers. The motels themselves were welcoming enough, but so were the students. If the Wildcats stayed in Starkville, they were guaranteed a dusk-to-dawn serenade of horns, shouts, and cowbells as dedicated hecklers circled the block. As a result, Kentucky spent Friday nights before Saturday MSU games far from the madding crowd in undisclosed motels forty or fifty miles away.

There was no escaping the game-day crowd in the Rupp's Runts' season as Mississippi Staters did their best to upset Coach Rupp's equilibrium. Always when the team went back to the locker room for the pregame pep talk, Slim made sure the bench was cleared of water cups and towels and was shipshape when they came back to start the game. As he went about his task, he tried not to pay attention to catcalls from the behemoths occupying the front row of bleachers directly behind the bench. They were either the interior line of State's football team or sumo wrestlers or both. Their taunts and jibes were only words, but they looked like sticks-and-stones guys, not the sort to be challenged by a guy called Slim.

His mission accomplished, he went back under the stands to see if there was anything else Coach Rupp needed. That was usually the right thing to do. This time it wasn't. By the time the team came back out to start the game, the bench had undergone a transformation, as if unruly children had used it as a staging area for Mud Pie Mania. During the game, every time Rupp jumped up to challenge a call or berate a player, the sumos would shout and jeer and do whatever they could to disrupt him. He gave no indication he heard, and the Runts squeezed out a narrow 73–69 win. Were the sumos there by direct invitation of Babe McCarthy? Probably so.

When opposing coaches weren't successful in raising Rupp's anxiety, he would be obsessing about things like his film budget. "Slim, tell them if we get a comfortable lead to only film the first half." Five minutes before he might have been looking dark defeat squarely in the face. Now he was the pragmatic planner, the diligent guardian of things financial. No sooner had a manager been dispatched to report the decision to the cameraman at the top of the coliseum than the coach had second thoughts. "No, Slim, tell him to do it all but the last three minutes. Then, if we're twenty points up, he can stop."

Once the game started Rupp's intensity was most often on display when he came off the bench to protest a referee's call with a resounding "NO!" Because Wildcat basketball fans are among the most knowledgeable in the country, the ref's whistle served to mute the crowd. Twelve thousand voices hushed to learn whether they should cheer or jeer. And just when the crowd got quiet, Rupp's "Goddamn it!" reverberated through the coliseum. He couldn't have done it better with a loud speaker. When a player took a shot Rupp didn't want him to take, he came off the bench screaming, "No, goddamn it!" If the shot didn't go in, he'd continue to chew on the guy. "Jesus, Dampier, what the hell were you...," fading out as the teams reached the other end of the floor and he realized Dampier could no longer hear him.

Only the most ill-conceived shot or defensive blunder would convince Adolph to call a time-out in the first half. That's why one he called in a game against Georgia two years before Rupp's Runts was so memorable. The teams had been going up and down the floor for five or six minutes. Kentucky scored, Georgia scored, Kentucky scored again, with neither team gaining an advantage. The Wildcat defense looked solid, the offense a little less so. For one thing, Cotton Nash, UK's three-time All-American, had yet to touch the ball. Charles Francis Nash got his nickname from his white-blond hair, but it was his extraordinary skills that had sportswriters hitting the thesaurus in search of superlatives and Rupp dreaming of a fifth national championship. "You will seldom, if ever, see a boy so big with so much grace, so much agility," gushed Atlanta sportswriter Furman Bisher, who was even more impressed by "his soft and velvety touch."

Cotton Nash's Robert Redford looks and Jordanesque skills put him on the cover of *Sports Illustrated* and once, when a lapse from perfection cost Kentucky a home game it should have won, earned him a Rupp tongue-lashing. "You're not a goddamn All-American," Adolph shouted in a postgame critique. "All-Americans don't miss the front end of a one-and-one."

On this day the coach was focused on Nash's teammates. Five minutes into the game, Adolph suddenly leaped to his feet, making the T sign. "Time-out!" he shouted as Georgia lost the ball out-of-bounds right in front of him. Kentucky players, halfway up the floor, stopped in midstride and turned toward the bench with puzzled expressions. Usually, a first-half time-out brought with it a rush of invective against the player who'd upset the carefully ordered balance of Rupp's universe, but this time the coach stood by the bench, waiting.

"Gentlemen," he said, as his mystified team gathered around him, "I want to introduce you to someone who is here tonight." The players exchanged curious looks. *This is weird. He called time-out to make an introduction?* "This is Cotton Nash," he said, calmly. "GET HIM THE GODDAMN BALL!"

On campus in Lexington the eat-rest-eat pregame routine was totally predictable. The team always ate in the same room at the Student Center. Just one block and across the street from the coliseum, it was a perfect little walk to settle your meal with no reason to concern yourself with mundane logistical considerations.

On the road logistics were a constant irritant, especially for a coach whose patience meter spiked to hyper with even the slightest delay. That same season—Cotton Nash's senior year—Kentucky played in the basketball double-header that accompanied the Sugar Bowl in New Orleans. With two schools' worth of football fans—Alabama and Arkansas—on hand for the next day's game, hotels were slammed. Coach Rupp always left ample time for contingencies but was never in a mood for even a minute's delay waiting for buses or taxicabs, and certainly not for elevators. With the team around him on the top floor of the Royal Sonesta Hotel, he looked first at his watch, then at the light above the elevators indicating they were all either in the lobby or heading that way, leaving him and his basketball team stranded. "Jesus!" he sputtered. "What the hell's going on?" Rupp needed another means of exodus and needed it fast. Pacing back and forth, he spotted a service elevator. "I've got it boys," he said triumphantly, heading toward the lifesaving alternative halfway down the hall. "Follow me."

The walls of the elevator were padded, which might have come in handy if some hotel employee on a lower floor had the temerity to press a button halting the escape, but that didn't happen. Another thing that didn't happen was a stop at the lobby level. When the elevator reached the basement, Coach Rupp charged out into a grungy hallway that was completely devoid of signage. No direction arrows. No exit signs. Nothing. Rupp looked both ways, made his decision, and started off to his right, past storage closets and locker rooms. He stopped, turned around, and reversed course, past the elevator and down the hall in the opposite direction. His team followed in bemused silence as the most famous coach in America led them past a furnace room, more closets, and storage areas into the gleaming hotel kitchen. Stepping gingerly around bustling waiters and cooks, Rupp strolled purposefully through the heart of the kitchen until he came face-to-face with a massive man in a blood-spattered tunic who was whacking away at a side of beef with a meat cleaver. "Excuse me, sir," said Adolph, with the beginnings of a courtly bow. "How do we get out of here?" The cleaver stopped in midchop. "That way," said the man, using the blood-covered instrument as a pointer. Rupp nodded his thanks and led the way out of the kitchen and down the hall to the safety of the back alley behind the hotel.

If they were using a bus to get from hotel to game, Slim made sure it was there an hour ahead of time so there would be no delay. If they were using cabs, and there was even the slightest hiccup, he was sure to hear, "Manager, where's the goddamn cab? I need to get out of here." From experience Slim knew a failure to get Rupp in the first cab would lead to one of the most intense thirty seconds of his life. Once when Rupp got into the front seat of the first cab, the driver flipped the arm on the meter while a couple of the players were getting into the backseat. "Slim," said Rupp, "you better hurry the hell up. He's already charged us fifty cents."

12

The Haskins Way

"Turn him to the middle!" shouted Haskins in frustration as New Mexico State's fleet-footed guard—a sprinter on the track team—flashed down the left sideline, dribbling past a slipping, sliding Steve Tredennick. Moments later Steve was out of the game, replaced by his roommate, Bobby Dibler. Before Steve found his place on the bench, Haskins shouted, "Tredennick! Get in there for Dibler!" Usually when the Miners played New Mexico State, dust wasn't a factor. Tonight it was, and Coach Haskins was exasperated.

A year before the championship season the NMS game was played in the Las Cruces High School gymnasium, where gaps between floorboards rendered the custodian's attempts at mitigation useless. Before the game, at halftime, and in time-outs, the guy wielded a wide white mop, pushing piles of dust before him. *There we go, clean as a whistle.* Or not. By the time basketball players ran up and down the floor a couple of times, dust was swirling again, giving them the sure-footed traction of a puppy on polished linoleum. As dust continued to swirl, Haskins got more and more exasperated. The Miners were winning handily, but Fleet-Foot kept sprinting by them on the sideline no matter who was guarding him, first Steve, then Bobby, then Steve again. In and out they went.

Haskins stood in front of the bench, a rolled-up program in his hand, his face getting redder by the moment, shouting at whichever point guard was in the game at the moment. Beyond an occasional *hell* and *damn*, his working vocabulary included few expletives stronger than *knucklehead*. But when he berated a player, his intensity was epic. Defense, as he taught it, was nothing more than making your man do what you wanted him to do and go where you wanted him to go. Tonight, rotating guards weren't making that happen.

As Fleet-Foot shot past a slipping, sliding Bobby Dibler, Haskins turned away in disgust. *Damn dust!* The effort was there, if not the execution. What he could never accept, as the team learned from the start of practice his first season, was a player who failed to give the kind of full-out effort he demanded.

Effort was never an issue with his alternating guards, but both were in constant danger of running afoul of another Haskins bugaboo, girl-friends. Married players? No problem. Girlfriends? Distraction. And because Bobby and Steve were both dating girls they would one day marry, the girls waited in the shadows after home games until Haskins left the building. It was another of *Mr. Iba's* rules and one that Haskins, the player, honored in the breach. Mary Haskins tells the story of the game-day afternoon at Oklahoma A&M before she and Don were married. They were spotted coming out of a movie theater by a preteen Moe Iba. "Haskins," shouted Moe as he rode by on his bicycle, "I'm going to tell my daddy I saw you with a girl!"

A dozen years later, Moe, who inherited *Daddy's* basketball genes, became Haskins's first assistant. Their personalities were different—Moe was the softer side of Haskins's brusque—but because both had been forged on the solid steel of Hank Iba's basketball anvil, theirs was an almost preternatural connection. A handsome young man with dark hair and horn-rim glasses, Moe had the look of a GQ professor more likely to be found discussing Kant's categorical imperative in an oak-paneled faculty forum than the intricacies of the motion offense in a sweaty gymnasium. Behind his back the players called him "Squeaky" because his normal speaking voice soared to a higher octave when he was excited, but everyone respected his basketball smarts if not always his passion for detail. Once, when he was in the middle of an animated pregame *X*s-and-*O*s chalk talk based on his most recent scouting trip, Haskins interrupted. "Oh, hell, Moe, we don't care what *they* do. Let's just go out there and play *our* game."

During practices Moe spent most of his time as a silent observer of the Haskins techniques both had learned from Moe's father. When Haskins blistered a player for some lapse in energy or execution, Moe became the soother, bridging the gap between angry coach and frustrated player. As father-confessor, junior grade, he'd explain it was only when the old man stops taking the time to get on your case that you need to be concerned.

When the whole team seemed especially lethargic in practice, Haskins would sometimes stop things abruptly with a command: *Run the lines* or *To the bleachers*. "And we sometimes ran for a solid thirty minutes," said Jerry Armstrong, one of four white players on the championship team. "Up and down, up and down. Somehow he knew when to push the button. I know I couldn't make spit, and my legs were just about gone when we stopped." Haskins would say, "Moe, call the cafeteria and tell them to hold dinner, 'cause we're going to be late."

One day when he got really mad he put his team in a zone. A zone? Everybody on the team knew how much their coach loathed a zone defense and had come to share his feeling. To them the zone was a slap in the face. A few days later, when effort wasn't there, Haskins had a different approach. "Y'all aren't really ready to play," he said. "Just go on home." They didn't. Instead, they turned up the energy, intent on proving him wrong.

At the beginning of practice his first year at Texas Western, five years before the championship season, Haskins's focus was on one player: Ted Sterrett. "Damn it, Sterrett, you've got to move your feet," he said, as shorter, quicker Nolan Richardson rolled around six-foot-eleven Ted Sterrett for an easy lay-up. Sterrett was the only authentic big man he'd inherited from his predecessor, and Haskins decided the key to success was to turn him into a player. It wasn't working. In a game demanding quick reactions, the big center seemed contemplative. In a game where big men block shots, he had all the vertical leap of Michelangelo's marble *David*.

In the first week of practice Ted Sterrett went from project to whipping boy, with teammates wondering how long he could take the abuse Haskins was heaping on him. The answer came in a scrimmage a few weeks later. Haskins had been wearing him out as usual when Sterrett attempted a dunk. With no chance to block the shot, the much smaller defender caught him shoulder to butt, moving him laterally so the dunk was up through the basket, inside out.

"What the hell's going on, Sterrett?" shouted Haskins. "You got a gimme over a guy half your size, and you blew it."

The big man started to explain himself, but Haskins kept ripping at him until Sterrett stormed off toward the locker room. When he got to a folding chair at half court, in what seemed like a moment of indecision, it looked like he might use it as a weapon against his tormentor. Instead, he picked up a reversible practice jersey from the chair, wadded it up, and threw it toward Haskins before turning to leave. The jersey fell to the floor thirty feet shy of its target.

"Sterrett!" shouted Haskins, his voice reverberating through the nearly empty gym in pure intimidation. "You get your ass back here and pick that up."

Sterrett turned around, walked half the length of the floor to the shirt, picked it up, put it on the chair, turned, and left. He just walked out. Gone. The next day he was back again, and Haskins, displaying a penchant for forgiveness that was almost biblical ("seventy times seven"), acted as if nothing had happened.

In one preseason practice in the championship season, the target of the coach's frustration was Dick Myers. Myers, a six-foot-four forward who transferred in from Hutchinson Junior College in Kansas, collided with David Lattin at midcourt. The big center's knee caught him in the right thigh, causing what could have been a season-ending injury. It was his first year in El Paso, and Myers, anxious to earn playing time, was back at practice the next day, moving at half speed with a football thigh pad as protection.

"What you got there?" demanded Haskins, in a tone suggesting Myers was dogging it.

"It's a bad bruise, Coach."

"Let me see." What he saw was a bloody mass, a complete blood contusion. The coach recoiled, then patted Myers on the shoulder, apparently satisfied he was doing his best.

That wasn't always true of Nevil Shed, who became Haskins's whipping boy after Ted Sterrett graduated. During a film session one day Haskins ran a scene of Shed reaching down, almost casually, to retrieve a ball rolling toward him. Running the film backward and forward again and again gave the team a good laugh at Shed's expense while underlining a teaching point: on a Haskins team, when the ball comes loose from a scrum, you dive on the floor to get it. Later that week, when Shed was coasting through a drill, the coach set him to running the bleachers. Thirty minutes later Haskins had forgotten all about him. "Where's Shed?" he asked trainer Ross Moore. Leg weary, Shed was still running up and down, up and down stairs so steep if he leaned toward the court, he had a better than even chance of falling twenty rows to the floor.

Over time it seemed that Shed had a way of getting under the coach's skin no matter what he did. One day after making an aggressive slam-dunk recovery of a missed shot, he headed back up the court with a cocky, self-congratulatory attitude. "Shed, get the hell out of here!" shouted Haskins, for whom any kind of showboating was a major sin. Shed hit the showers and was back in the dorm thinking *No big deal* when the coach came to his room. "Nevil, I can't take any more of your facial contortions," he said. Reaching into his pocket, he brought out an envelope. "I thought it said Continental 144 from El Paso to Dallas to LaGuardia," Shed would recall. "All I could think about was my mother was going to whip my ass." The threat was real enough that night to convince him to change his behavior. At practice the following day the coach gave no indication there had been a problem between them.

Along with defense and conditioning, Haskins's emphasis in every practice was free throws. "Coach Haskins was a free-throw fanatic," said David Lattin. "You had to make ten in a row before you could leave the gym. You don't make ten in a row, you stay all night. His theory was when you get up to the line to shoot a free throw, you don't have to think about it. You've done it hundreds of times, over and over. You know you're going to make it; you don't have to guess about it."

Each player had his own routine, but Haskins, who could make nine out of ten free throws while looking at the floor, insisted right-handed shooters put their weight on their right foot while lefties—Bobby Joe, Harry Flournoy, Willie Cager, and Lou Baudoin—put their weight on the left. Always his players shook their arms to relax before the referee handed them the ball. Always they bounced it a set number of times before shooting. "I bounced the ball three times," said Lattin. "Bobby Joe bounced the ball two times."

When it was time to shoot free throws in practice, Shed and Willie Worsley usually shot at a smaller basket in the corner of the gym. To make ten in a row required greater concentration and more arch on their shots. It was a Haskins fix that helped them both. "When I got on the free-throw line in a competitive mode," said Shed, whose jumper was flat as a pancake, "I felt very comfortable. I never saw anything but the basket." For Willie, whom teammates called the second-most competitive player they'd ever seen, practicing on the corner rim made full-size rims seem enormous. "I was throwing the ball in the ocean," he said. "You can't miss the ocean."

Haskins wasn't particularly superstitious as coaches go, but during games, when it came to free throws, *his* preshot routine was as predictable as the routines of his players. He would watch intently as Shed or Willie Worsley or one of the others toed the line, shook his arms, and bounced the ball. Then, as the player started into his shooting motion, Haskins covered his eyes, sometimes sneaking a peak between his fingers, sometimes waiting for crowd reaction to tell him when to look up.

Having been schooled in Canonical Basketball by Hank Iba, one of the coaching legends Nolan Richardson calls the Old Cowboys (Iba, Phog Allen, Branch McCracken, and Adolph Rupp), Haskins was not inclined to venture into the unknown. In his college days the movement from black to white shoes seemed pretty radical, but at least they looked like basketball shoes were supposed to look. The brand-new Chuck Taylor Converse All-Stars Low-Cuts didn't, not at all. On the other hand, his guards were convinced the Low-Cuts would improve their quickness. "Okay," said Haskins. "We'll see."

Whether the Low-Cuts could have lived up to their billing was never determined, at least not by a Haskins-coached team. In one of the first new-shoe practices, somebody got the back of his shoe stepped on, and it came off. Haskins, who didn't like anything or anybody interrupting his practice, fumed as the shoe was retrieved and restored to its owner. Shoe back on. Start up again. It happened again. "That's it!" shouted

Haskins. "Back to the locker room and get those things off and *real* basketball shoes on." Sanity restored.

One of Coach Haskins's duties that went along with the *privilege* of living with his family in Miners' Hall during his early years at Texas Western was to act as something of a Dorm Daddy. And because there was a mixture of footballers and basketballers in his charge, that meant enforcing football coach Ben Collins's 10:00 p.m. lights-out. Haskins wasn't a curfew guy, but on a dark night it was hard to determine who was in which rooms, so it was lights-out for everybody. One night when he came back to the dorm, he saw a faint but unmistakable light coming from the room Steve Tredennick shared with teammate Ron Shockley. Steve was studying with a flashlight under his pillow.

"Get that light out!" Haskins hollered up at him.

At breakfast the following morning, Haskins confronted Shockley, who pleaded his innocence. "That must have been my roommate, Coach. I was sound asleep." Nonplussed, but only for an instant, Haskins regained his form and backed the six-foot-five forward up against the cafeteria wall, where he continued to berate him in most emphatic terms, adding the clincher "Damn it, Shockley, you're responsible for what your roommate does." The incident was quickly forgotten by Haskins, but not by Shockley when he encountered his roommate later that day.

To fully appreciate the Haskins approach to basketball, you had to see him on the sideline standing with a rolled-up program in his hand, shouting instructions. When a player made a bad play, he would hear about it all the way back up the floor. For Nevil Shed the solution was obvious. Bad play, run up the opposite side of the court, out of range of Haskins's voice. Good play, run so close to the bench you almost trip over the coach's feet.

Another aspect of the coach's game-time demeanor involved his complicated relationship with referees. There were only two in those days, and Haskins often felt the need to critique their performance as well. Usually, he showed enough restraint to avoid unwanted technical fouls. Sometimes he didn't. Once when he was coaching the girls' team back in Benjamin, the referee called a foul in the first minutes of the game that was so egregious that Haskins, flushed with anger, charged half the length of the floor to plead his case. Towering and glowering over the diminutive official, Haskins shouted down at the little man, who stood, arms folded imperiously across his chest, waiting for the uproar to stop. Then it was the ref's turn. "Coach," he said, in a high-pitched voice loud enough to be heard at the far end of the tiny gym, "you get one technical for every step it takes you to get back to your bench." "You don't have the guts," scoffed Haskins. As he turned to go the referee started counting: "One, two, three . . ." Sixteen altogether. The opposing team's free-throw shooter stepped to the line and made fourteen of sixteen. With the game barely under way, the Benjamin girls were behind 14–2.

At the college level Haskins often thought officials needed his critique. One night after Haskins had complained for most of a half, the official said, "Sit down, Coach. Next time I see you up, I'm going to run you out of here." Haskins's reply: "If you do, that will be the best call you've made all night." In a game against the University of New Mexico at Albuquerque, Haskins took all he could stand from a referee who seemed incapable of calling a foul on the home team. Finally, Haskins got up, walked past the scorer's table, and sat down on New Mexico's bench. Startled, the Lobos' coach said, "What are you doing here?" "I wanted to see if it's as bad down here as it is where I'm sitting," said Haskins.

Ross Moore, the Miners' trainer and a first-magnitude character in his own right, always had a towel in hand during games. When things went wrong, he'd throw the towel on the floor. One time he was so frustrated, he threw it in the air. His timing couldn't have been better. The towel floated up and draped over the head of an official who was running past the bench at that precise moment. Suddenly blinded, the ref yanked the towel away, turned toward the bench, and gave the trainer his first and only technical. On another occasion, when a referee named Curley Hayes made a call Moore didn't appreciate, he shouted out, "Damn you, Curley Hayes! I've known you for twenty years. You couldn't see back then, and you can't see now." Curley just turned and laughed.

There were times when Haskins felt he needed a technical to change the momentum of the game. "I just can't take it anymore," he'd say. "I'm going to get a technical." When the rule changed so technicals against coaches were two-shot fouls, the stakes were higher. Once when Haskins wanted a technical but not one of the two-shot variety, he sent one of his players, Luster "Pony" Goodwin, to argue his case for him. To no avail. Legendary ref Irv Brown listened patiently and then told Pony, "You tell Haskins if he wants a technical foul, he'll have to drag his sorry ass out here and get it himself."

Not all contacts with the referees were acrimonious. Once when Brown was refereeing one of those ugly early-season games, the ball came spurting out of a scrum toward the Texas Western bench. Haskins kicked it high into the bleachers. Smiling, Brown threw both hands into the air, signaling a made field goal. Before assessing the mandatory technical, Brown sidled over to Haskins to ask what he was doing. "Aw, hell, Irv. Everybody else was kicking it. I figured I should, too."

13

"Quite Improbable"

"On the face of the matter," according to that year's UK *Basketball Facts Book*, "the chances of Kentucky's Wildcats executing a marked reversal in form this year seem quite improbable." On the face of the matter, that was all too obvious. The problem, according to *Facts Book* and nearly anybody else who opined on the subject, was "no proven big man." John Adams, the team's top rebounder the year before, was lost to graduation. And the only man on Rupp's roster with height to match other conference big men was six-foot-eight Cliff Berger. A sophomore from Centralia, Illinois, he was destined to spend most of the season in a backup role. Tommy Kron and Larry Conley were solid, Louie Dampier and Pat Riley could score the basketball, but the man projected to play center was Thad Jaracz. Local sportswriters had followed his outstanding career at Lexington's Lafayette High School, but nobody expected the six-foot-five sophomore to be strong enough to hold his own against the giants who populated the low post on teams across the conference. Nobody with the possible exception of Adolph Rupp.

Coach Rupp was optimistic, or at least said he was. "I honestly believe that man-to-man we might have the makings of a better team than we had in 1958," said Rupp in a preseason interview. Fans ardently hoped he was right. But even though there had been dramatic improvement over that grueling Thanksgiving weekend, it was hard to believe this was a team to rival the Fiddlin' Five, who, after all, had fiddled their way to a national championship. Rupp said he expected a "fast, experienced, good-shooting team" and that ball handling would "solve [our] rebounding problem." It might, but, as the *Basketball Facts Book* writer helpfully pointed out, "You've got to have the ball to play with it."

With the season about to begin, Coach Rupp brought in regular referees for some of the final Blue-White scrimmages. One of them was Larry Conley's dad, who had officiated ACC and SEC games for more than a decade when Larry was growing up. George Conley's SEC career came to an end when Larry started playing for Kentucky because of concern he might have a pro-Kentucky whistle, even if he was never assigned to UK games. On this day he was calling them down the middle until late in the game when he whistled Larry for a blocking foul. It was one of those fouls that could have gone either way, and Larry was not happy. Larry said something to his dad, and referee George blew his whistle again, this time even more emphatically. "You're out of here!" he shouted. "George, you can't do that," said Rupp. "That's my player." "Coach, that's my son, and he's out of here." Larry was gone. Out of the scrimmage. Out of the coliseum.

Another father-son conversation around that time remained private until I interviewed Bob Tallent for this book. "I was all confident I was going to be a starter," he said. "Of course, I was a little bit naive." On the stat sheets Rupp kept for all scrimmages, Tallent was a statistical leader, with a shooting percentage right up there with Dampier and Riley. "I know you think you're doing good," said his father, "but those guys ahead of you are pretty damn good, and they've got experience. You're going to have to bide your time."

After forty-five days of practice, the 1965–66 edition of the Kentucky Wildcats was more than ready for the season to start, but it was a little hard to get up for the first game against Hardin-Simmons, a tiny Baptist college from Abilene, Texas. It was surprising somebody had shot film of one of their games and even more surprising that anybody thought it would be worth watching. As Slim threaded the film through the projector, he looked around the room. Every one of the players had faced stiffer competition in high school and in Blue-White scrimmages all fall. They could have had a more competitive game by suiting up against UK freshmen or even Thad's Lafayette High School team. But Adolph being Adolph, they watched, and he dissected every aspect of the film as if this Division III David might actually stand a chance against even a minor-league Goliath, let alone the University of Kentucky. The problem for the players was concentration.

They had watched about two-thirds of the film when the coaches left the room to tend to another matter. Everyone took a deep breath. Into the lightened atmosphere Slim said what everyone else was thinking. "If you guys can't beat this piece of crap, we're in for a long season." The laughter that followed stopped abruptly when Coach Rupp suddenly reappeared. "What's the laughing about?" he asked, looking around the room at his now silent team. For him there was nothing to laugh about. Somehow, he had to move them from casual to concentrated, from confident to concerned. He knew the film showcased serious Hardin-Simmons weaknesses. He also knew how important the first game was to setting the tone for the season. "Slim," he said, "roll film."

Two days later, when the Hardin-Simmons Cowboys held their morning shootaround in Memorial Coliseum, Slim watched through a crack in the door in a room at the top of the stands, the way he always did. If teams were naive enough to run their plays on Kentucky's floor, they deserved to be spied on. Usually, he would report to Coach Rupp on a particular offensive or defensive pattern he'd seen. Sometimes, he'd diagram the plays for the team on the blackboard. This time his notebook remained empty. The game that night was a nonevent except for the fact that there was a pretty good crowd of basketball-hungry fans anxious to see this year's Kentucky Wildcats in action, even if the starters would barely break a sweat. The Cowboys looked like a basketball team in their purple and gold uniforms, and, when defense slacked off, a few of them were okay shooters. But as predicted, they were never really in the game. Tommy Kron and Larry Conley had fourteen and twelve points, respectively; Pat Riley and Louie Dampier had nineteen and twenty-three; Thad Jaracz and Cliff Berger cleaned up the boards. Jaracz got only six points in his varsity debut, but it was hardly a test, since the starters spent most of the second half on the bench.

With game 1 safely tucked away in the win column, it was time to leave the friendly confines of Memorial Coliseum for a first road trip to Charlottesville, Virginia. The University of Virginia Cavaliers had a pretty good record the previous season, and their starting center, six-foot-nine John Naponick, would give the Wildcats their first experience against an authentic big man. But the real story that day wasn't basketball per se but the fact that this would be the inaugural game in Virginia's spanking-new John Paul Jones Arena. Local reporters crowded in as the team arrived for a morning shootaround. "What do you think, Coach?" they asked excitedly as Rupp stepped down off the bus. "Isn't she a beauty?"

"Well, boys, it looks like a mighty fine facility," he said, looking at the new building with an appraising eye. While the players headed for the locker room, Adolph, who considered himself an expert on the modern basketball arena, was in his element. Memorial Coliseum, built to his exacting specifications fifteen years earlier for a then astronomical four million dollars, was still considered one of the finest basketball facilities in the country.

The team didn't hear the rest of his evaluation, but they made their own. The floor gleamed with fresh varnish, a navy-blue block V in the center circle. The stands stretched up from the playing surface, providing an unrestricted view for some ten thousand fans. There was an orange and blue UVA banner up near the ceiling, hanging proudly alongside the red, white, and blue of the American flag. Nice, really nice. All that gleam and glitter left them unprepared for the locker room. Painted an industrial gray, it looked like a holdover from dusty old University Hall that had served Virginia's hoopsters since 1925. The transition from Technicolor to black-and-white wasn't a problem. The size of the room was. It was minuscule. About a third the size of the locker room back in Lexington, it was better suited for Lilliputians than Gulliver-size basketball players, even ones soon to be nicknamed Rupp's Runts.

Everyone knew Adolph's reaction would be instant and visceral. What they didn't know was that he would sweep into the room ten minutes later trailed by those same reporters still intent on capturing—in recorders and notebooks—every word of Rupp's ongoing critique.

"Now why in the world would anybody build a goddamn locker room this fucking small?" he asked, looking around in disbelief. "What the hell were they thinking of?" Reporters usually liked Coach Rupp because, unlike most coaches then and now, he always said exactly what he was thinking and often in the most colorful language. This time, looks of horror, as if Adolph had just pissed in the Holy Water.

After the shootaround and the regular game-day lunch, everyone expected routine rest-in-the-room time. Not today. Rupp was something of a history buff, and Virginia's campus was hard by Thomas Jefferson's Monticello. The visit nearly died aborning. Nobody was in the ticket booth by the entry gate, so the bus drove on up the hill to the parking lot near the mansion. When the door opened an officious-looking young man (standard-issue blue blazer, gray slacks, oxford shirt with UVA school-color orange-and-navy-striped tie) stepped onto the bus, shaking his head officiously. "I'm sorry," he said, looking at Adolph and Harry, seated, as always, right behind the driver. "You're going to have to go back down the hill and get your tickets."

"Oh hell no," harrumphed Adolph, fixing the young man with the look of a blood-starved Dracula. "No damn way we're going back down that hill. Turn around, driver. We just won't stay."

"Ah, no, I didn't mean . . . I mean . . . I can get 'em," stammered Officious, backing out of the bus as if the Baron were a rabid rottweiler.

With Rupp in the lead, the team toured the eleven-thousand-square-foot architectural marvel before returning to the regular Rupp routine, which, on this night, involved a shocking abnormality. In the locker room before the game, Coach Rupp said, "Slim, there's a photographer going to be shooting around the bench during the game." Seeing the look of disbelief on his student manager's face, he added: "*Charlottesville Daily Progress*. It's okay."

Ever since his freshman year Slim had been preventing what was about to happen from happening. That was when a photographer cut through the crowd, got right up behind the bench, and said, "Hey, Adolph!" When the coach turned, the guy fired off his flash from point-blank range, throwing Rupp into a rage. "Keep those damn people away from me," he said, brimming with anger. "Don't ever let that happen again." For three years Slim made sure that he or another manager was behind Rupp whenever he was on the bench. Now he felt like a guard at Fort Knox suddenly told, "Let them take the gold."

For the entire first half there was a click and a flash every time Adolph got to his feet to shout instructions or complain about an official's call. During time-outs the guy was in the huddle, sometimes on his back shooting up, sometimes on a chair shooting down, always in the way. By halftime the shutterbug had clicked and flashed his way through a couple of rolls of film, but the team was playing well, and, somehow, Adolph wasn't bothered.

At the start of the second half Larry Conley spotted Pat Riley open on the baseline and shot him a no-look pass that sailed over his head and into the stands. "No, goddamn it!" screamed Rupp. Leaping to his feet, he tripped over the photographer. Staggering to regain his balance, Rupp ended up in a semicrouch, face-to-face with the kneeling photographer, barely six inches apart. "Haven't you taken enough goddamn pictures?" he snarled.

With photographers now off the radar, the game came back into focus, and a Jefferson quote seemed apt: "Nothing can stop the man with the right mental attitude from achieving his goal." With Larry Conley in the role of facilitator, Dampier and Riley had twenty-three and twenty-nine points. No surprise there, but Thad Jaracz was a revelation. In only his second game as a varsity player, Thad had a coming-out party. "What happened early on was there was a lot of emphasis put on the players they knew," said Thad. "There were some things that I could bring to the table which they hadn't seen before, and we were unselfish enough to take advantage of that." Thad not only held his own against his six-foot-nine counterpart, but also hit for twenty-two points and pulled down thirteen rebounds. Meanwhile, Tommy Kron and Larry Conley were settling into the roles they would play for the rest of the season: Conley the facilitator, Kron the defensive specialist and matchup nightmare. Final score 99–73.

Two down and twenty-four to go.

Now the games came hard and fast, and things were getting rougher. The third game in seven days was on the road against a University of Illinois team coached by Harry Combes. It had been more than a decade since the Illini had three third-place finishes in four NCAA Tournaments, but Adolph respected Combes as a coach and the Big Ten as a conference. "Damn fine play," he would say in practices. "That might even work in the Big Ten." With only three days to prepare for the trip to Urbana, the intensity of practices ratcheted up another notch. "Fellas," Rupp said more than a few times, "patty-cake is over and done with. If you don't play way better than you have so far, those Illinois boys will eat your lunch." This time the film session was deadly serious. This time the guy running the projector kept his mouth shut. Rupp knew Combes's offensive and defensive schemes almost as well as he knew his own. Illinois had beaten him in the Christmas tournament the year before, and this game promised to be a chess match. It wasn't.

Kentucky was up 4–2 in the first minute of play when Jaracz's man beat him down the floor for a lay-up, plus one. While the teams were lining up for the foul shot, Conley, usually the calm one, got in Thad's face. "Jaracz, goddamn it, you get your ass back on defense and quit screwing around." Flushed with anger, Thad said, "Fuck you, Conley." Larry's words seemed to flip a switch.

The next time down the floor, Thad came off a pick-and-roll, and Larry fired a pass that hit him in the belly. Demonstrating the quick hands that made him Conley's favorite in the Berger-Jaracz contest, Thad gathered it in and made an easy lay-up. "They just forgot about Thad," said Conley. "They looked at four of us, two juniors, two seniors. They thought, 'We'll shut down Riley and Dampier, and Kron and Conley aren't going to score that much.' Every time I looked up, Thad was wide open. I thought, 'What's going on here?'"

Kron hit Thad cutting across the middle, and he put up a little left-handed hook that floated high over the outstretched arms of the Illinois center—six-foot-eight Ron Dunlap—and settled softly through the net. An unorthodox shooter, Thad Jaracz was using the technique he'd used against six-eight Cliff Berger in all those Blue-White scrimmages. He leaned into Dunlap, creating room for a baby hook off both feet.

Later in the season, there would be scouting reports and opponents would know that Thad was, as he put it, "totally lefty," but he hit three more hooks—one jumping off both feet and two off his left foot, "one step sooner than they'd think I was going to shoot"—before Dunlap made an adjustment. When he did Thad showed his versatility by stepping back for a neat little twelve-foot jumper.

Late in the first half, with the Illini falling further and further behind, 210-pound Preston Pearson battled 175-pound Bobby Tallent for a loose ball. It was no contest. Pearson, who would go on to a fourteen-year career in professional football with the Colts, Steelers, and Cowboys, drove Bobby to the floor with a resounding thud. Coach Rupp grabbed Riley. "Don't let him treat Red that way," he demanded. Riley looked at Pearson, who would spend his pro career plunging into (and around) 300-pound linemen, then back at Rupp. "What do you want me to do?"

"I got a lot of points that night," said Thad, recalling the biggest scoring night of his basketball career. "Just being on the high post, ball going to the side, and just wheeling off the high post and going down the lane and the guy not being able to follow me fast enough and just laying it off the board."

"He almost scored at will," said Conley. "I would have loved to be in their locker room after the game was over to see the shock on all those guys. 'Where did this guy come from?'"

Kentucky was so far ahead with a minute and a half to go that Slim was already halfway to the locker room when he heard Thad coming down the hall behind him. In only his third varsity game, Jaracz had led the team with a masterful thirty-two-point performance and was flying high. "We really kicked those sonsabitches' asses tonight!" he shouted. Just then two nuns came around the corner. Thad turned as red as the sun, while Slim was so doubled over with laughter he could barely get the key in the locker-room door.

The celebration after the game was muted, as it always was, but team confidence was real. Kentucky had gone on the road and won by a comfortable margin—86–68—against a Fighting Illini team with four starters, including All-American Don Freeman, who would go on to play professionally. Their brand of basketball *did* work against a Big Ten team. The feeling was palpable. We can play this game.

After beating Northwestern at Memorial Coliseum, the Wildcats headed into the UKIT (University of Kentucky Invitational Tournament) against Air Force Academy. The flyboys put up a pretty good fight before losing by twenty points, setting up the championship game with Indiana. It was that game that put Kentucky in the national spotlight for the first time. The Hoosiers were a different team than their 1964–65 version, when the Van Arsdale twins, Dick and Tom, led the way to a 19-5 season, fourth place in the national rankings. But Indiana had been a basketball powerhouse for two decades, picking up four Big Ten titles and two national championships under Coach Branch McCracken. Rupp had faced off against McCracken a number of times down through the years, but he knew nothing about McCracken's longtime assistant, former IU All-American Lou Watson, who succeeded McCracken when he retired.

Indiana's defense was as predictable as it was ineffective. The focus was on Louie and Pat, just as it had been the year before. They paid some attention to Tommy Kron, an Indiana schoolboy they'd tried to recruit, but apparently forgot about Conley. A couple of fast breaks, a couple of jump shots, and he had a quick eight points. By the time the Hoosiers called their first time-out, they were down 13-2 and Larry had scored all of Kentucky's points. "Some nights things happen a certain way," he said. "You don't know why, but they do. So we go over to the bench to sit down, and Riley is sitting next to me. 'All right, you've got yours,' he said. 'Now let the rest of us get ours.'" Larry looked at Riley. "You sonofabitch, I just happened to be in the right position to do that." Conley didn't score again.

Coach Rupp prided himself on being able to predict adjustments opposing coaches would make as the game progressed, but with Watson his prognostications proved faulty. After the time-out Watson switched to a zone defense that opened things up for Riley in the corner and Dampier at the head of the key. Four quick baskets put Kentucky up by 22-8, and Watson called a time-out again.

"Fellas, they're going to come out of that zone now," said Rupp, setting up the plays he wanted to run against their man-to-man. Wrong again. "You walk out there and you go, 'All right!'" Conley recalled. Still the zone, still wide-open shots, and five more quick baskets, stretching the Wildcat lead to 32-8. Another time-out. Coach Rupp blew his nose and shook his head. "By God, fellas, they're coming out of their zone now." They never did.

"I think they were afraid to go man-to-man against us," said Conley. "They didn't have the quickness that we had, and they were afraid of being blown out," which happened anyway. The margin of victory was thirty-five points.

An interesting aspect of the game was Louie Dampier's defense. Only six feet tall, Louie was quick as a cat, but defense had never been his thing. During practice that week Coach Hall said, "Louie, you couldn't play for me at Central Missouri or Regis." When Louis asked him what he meant, Hall responded, "Hell, you don't guard anybody." Against Indiana not only did Dampier get his twenty-eight points, but he virtually shut down the Hoosiers' flashy point guard, Vern Payne. After the game Louie asked Hall, "Could I play for you at St. Regis now?"

Kentucky had been overlooked in the preseason polls, but that Indiana butt-kicking put them in the top ten for the first time. The players were supporting each other, spitting out baskets like a machine stamping out ingots. "When you're playing like a team and winning," said Coach Hall, "there's enough glory for everyone."

14

The Games Were the Break

A month and a half after the start of official practice, the Texas Western Miners were like their counterparts in Lexington. They needed a break from the unrelenting repetition of practice. They were ready for the real thing.

"If we could have played a game every day . . . fifty or sixty of them, it was better than going through those practices," said Harry Flournoy. "The games *were* the break." Most of them, in the early going, were also a walk in the park. After trouncing Eastern New Mexico by fifty-one points, the Miners breezed through an early-season schedule where the main obstacle was boredom. Yet "I think there was just as much pressure because you had to really perform and really execute those things [Coach Haskins] taught you in practice regardless of the competition. If you didn't, you caught hell the next day."

No matter how big the win—whether by forty-six against South Dakota or thirty-seven against Nevada and Loyola of New Orleans—Haskins was always coaching. "The worst chewings you would get were after a win," says Steve Tredennick. "If you won and were in there goosing and giggling, he'd make it clear in a hurry he saw a lot of problems with the way we played."

The single biggest problem Haskins saw during the championship season was his team's tendency to play in spurts, driving their coach crazy. They would start games playing defense with the intensity he demanded. "They just swallowed up other teams," Haskins wrote. "Eventually we would have this huge lead and they'd stop trying." Instead of the disciplined team they could be, it would be "playground ball" with "crazy passes" and "wild shooting." Defensively, they became "lackadaisical."

Haskins would "go crazy on the sideline" with every easy basket. His players "would just smile and look at the scoreboard. We'd be up thirty, so why should I care?" Once, when team defense wasn't up to the coach's standards, he hit on a surefire solution. "If your man scores," shouted Haskins, "you're coming out of the game!" It took only one benching to recalibrate defensive intensity.

In the early going everybody played, until, game by game, Haskins settled into a rotation that featured his seven best players, who just happened to be black. By starting five blacks Haskins was defying a de facto quota system adhered to by even the most liberal universities, *two at home, three on the road, four if you're behind*, but never five black players on the floor at the same time. "It went back to the slave mentality," says Flournoy. "You had to have the master—to be a straw boss, so to speak—making sure that everybody stayed in their place, that everyone was doing what they were supposed to do, because they couldn't think that well to do it on their own." Loyola University of Chicago had won the 1963 NCAA Championship starting four African Americans, but conventional wisdom had it that their white point guard, John Egan, was the glue that held the team together. The glue for Haskins was preparation and the character of his players. They had discipline and grace under pressure with or without a white player on the floor.

Nine games into the season, Texas Western was beating their opponents by an average of twenty-seven points per game, with only Fresno State raising a challenge. The Fresno State Bulldogs had never made it into an NCAA Tournament and wouldn't for another fourteen years, but on that Friday night they were on fire and the Miners were flat and almost flattened. With three minutes to go, behind by five points, Haskins called time-out. Unlike Adolph, who often spent time-outs shouting, Don stood there saying nothing. "Everybody knew exactly why there was a time-out," said Lou Baudoin. "A lot of it had to do with not getting caught up in the pace, and that's critical for a team that doesn't run. He needed us to control the game."

They did, barely, winning by a scant two points, 75–73, despite the fact that Bobby Joe Hill missed the game because of a charley horse that wouldn't go away.

Haskins was livid. In an earlier season he vented his anger after one game by kicking a locker-room garbage can, breaking his toe. There was a time when he said, simply, "You don't need to shower, boys." Everyone knew what that meant. They were in for a long, grueling postgame practice. This time all he said was, "You guys were damn lucky."

They weren't so lucky the following morning. There was another game that night against the same Fresno State Bulldogs, but the regular game-day shootaround morphed into a full-scale practice. As always the emphasis was defense.

"What have we been practicing all season?" said Haskins, after the starters assumed their defensive positions. "When their guard passes down to the forward and you're on the opposite side of the court, on the weak side, where are you supposed to be . . . Shed?"

Nevil Shed moved off his man into the lane.

"Right! And where were you last night when number 24 came down the middle?" Shed drifted back toward his man. "You were so busy being *the Shadow,*" Haskins said, lowering his voice to emphasize Shed's nickname, "you gave him a clear path to the basket." Shed nodded. "I've been telling some of you guys for four years now: you've got to keep an eye on your man, but, damn it, we play a helping man-to-man. When Artis pushes his man into the middle, you have got to be there with the weak-side help. Got it?"

"Yes, sir," Shed replied.

For the next forty-five minutes Lou Baudoin became Fresno State's number 24. It was a familiar role for Lou, a left-handed, six-seven forward his teammates called Flip. An excellent jump shooter with range, Flip didn't fit the Haskins system, but on days like this he became an invaluable stand-in for an opponent's best man. Now, cutting off screens by Jerry Armstrong and Togo Railey, he shredded the Miners' defense with a combination of jumpers and driving hook shots with either hand. He put up numbers the way he had back in Albuquerque High School, until Haskins made his adjustments. The coach shrugged when Flip hit a twenty-foot jumper from the left baseline, but then the shutdown started. It ended when Flip came across the middle, took a pass from Worsley, hit the brakes, and put up a fifteen-foot jump shot. David Lattin slammed it back in his face. Haskins nodded his satisfaction. Practice was over.

Eight hours later the real number 24 made the same cut, got the same timely pass, and ate leather. David "Big Daddy" Lattin got credit for another blocked shot, but Flip Baudoin and his second-five teammates got the satisfaction of knowing they'd made their contribution.

On the offensive end the cold-shooting Miners of last night suddenly found their range. The box score shows Lattin with eighteen, Orsten Artis with sixteen, and Nevil Shed and Harry Flournoy with twelve and eleven. But the difference maker was Bobby Joe Hill. Still bothered by the charley horse, he watched from the bench as his lifeless teammates ground out a 34–32 lead at the intermission. After a halftime of manipulation of his cramped thigh by trainer Ross Moore, B.J. declared himself ready to go. With seventeen second-half points, and his signature stifling defense, Bobby Joe provided the spark that made the difference. Instead of the Friday-night squeaker, the Miners beat Fresno State by a comfortable eighteen points, 83–65.

With a limited travel budget, Texas Western drove to neighboring-state games in station wagons on loan from a local Chevrolet dealer. For longer trips they usually flew commercial. Because commercial airlines didn't fly directly from West Texas to Rock Island, Illinois, where Haskins had scheduled the Miners in a pre-Christmas tournament, it was time for a charter. So there they were at El Paso Municipal Airport at six in the morning on December 20 . . . waiting. They waited and waited and waited. Six o'clock became six thirty, then seven, then seven thirty. Finally, they saw it, a vintage gray DC-3 rolling toward them across the tarmac. It was not a sight to inspire confidence in even the most fearless flyer. The World War II relic was coming at them tail first, pulled by a sturdy yellow tractor that looked more airworthy than the plane itself.

As the crow flies, the trip from El Paso to the Quad City airport, four miles from Rock Island, is just under thirteen hundred miles. On this particular day crows were not flying. The ancient airplane bumped along through the sky like a june bug on a pogo stick. Before clearing Texas it made a refueling stop in Wichita Falls. Winter headwinds forced another landing just over the border between Kansas and Missouri. With all the bumps and rattles along the way, would-be nappers were jerked and jolted into white-knuckled wakefulness. Those who ventured a look out the window swore the limping machine was in imminent danger of scraping its underbelly on tree limbs and power lines. The few hardy souls who attempted a game of hearts spent their time retrieving playing cards from the floor. Finally, they touched down in Illinois.

For Dick Myers, a six-four junior college transfer in his first year as a Miner, the trip was more than worth it. Having grown up in Kansas, the icy cold didn't bother him, and it would be a first chance in three months to spend time with his fiancée. He was hoping for playing time he'd missed because of a preseason run-in with David Lattin that left him limping badly through the early season, but he was worried about his haircut. Damn you, Baudoin! Flip, who'd performed tonsorial services for teammates at twenty-five cents a pop, knew this would be the first time Myers would be spending time with his future in-laws. A cutup with or without his scissors, Flip performed a scalp job that sent Myers searching for a stocking cap.

The games that weekend were old-fashioned butt-kickings: forty-six points over South Dakota and thirty-seven over Nevada. Myers, Armstrong, Baudoin, David Palacio, and Togo Railey got playing time that would be in short supply going forward. When the tournament was over, Myers approached Haskins. "My uncle lives in Chicago," he fibbed. "He asked me to spend Christmas with him. I can be back for practice on Sunday [the twenty-sixth]."

If Haskins had happened to spot Myers as he rode away from the team hotel, he might have figured the man at the wheel was Dick's uncle instead of his future father-in-law. And had he been a little more observant, he might also have wondered about the extraordinary affection Myers was lavishing on his alleged kissing cousin, a very attractive brunette who was actually his fiancée and future wife, Elsie.

15

Seeing Things I Really Like

It was three days before Christmas when the Wildcats headed for Lubbock, Texas, to take on Texas Tech. Most road trips were on a charter DC-3 the university leased from a Purdue, Indiana, company named, of course, Purdue Airlines. On this trip, because of the distance involved, the team was flying commercial. The plane was nothing like the World War II relic Thad described as "a bus in the sky with not as many stop signs." On one very bumpy flight that fall, Harry Lancaster's seat was turned around so he could play poker with Billy Thompson, a Lexington reporter. Flying over the mountains at twelve thousand feet, the plane started shaking like an Oklahoma earthquake. Billy got a frightened expression on his face. "Bend over and put your head between your legs," Slim said, trying to be helpful. Billy looked like he was about to follow the suggestion. "What good will that do?" he asked. Slim answered, "You can kiss your ass good-bye."

While Billy shot Slim the bird, Harry was cracking up, but his enjoyment came to an abrupt end a minute later when he sneezed and threw up all over Billy. By that time everybody on the plane was looking a little green around the gills and was searching the seat-back pockets for barf bags. Riley was next to lose his cookies, and before the pilot found smooth air, most of the rest of the team had done the same.

The sleek, new DC-9 that lifted out of Louisville's Standiford Field on this day was bigger, the flight smoother, and smiling stewardesses in their honey-beige shirtwaist dresses, orange ascots, and three-inch stiletto heels were on hand to flirt with the players and serve up elegant meals: cornish hen or beef stroganoff. "If we don't have your choice when we get to you, don't worry about it," said a statuesque blonde with a dazzling smile. "They both taste just the same." Maybe, but for college students accustomed to cafeteria grub, they were delicious. The entrée was served with salad, rolls, and chocolate sundaes. It was beyond finger-lickin' good, but there was a problem. Rupp's Runts may have been small by basketball standards, but they could eat like horses. By the time they got to the hotel it was early evening, and these horses were starving.

Rupp asked his usual question: "What do you think the boys would like to do this evening, Slim?" Often on the night before a game, the answer was go to a movie. This time it was EAT.

"My God, Slim," said Rupp. "We already had the finest airline food I've ever tasted. Cornish hen is pretty high on the food table."

"Just not enough of it," Slim responded.

Coach Rupp nodded, handing him two crisp new hundred-dollar bills. "Take them out and get them some hamburgers."

The weather on game day was raw and blustery, and everyone was half expecting Coach Rupp to try to bring them down from the artificial high of being nationally ranked for the first time in recent memory. Instead, after the noon meal, he started his usual talk by going around the country, ticking off the teams above them in the rankings. One by one he went down the list, dissecting each team's pluses and minuses. "Michigan's got Cazzie Russell. He's probably the best damn player in the country," said Rupp. "But he's their only true scorer, and a good team can beat a great player every time."

The players exchanged looks, wondering where this was going, as he moved on to Duke, UCLA, and Dayton. "Dayton's got that big guy, Henry Finkel. A goddamn giant—seven feet something—and the guy can move. But you can double up on him, block him out, and make it hard for him to get to the basket." Next on his list was the University of Kansas.

Everybody in the room knew that Rupp had played for Kansas and the legendary Forrest Clare "Phog" Allen, who had played for Dr. James Naismith, making Adolph two degrees of separation from basketball's founding deity (*In the beginning was the word*). "We can beat Kansas," he said. Heads nodded. "They don't play good defense, and they never have." Eyebrows rose. *Does he know what he just said?* "Kansas has a couple of All-Ameri . . . Wait a minute," he sputtered. "We played good defense when I was there." Even though there was a no-laugh rule, the room lost it. Surprised at first, Coach Rupp joined in.

When the laughter subsided Coach Rupp turned serious again. "Fellas, you've been working hard in practice, and you're starting to really play as a team." Again the questioning looks. "I told you on the first day of practice that I was going to get things out of you that you didn't know were in there, that if you work at it every day, you can be a really good team." He paused and looked at the players sitting around the table. "We're only six games into the season—seven tonight—but I'm seeing things in you I really like." Another pause. "Fellas, if we keep on working, keep on running and blocking out and playing as a team, I think we can win the national championship."

With less than a minute to go in the first half that night, Louie Dampier suffered a knee injury and had to be helped off the court. It was a big letdown. Kentucky was up by two, but the game was tight as a tick, and Louie, scoring thirteen points in the first half, was on his way to a typical Dampier night. His replacement was Bobby Tallent. Despite impressive performances in Blue-White scrimmages, Tallent had played only limited minutes in the first six games. The way Louie limped into the locker room at halftime, it looked like that was about to change, but Harry Lancaster had a different idea. Jim LeMaster.

LeMaster, a sophomore from Paris, Kentucky, was an inch taller than Tallent at six feet two but had played even fewer minutes. He was a good all-around player, but, with Louie down, someone needed to step in and score Dampier-like points. Everyone in the locker room knew Bobby was a better shooter than Jim, everyone except Harry, who kept saying, "Coach, you need to put LeMaster in."

Bobby was staring at the floor with a look of resignation. He'd been a starter and star on every team he ever played on since his dad first introduced him to basketball as a kindergartner. As a high school senior he'd averaged forty points a game and never missed a beat when he arrived in Lexington, leading the UK Kittens freshman team in scoring and assists. Now there were whole games when Kentucky's starting five played all forty minutes, when Bobby Tallent, former *Parade* High School All-American, never left the bench. And now Bobby knew what his teammates knew: Adolph usually follows Harry suggestions. Not this time. "No, Harry, goddamn it. I'm going to stick with Red."

Biding his time was about to pay off. Bobby Tallent would have an entire half of basketball to show Adolph the skills that produced nineteen points a game on the freshman team were still game ready. He felt the same little flutter in his stomach and surge of adrenaline that always told him he was ready to play.

"What do you want me to do?" he asked Conley. Larry had been his hero since his freshman year in high school. That was the year Tallent watched Conley drive the baseline in the state championship game against a pair of Lexington Dunbar behemoths. "You could see four hands on the backboard. He went underneath and laid it in with a soft hand. I said, 'Wow!' That was pretty impressive." Now, as they took the floor at Lubbock's dome-shaped Municipal Coliseum to start the second half against Texas Tech, Conley said, "You can play just like Louie."

While Harry was overruled on LeMaster for Tallent, Adolph took him up on his suggestion to switch to a one-three-one defense: Tommy Kron out front, Thad Jaracz in the middle, Larry and Tallent on the wings, with Pat Riley down under. They'd been practicing it on and off since mid-October, but Texas Tech was its first test under game conditions. In the man-to-man Tommy's height and wingspan made him a matchup nightmare for opposing point guards, but it was his quickness that gave him his biggest advantage in the zone, the "stratified transitional, hyperbolic, parabolic man-to-man."

In a hundred-yard dash, Tommy would probably lose to everyone on the team except Berger, Lentz, and maybe Thad. But in fifteen to thirty feet he was greased lightning. Against Texas Tech it was cat and mouse, with the mouse looking alternately puzzled and perplexed. First Tommy played it soft, dropping back into the passing lanes. On the next possession he jumped the ball, forcing the befuddled Techie to the left, where Larry was waiting to clamp on the trap. "It was really something," said Larry. "They didn't score for the next eight to ten minutes."

Defensively, the Wildcats were devastating, but offensively, the precision that so impressed their coach in the first six games just wasn't there. Frustrated, Adolph called time-out. Always before when the team huddled around Coach Rupp during a time-out, it was Adolph or Harry who did the talking. This time Conley spoke up. "Like the coach said, now's the time we've got to pull together."

Less than a minute later, with the Wildcats running a high-post split, Tallent passed the ball to Thad, came off a Tommy Kron screen, and got the return pass in rhythm at the top of the key. Feet planted, shoulders squared. Nailed it! The next possession Kron to Larry to Tallent. Swish! At this point in his basketball career Bobby Tallent was no Louie Dampier. He was tonight. Tonight, back in his freshman groove, he hit three more in quick succession. It was *feed him and fan him.*

Suddenly, the team was in perfect sync, rebound, pass, pass, score. The photographer with his constant-click camera could have made his time-lapse series in a single second, okay maybe 1.9. Riley led all scorers with twenty-nine points, but it was Tallent, coming off the bench for thirteen second-half points, that sparked the team to an 89–73 win and prompted Rupp to say, "When Red's having a night like that, you could put a lid on the basket and he'd still score."

16

Things That I Can't

When Kentucky got back from the Texas trip two things had happened. First, and most obvious, the campus was virtually deserted. It was two days before Christmas, and everyone not connected with the basketball team was enjoying home and hearth, if not chestnuts roasting on an open fire. The other thing that happened was a new national poll. In seven games, capped off by a decisive win over Texas Tech, Kentucky had risen to number five in the country. Somehow that made the lack of a Christmas break more bearable. Another thing that helped was the generosity of a local alum.

Coach Rupp had given Slim a list of some twenty "friends of the team" who were allowed into practices "because they can do things that I can't." He'd seen one of the things they could do when he accompanied a player to Lexington's finest men's store. While Slim bought a much-needed belt, the player went around the store selecting shirts and pants, socks, and underwear and on and on, something north of $300 worth of clothes. When it came time to pay up, the belt cost $2.95. The player's stash came to a total of $19.95. It paid to be a Kentucky basketballer on another level. While Slim drove around campus in a beat-up 1949 Chevrolet, the players all drove late-model cars "purchased" from a local car dealer. Either their parents were a lot richer or . . .

One man on the coach's "allowed list" was a wealthy Lexington businessman who took his family on vacation every Christmas, giving the keys to his enormous house, several fine cars, and a pair of well-stocked refrigerators to the basketball team. So while daytimes were devoted to basketball, nights were Party Time. Usually, the interval between one and the other was like the airline pilots' slogan: "Eight hours from the bottle to the throttle." One time it wasn't.

At both ends of the practice floor—attached to the support frame for the backboard—the janitors had put what the players called the Up-Chuck Bucket. If you had to spit or throw up, you were supposed to use the bucket. It was the day after the night before when Thad Jaracz pointed at the bucket. "I'm probably going to need that today," he said. "You can call a foul every time down the floor, and you won't hear one damn word from me." One minute into the scrimmage, Thad pushed off on his man and broke to the basket for an easy lay-up. It was the kind of rinky-dink foul a referee might let pass, especially that early in a scrimmage, but this time Slim blew his whistle. While Thad nodded his thanks, Harry called out, "That figures, Jaracz. Best damn break you ever made. It had to be cheating."

Slim had a "whistle happy" scrimmage, but to avoid the coach's ire he kept a careful balance of calls against the White and Blue Teams, all the time expecting Rupp to say, "Let 'em play, Slim." It didn't happen.

What did happen that day and every other day during the Christmas break was a rerun of what happened in every other Rupp practice: silence. "You'd go to our practices, and you wouldn't hear squat," said Thad. "No one ever said, 'Hey, good shot or good job or let's play some D.' All you heard was tennis shoes squeaking, and that was it." "It was very clinical," Larry Conley recalls. "None of this rah-rah stuff that you see today. It was very much a classroom environment. Coach Rupp had a certain number of things in his head he wanted to get accomplished that day, and we went out and did it. Once we got it done we'd move on to something else."

Every day they ran and reran plays. Every day Rupp railed against the most minor deviation from perfection. "Goddamn it, Dampier, you think you could make a decent pass?" Or "Riley, the play was Seven and Go Backdoor. Where the hell were you?" Years later Larry Conley said two things about those practice sessions the others had to be thinking. "They were boring." They certainly were boring. And "sometimes I hated that sonofabitch." So did they all, sometimes.

What Tommy Kron hated most about Christmas break wasn't the

practices (they were what they'd always been) but Rupp's ironclad rule against out-of-town travel. In normal circumstances Tommy tooled around town in his late-model greenish blue Ford Fairlane convertible, top down, radio volume up, highly visible. During Christmas break, with his pin mate and soon-to-be fiancée home with her parents, it was a different matter entirely. After the day's final practice Tommy would slip away to Frankfort, top up, volume down. Willing himself invisible, he drove along the less-traveled two-lane Old Versailles Road instead of the interstate. His clandestine thirty-mile trips, winding between picturesque wood-fenced horse farms, took more time but were a lot less likely to be reported back to Adolph. They never were. Or if they were, the coach chose to ignore them. After a few hours with Dianne and her family, Kron was rejuvenated and ready for another day of practice.

Looking back, Rupp's Runts all agree, the reason Kentucky teams were known for their calm under pressure was their daily experience with pressure-packed practices. "The biggest battles you had were on Thursday afternoons," said Thad. "That's where the war was. You had to beat out the other guys on your team, or you weren't going to play." Another factor in the pressure equation was that in practice a miscue could bring down the wrath of God on a player for what seemed like an eternity. In the game, whatever you did, Adolph wouldn't come charging out on the court and dress you down in front of your teammates. He would yell, "No, goddamn it!" but play would go on.

Reporters, aware that Wildcat players seldom "improved on silence" during practices, concluded they were passionless robots who went through their Rupp-ordained paces but weren't having any fun. They were right about the repetitive nature of the practices (they *were* often boring). They were wrong about the fun. Even when the coach was being a sonofabitch, most players who stuck with the program came to understand that his methods led to winning basketball games. They might not be as dedicated to winning as their coach—few mortals could (or wanted to) aspire to his level of commitment—but they knew that winning was where the fun was.

Most players arriving on the University of Kentucky campus had never experienced the level of intensity demanded at the college level and certainly nothing like the Rupp practice routine. They thought of themselves as good players (after all, one of the top basketball programs in the country had recruited them), but they didn't know what they didn't know.

On the freshman team, using Adolph's tried-and-true techniques of constant repetition, Harry started the process of helping players focus on the vast areas of what had always seemed a simple game that they didn't really understand. The next step was to learn how the complexities of the game were supposed to be played. The spontaneity with which they'd played the high school game became a thinking process, as if they were back in grade school learning their times tables. Six times nine is . . . ah, fifty-four. They really did know what to do if they thought about it, but thinking slowed reaction. To be truly successful in the Rupp system, a player needed to reach the final level when nearly every situation on a basketball floor triggered an automatic response. When five players play with automatic responses, it is like the New York Philharmonic playing the "Hallelujah" chorus for the hundredth time while the conductor is on a coffee break. It is, as the saying goes, "a thing of beauty and a joy forever."

There wasn't a lot of pure joy in those Christmas practice sessions that year, but little by little the team was getting to the point where they really meshed. In the half court, Rupp polished each play by having the starters run it twenty or thirty times and then run it another fifteen times for the subs. When Tommy Kron made a chest pass to Pat Riley, it triggered something. If it was a bounce pass, that triggered something else. A bounce pass to Thad Jaracz in the low post set a different pattern in motion. There were only six or seven plays, but each came with prescribed variations depending on the reaction of the defense. If opponents started overplaying on one side, the reaction was automatic. There was one play—Seven—where Tommy Kron would pass to Louie Dampier and set a pick on his man. If their guards switched instead of trying to work through the pick, Seven would become Seven and Go Backdoor, with Kron rolling and then streaking to the basket. In practices they ran Go Backdoor as often as they ran Seven. In practice everything would move seamlessly, from blocking out to rebounding to setting picks until somebody screwed up.

"No, goddamn it!" Rupp would shout, stomping onto the floor to rail against some failure of execution. "When you set a pick, you don't sashay like some fucking flamenco dancer," he'd say, going into a demonstration flounce. "You SET a GODDAMN PICK!" If Jackie Gleason performed it on *The Honeymooners*, everybody would have been rolling on the floor. But this was Coach Rupp. And in a Rupp practice nobody laughed.

Harry Lancaster was equally serious, but usually not as outrageous. One day during practice he pointed out an interloper up in the top row of the coliseum. Because all basketball practices were closed to the public, Slim hustled up there to perform the extraction. "Excuse me, sir, but this is a closed practice." The man responded with a shrug, but said, "I'm going to leave, but you go down there and tell that Lancaster guy to kiss my ass." When Slim got back down to the court, Harry said, "What did that guy say?" "Well, Coach, he said to kiss his ass." "Yeah, I thought he'd say something like that," said Harry. "Go see if you can find him and tell him to come down here. I'll kiss it, but he won't like it when I do."

Because Rupp practices were the sixties equivalent of a Central Intelligence Agency black-ops site, how that guy got in was never known. Gates were locked. Doors were locked. Everything was covered with yards and yards of thick, totally opaque gray canvas. Blinds were down on the windows at the top of the coliseum.

Once the players were on the court, the gate was locked behind them and then covered, top to bottom, with canvas. To say Rupp was paranoid about privacy understates his obsession by half. He was certain there were hundreds if not thousands of people who would go to any lengths to discover what went on during practice sessions.

Down on the floor Rupp was polishing the fast break that had worked with such devastating effect from Virginia and Illinois to Indiana and Texas Tech. Pat Riley rebounded the ball, with Conley streaking up the floor on one side, Kron on the other, and Dampier in the middle. Riley to Kron to Dampier for a lay-up.

There were two essentials to a Rupp's Runts fast break. Nobody had assigned lanes, and whoever got the rebound would bring the ball down the floor as fast as they could. "If I got the rebound," said Conley, "I brought it all the way down. If Tommy [Kron] got it, he'd bring it. If Louie got it, he'd bring it. If Pat got it, he'd bring it. There weren't four guys on the floor faster than the four of us. One of the things we had was a lot of speed. Not Thad. Thad was slow as shit. He ran fast enough to outrun any centers because the centers were really slow back then. On a comparative basis, he was really fast."

No matter who got the ball off the backboard, what happened next was, in Larry Conley's words, "instinctual, almost robotic." It was all about spacing. Too close together and one defender can guard two men. It was about filling gaps.

If there was a lane that was not filled, I'm over there getting into that lane. If you didn't get [the ball], you'd go under the basket, which made it hard for the defense. There were times when Tommy had the ball, and I'd look up in front of me and I might see Dampier over here and Pat over there. I would back off because they were filling the lanes to the basket. And then if we were stopped, I'd immediately go to my spot and get ready to start our offense.

Every time down the floor on the break, you see that initial push of the players running and the defense retreating and trying to pick up the players coming at them. And all of a sudden, those players kind of slow down and stop. The defense relaxes. When they relax, here comes that trailer right down the middle. And all of a sudden they realize they haven't covered that easy lay-up. Riley used to get a lot of baskets like that.

Rebound. Pass. Pass. Run.

Out-of-bounds on the side against a pressing defense set up one pattern, under the basket another. If Adolph thought they might have to play against gorillas, there would have been a banana plan for sure. Rupp had been playing and coaching, living and breathing basketball for going on five decades. For him, the game of infinite permutations and manifestations was a matter of a few basic fundamentals. Practice them enough, and most of it becomes as predictable as grandma's apple pie on Thanksgiving Day. She might surprise you with a new cranberry salad she picked up from Betty Crocker, but the apple pie was a lock.

One day Rupp had the team practicing their under-the-basket out-of-bounds play where Riley, Dampier, and Jaracz lined up along the three-second line at the side of the key as if somebody were shooting a free throw. When Conley, the out-of-bounds man, slapped the ball, Dampier dropped back and Riley and Jaracz set a screen. If Dampier wasn't open, the second option was for Conley to hit Kron in the corner, run around the screen, and get the ball back. They ran the play maybe twenty times, with a few extras for subs who might be in the game down the stretch. As always Coach Rupp stepped in again and again with minor adjustments, making sure each player was exactly where he needed to be. After they'd run the play to death, Adolph flashed back to his 1949 championship team and probably his favorite player of all time, Clifford Oldham "Cliff" Hagan. "When Cliff was here, he would take the inbounds pass, go to the corner, and shoot a hook shot."

Coach Rupp was always citing Hagan as an example. His favorite Hagan story was about his first varsity season, warming up for a game in Madison Square Garden. In Rupp's telling Hagan came back to the bench and told him the basket was too high. "Here was this little shit from Owensboro telling me that they didn't know how to fix the goals in downtown New York City," Rupp would say, warming to his story. "I told him to get his butt back out there and shoot the basketball. After a few minutes he came back to the bench again and said, 'Coach, I don't care where we are, the basket isn't the right height.' So I got the people there in the Garden to check, and sure enough it was off by a quarter of an inch."

Now Rupp was waxing nostalgic about the Hagan Hook. Cliff Hagan did have the most beautiful hook shot ever seen. He could hit it from almost anywhere within twenty feet of the basket. "Now I know some of you fellows don't know how to shoot a hook shot," Rupp continued. "You should learn from those who can."

Standing off to the side, Conley and Riley contemplated the question. "Which one of you guys will be the first to shoot a hook shot from the corner?"

"Yeah, right," whispered Pat. "Good way to get yourself killed."

17

Give Iowa a Try

For his Broadway musical *The Music Man*, Meredith Wilson wrote a song about Iowa's "chip-on-the-shoulder attitude." That attitude was very much on display when the mighty Iowa Hawkeyes came to town to participate in El Paso's annual Sun Carnival Tournament. The new issue of *Sports Illustrated* had Iowa center George Peeples on the cover with the headline "Iowa Challenges in the Big Ten." The six-foot-seven center, a prolific scorer and dominant rebounder, promised to be a handful for Nevil Shed, who'd drawn the assignment to keep him in check.

At the kickoff luncheon for coaches and players of the four competing teams, Iowa coach Ralph Miller made no mention of the Texas Western game. Instead, looking ahead, he talked about the tough schedule his team would be facing in January and how they were going to overpower everyone. Coach Haskins was a gifted speaker known for his off-the-cuff, often humorous remarks, like the time he introduced team doctor Bill Dickey as "our pecker checker." This time he was both brief and serious. Looking at Coach Miller he said, "When you walk out of the hotel, don't be surprised to see us waiting because we're going to start guarding you at the hotel door." Miller just smiled.

There was something of a murmur going around the room. Detractors had been saying that finally Coach Haskins would get his comeuppance.

Haskins was never much for talk in the locker room before a game, but once the players were taped, dressed, and ready, he took chalk in hand. On the blackboard he wrote the number 35. He'd done that before other games, so everybody knew what it meant. Tonight they were supposed to hold the Iowa Hawkeyes, a Big Ten powerhouse ranked fourth in the country, to thirty-five points. Tonight Ralph Miller would not be smiling.

Don Haskins didn't smile either. Always, no matter what was happening on the floor, he had a game-face intensity. Less than a minute into the game, his clip-on tie came off, as it always did, and he stood on the sideline clutching a rolled-up program, watching his team demonstrate the smothering defense he'd been drumming into their heads in practice.

"We overwhelmed them," said Harry Flournoy. "Once they crossed the half-court line, they were ours. That basket we were defending—that they're trying to score baskets on—that's our basket. That's how we looked at it."

Before the mighty Hawkeyes and their arrogant coach knew what hit them, they were on the down side of a 21-4 score. Two of their points came when Nevil Shed, battling for a rebound, slapped the ball into Iowa's basket. It might have been the *SI* jinx, or it might have been Shed living up to his reputation as the Shadow, but cover-boy Peeples had yet to touch the ball. It wasn't until Haskins started subbing midway through the second half that Iowa managed to avoid an embarrassing bloodbath. The home crowd loved it, but Haskins, watching from the bench, was disgusted. "We didn't play a lick" in the second half, he wrote. "So even though we crushed the number four team in the country, at home, in front of an overflow crowd . . . I was sitting on the bench miserable. I just could not accept anything less than a complete and total effort."

His team, true to form, reverted to what their coach called "street ball" on offense and a lackadaisical defense that let Iowa outscore them in the second half by three points. Instead of the 35 Haskins had written on the blackboard, Iowa managed to slink out of town with a respectable-looking sixty-eight points. The final score, 86-68, left Haskins shaking his head. "We should have beaten them by thirty-five or forty. I wanted to hold their asses under forty."

The handshake between coaches after the game was perfunctory, but Haskins now knew what he'd suspected from the beginning: his team was special. In the locker room the team knew it too. "It was really the game where I think we all realized we had a pretty damn good team," said Dick Myers. "We literally blew them out of the gym. And, at that point, we figured, hey, we can play with anybody."

The Miners had arrived, but their coach was still mad about their second-half letdown. Years later he would say, "We'd win and I'm mad. We'd lose and I'm mad." Win or lose, if it was a home game, Haskins would get into his pickup and drive off into the night, away from the lights of the city, out across the arid desert for a round-trip he described as "four Buds each way," reliving the game's ups and down and pondering how to motivate his charges to play forty minutes of in-your-face basketball.

18

Neutral-Court Advantage

The Kentucky–Notre Dame game was always special because it was played at Louisville's Freedom Hall, giving eighteen thousand Kentucky fans who couldn't find tickets for games at Memorial Coliseum in Lexington the opportunity to see Big Blue in action. Because Rupp never scheduled a game against any other Kentucky colleges and home games were sold out, two or three thousand fans who couldn't find tickets for the game itself showed up to see the Wildcats shootaround the morning of the game. The game was also special because of Rupp's history against Notre Dame. In his early years the Fighting Irish never had to fight all that much (Rupp was 5-11 in his first sixteen Notre Dame games), especially on their home court.

Rupp's complaints after losses in South Bend included the Notre Dame band that occupied the bleachers right behind Kentucky's bench, making it impossible for him to hear the whistle or talk to his players. He was even more discombobulated by the three hundred black-robed priests on the opposite side of the court. "No way can we win at Notre Dame," said Rupp. "Impossible."

The Louisville series, inaugurated in 1960, gave Kentucky a chance to meet Notre Dame on a neutral court, although Freedom Hall was about as neutral for the Wildcats as playing at the Vatican would be for Notre Dame. Still, in Rupp's mind at least, there was *the Catholic problem*. He didn't face a phalanx of black robes in Louisville, but it bothered him that Notre Dame players crossed themselves before shooting free throws. In 1958 Rupp's antidote had been a six-foot-seven forward from Fort Valley, Georgia, named Ed Beck.

Beck was the SEC defensive player of the year, but, more important, he was a Methodist minister. Beck recalled Rupp's pregame speech. "Boys, I don't want you to get upset or feel outnumbered when Notre Dame boys cross themselves. Now don't worry about all those priests that they have on the bench because we have them outnumbered. We have Ed, and I know he has been praying." Beck recalls how Rupp pulled a small carved Madonna out of his pocket with a sly grin. "The last time I was in Rome, the pope blessed this, and I have put a hex on Notre Dame."

During three years of the Louisville series, from 1961 to 1964, Rupp's hex, aided no doubt by a pro-Kentucky priest on his bench, worked out well. A contributing factor may have been Cotton Nash, who racked up thirty-one, twenty-six, and thirty-three points in three successive Notre Dame outings. There would be no Cotton to lead the way this season, but Rupp's competitive juices were stoked by his long and continuing animosity toward Notre Dame coach Johnny Dee. A decade earlier Rupp told reporters his 1954 team was "the finest team ever assembled in the United States." Dee, then coaching at the University of Alabama, responded by asking reporters, "How can he tell? He hasn't played anyone." After leaving Alabama Dee questioned Rupp's eight-hundred-plus wins because so many of them were against SEC opponents. "That's like me going down to Texas with six kids from Canada and starting a hockey league." Rupp's NCAA Championship–bound team answered for their coach by beating Dee's Crimson Tide by twenty-five points that year and fourteen the next. Dee got his revenge the year after that by administering an old-fashioned twenty-four-point butt-kicking, 101–77. After that game Adolph told reporters, "Boys, back when I was playing we would have taken that ball and eaten it—chewed it up and swallowed it—before we would ever let them score 100 points on us."

It was a decade later when Dee, by then at Notre Dame, not only beat Rupp's Wildcats 111–97, scoring the highest total ever against a Kentucky team, but also outrebounded them 81–49, another record. "That was the story of the game," said Rupp. "It just proves that we're going to have to go out and get ourselves some big boys or we're dead." Some big boys *were* recruited, including six-foot-eight high school All-American Wes Unseld, but they didn't come (Unseld, an African

American, ended up playing many a game at Freedom Hall, all for the University of Louisville).

The Louisville motel where the team stayed was less than five minutes from Freedom Hall. They could have walked it in ten, so even when the bus failed to materialize at the appointed time there was no real problem. In a philosophical mood Rupp might say something like, "Time and tide wait for no man," but the philosophical Rupp was nowhere to be found on game day. He burst out of the hotel, fifteen minutes before the scheduled 6:00 p.m. departure, in a frenzy. "Where's the goddamn bus?" Slim didn't have an answer, but he did have a solution. Taxies to the rescue. Five minutes later they were on their way, with Rupp, as always, in the lead cab.

Freedom Hall, usually an impressive sight in the glow of evening, was dark when the cabs pulled up to the players' entrance. Nobody there except the cleaning crew and the vendors setting up booths in anticipation of the crowd to come. With the concern about a tardy arrival safely behind him, Rupp went on to his next concern. That would come soon enough.

The Double Five pregame warm-up drill, with its intricate cuts and passes, had UK fans whooping it up. Thad Jaracz was in the middle, passing to cutters on both sides, when Tommy Kron came through at warp speed. Kron's teeth caught the back of Thad's left hand, his shooting hand. "Damn!" he said, holding his bleeding paw. "That hurts like hell." When Thad and the team doctor left for the locker room, it looked like a Cliff Berger night, but Doc Jackson gave Thad a shot and bandage, and he was back. No way was he going to let a high-speed bite relegate him to the bench.

As always the crowd was highly partisan Kentucky, but the format of the Freedom Hall series called for alternating "home" teams. In the 1965–66 season Notre Dame was the home team. They wore the white uniforms. They furnished the game ball. For the most part a basketball is a basketball, just as a rose is a rose. On the other hand, there are slight differences in the width of the seams from one manufacturer to another. Not much but enough so that the visiting team used the game ball for its pregame warm-up.

Coach Dee had a reputation of switching balls at game time to gain whatever advantage that might afford during the first few possessions. So when Kentucky went to the locker room for Rupp's last-minute instructions, Slim handed the ball to the referee. Sure enough, just before the starting tip-off, Dee approached the referee with another ball. "No, sir," said Slim. "That's the ball you designated as the game ball." Dee shrugged and smiled.

The supposed advantage of practicing with the game ball didn't show. From the beginning Kentucky looked like the pre-Thanksgiving team that had people thinking they might turn out to be Rupp's worst team ever.

At halftime Adolph grumbled, but Harry Lancaster was livid. "I don't believe what I'm seeing!" he shouted. "What happened to your goddamn hustle? Don't let their white shirts fool you. They're the bad guys. This crowd came to see Kentucky basketball, and you're showing them . . . shit! That's what."

Not in the second half. Once again the Runts were dominating the boards, running the breaks, executing the plays, finding the open man, synchronizing their defense. Thad, bad paw and all, had one of his best scoring games, hitting for sixteen points.

"I was living the dream," Thad recalled, reflecting on the season. "I show up. Nobody thinks I'm going to play, and here I am. What do I have to do to continue to be successful? I've got to guard my guy. I've got to block out, get rebounds, and get out on the fast break. If I do that, Conley's going to throw me the ball. So who've I got to please? I've got to please Conley."

Conley *was* pleased. Displaying a passing wizardry that kept the "neutral" crowd on its feet for most of the second half, Conley saw Riley hit for thirty-six, Dampier for twenty-six. Only a rock concert combining the Beatles and Beach Boys could have matched decibel levels, as fans roared approval of their Wildcats' 107–69 victory.

Lost to history is the name of the wire-service reporter who dubbed that year's Kentucky Wildcats Rupp's Runts (there was no byline on the story). Earlier in the season *Lexington Leader* sports reporter Russell Rice had labeled the team the Selfless Six, including Cliff Berger in the mix. It didn't stick. Rupp's Runts did. After the Notre Dame game the alliteration became part of Kentucky basketball lore. The Big Blue Nation had embraced the Fabulous Five and then the Fiddlin' Five. Both teams won national championships. Rupp's Runts never did, but they caught the imagination of their basketball-obsessed state, joining the pantheon of Kentucky's greatest teams, over the years moving to the top spot in hearts and sacred memory.

19

The Break from Hell

After ending the year with the Iowa butt-kicking, the Miners started 1966 with a couple of fairly competitive home games. They won by nine against a good Tulsa team on January 3 and by twelve against Seattle three days later. Then came the three-week break in the schedule the team had been dreading since the start of fall practice. Part of the dread was the reason for the break: finals, never an especially happy time on a college campus. Most of the dread was Haskins. Twelve games in the past thirty days had given them much-needed breaks from the grueling, unrelenting daily grind. Now it would be wall-to-wall practices for twenty straight days, *the break from hell*. The team was on a roll, and their coach was not about to have them lose their edge.

With the easy part of the schedule behind them, there had been only one close game—the two-point win over Fresno State—to test their mettle. Years later Bobby Joe Hill was asked, "What was the toughest team you played in the championship season?" There were more than a few barn burners to choose from. "The toughest team I played against," he responded, "was every day in practice."

Like Kentucky, like any really good college team, the importance of the second five to Texas Western's success can hardly be overstated. On a game-by-game basis, having bench players who can fill in seamlessly when a starter is injured or in foul trouble is critical. As a unit they are even more important for the hard-nosed, gamelike competition they give the starters every day in practice. Togo Railey, who played only at Garbage Time that season, put it most succinctly: "Because you didn't play, you wanted to make sure the guy representing you out there was the best he could be. We had great players with great attitudes."

"Every single one of those guys could have gone to another school and started," said Nevil Shed. "Every day in practice Louis B. 'Flip' Baudoin gave me pure hell." At six feet seven Flip matched up well against Shed's six feet eight. He could also handle the ball, shoot from distance, and drive to the basket. "I remember one day he dunked on me several times," Shed recalled. "Haskins went crazy."

It was Jerry Armstrong who usually drew the assignment of guarding Big Daddy Lattin; the task was daunting. "He was so strong that he could hold you back with his elbow and arm," says Armstrong. "He could hold you back, catch the ball, and score." Jerry played to Lattin's strong side, the ball side, attempting, mostly hoping, to deny him the ball. Otherwise, "His strength against my strength? I couldn't handle that." But he could put up a fight that prepared Lattin for battles to come and earned Jerry playing opportunities that would be important in the final half of the season.

With the tough part of the schedule still ahead, Haskins redoubled his focus on conditioning and free throws. During the January break he combined the two. The ten-in-a-row rule before you could hit the shower was still in effect, and the lower your free-throw percentage the more times you ran the bleachers. "We learned to shoot properly, take our time, spin the ball truly," said Baudoin. With Haskins setting the standard with his no-look shooting, "We figured if he could pull it off, we could, too."

True to form, Haskins's concentration during the finals break was defense. Hour after hour the starters worked against the second team while their coach critiqued their every move. Sometimes he liked what he saw. More often, a failure of execution would bring out the Haskins-isms. "Damn it, Shed, you're playing like a girl again!" he'd shout when the big forward didn't fight through a screen. "I'm going to get you a pink dress." When David Lattin let Willie Cager get by him for a rebound that should have been his, Haskins said, "You didn't jump high enough to get a Kleenex under your feet." Once when the team seemed lethargic, he shook his head in disgust. "You can't beat your grandmother playing like that." Then the inevitable: "*Run the lines.*"

The Miners were bored and exhausted by the endless repetition of five-on-five defensive drills, but sometimes there was even more frustration on offense. With no shot clock, the Haskins principle was Pass and Move, Pass and Move, Pass and Move: Work the Ball until you found the weak link, the guy on the other team who didn't want to defend anymore, then take him to the hole. Especially against a team that wanted to run, his teams would work the ball into the post man and outside as many as three times, moving the ball until they got *the shot you should take*. And if you had an open fifteen-footer after only a single pass? "Oh, no, no, no, no, no, you don't do that," one player explained. "The idea was to work them to death on your end so it was easier to shut them down on theirs."

Coach Haskins wasn't much for pontificating, but he knew another thing that was likely to happen as the season progressed. It had to do with racial taunts. Most teams they played in the championship season had two or three African American players, but on the road their starting lineup of five blacks often fueled latent racism. The Miners were called everything from niggers to coons to burr heads. "My rule was if they ever saw me turn around and acknowledge some fan," Haskins wrote, "they can do it too. But if I don't ever do it . . . then by God they better not do it either. That kept them in check and kept me in check, because there were some necks I wanted to wring. But I knew if I did, half my team would be in the stands slugging fans and that would be that."

Although Haskins never responded to taunts, there was a time during one home game when a guy just five rows behind the bench was giving him a particularly vicious kind of hell. "Haskins, you stupid sonofabitch, what the hell you think you're doing playing a whole team of jigaboos? Get some white guys in there, you goddamn nigger lover."

"Can you find Stretch?" Haskins asked sports information director Eddie Mullens at halftime. Carlton B. "Stretch" Elliot was a six-foot-four, 250-pound University of Virginia graduate who went on to play tight end for the Green Bay Packers. At the start of the second half, with Stretch now dwarfing Haskins's nemesis with his hulking presence, Vicious unleashed another torrent of vitriol. When he paused to take a breath, Stretch leaned down and whispered something to him quietly. Vicious gave Stretch a wide-eyed, deer-in-the-headlights look and made a quick decision. Urgent business required his presence elsewhere.

20

"The Secret of Basketball"

With the decisive win over Notre Dame, Rupp's Runts still hadn't lost a game and may have been just a bit overconfident. Five days later was a home game against the Billikens of St. Louis University, the final outing before diving into their all-important conference schedule. St. Louis had gone to the Elite Eight fourteen years ago and produced a couple of NBA players—Easy Ed Macaulay and Bob Ferry—along the way. Two years before, when Tommy Kron and Larry Conley were sophomores, Pat Riley and Louie Dampier were on the freshman team, and Thad Jaracz was a high school senior, Rupp was so embarrassed by a loss in St. Louis that he got the team up at six the following morning and hustled them off to the airport so he wouldn't have to talk about the game with reporters and fans from western Kentucky who had driven over the state line to see their Wildcats in action. This season St. Louis was better known for their elf-like mascot with his pixie ears and pointy head (the Billiken) than for their prowess on a basketball court. But they were up for the game, and Kentucky wasn't. The Wildcats won by ten points, but if ESPN had been around in those days, there would have been nothing for the *SportsCenter* highlights.

Yet probably because of their dominance over Notre Dame, the polls that came out that Monday had Kentucky ranked number two. "The Runts look good," said former Kentucky standout Randy Embry, "but they haven't been on the road in the SEC. That will tell me whether they're really good or not." For Randy, and for UK fans everywhere, the game the following weekend—on the road in the SEC against the Florida Gators—would be critical.

The University of Florida had a reputation as a football school, but their young coach, "Stormin' Norman" Sloan (who would one day lead his alma mater North Carolina State to a national championship), was intent on bringing Gator basketball into the consciousness of Gainesville fans. That afternoon, with the high-flying Kentucky Wildcats in town, it happened.

Florida Gymnasium, otherwise known as Alligator Alley, seemed a totally different place than it had been at morning shootaround. Then the basketball court was a postage stamp in the middle of a vast earthen field house; its baskets—hung from the ceiling—seemed to be floating in space. Now as the team made their way from the locker room on the far side of the massive structure about a block away, they heard what sounded like a herd of stampeding elephants. It wasn't until they got to the court that they realized the cacophony was coming from Florida fans stomping on metal bleachers yelling at the top of their lungs, "GATOR BAIT! GATOR BAIT! GATOR BAIT!"

Not exactly. What they saw was a game effort by the Gators and a clinic by the Runts. Thad Jaracz lit them up for twenty-six points on eleven-for-fifteen shooting, and the Wildcats were the team future Hall of Fame coach Al McGuire was talking about when he said, "Kentucky has found the secret of basketball, that it's five guys playing together." With Florida concentrating on defending against Riley and Dampier, Conley hit for seventeen, as Kron became the playmaker. Five guys playing together won by a score of 78–64.

After the game Larry Conley came to Slim with a problem. Somehow he and Tommy Kron had lined up dates for that evening and didn't want to be constrained by Rupp's regular curfew. One of Slim's jobs as student manager was to make sure everybody on the team was in their room by eleven o'clock. Because Larry and Tommy were roommates, they made a bargain. "I'll bypass your room tonight if you guys promise to be on time for breakfast tomorrow morning. Agreed?"

The year before Larry and Tommy had been caught trying to sneak back into the motel from another Gator date. As Larry tells the story, "Just as Tom turned the corner, there was Coach Lancaster." While Harry is chewing Tommy a new one, "I'm up against the wall . . . I'm not even moving and not saying a word." Larry escaped detection that night, but

1. Having won four NCAA Championships in a single decade, Adolph Rupp was "a man of consummate pride," wrote Frank Deford, obsessively pursuing "the only challenge left, trying to top himself." Photo by Rich Clarkson.

2. Born the year Adolph Rupp started coaching at Kentucky, Don Haskins described himself as "kind of a punk" compared to Rupp. Asked if he had employed a special strategy in the championship game, he answered, "Yes, I prayed." Photo by Rich Clarkson.

3. An All-American in both football and basketball at Schenectady's Linton High School, Pat Riley (34) passed on an offer to play quarterback for Bear Bryant at Alabama to follow his dream of playing basketball at Kentucky for Adolph Rupp. Courtesy of Schenectady Athletic Hall of Fame.

4. David Lattin was a *Parade* High School All-American after leading Houston's Worthing High School to the Texas State Championship, averaging twenty-nine points a game. Courtesy of David Lattin.

5. With four returning starters—Conley, Dampier, Riley, and Kron—Kentucky
began the 1965-66 season in search of a center who could help make them competitive against their taller competition. Courtesy of the *Lexington Herald-Leader*.

6. (*top*) Harry Flournoy was stunned when he walked into Coach Haskins's office and found his mother with tears in her eyes. Disappointed by his failing grades, she stayed for a week, forcing him to study. Later, Haskins had a phone at courtside labeled "Harry's Mom." Courtesy of Harry Flournoy.

7. (*bottom*) Steve Tredennick ended his playing career the year before the championship season still disliking Coach Haskins. Later he became Haskins's lawyer and friend, playing a pivotal role in helping TWC become the only college team admitted to the Naismith Memorial Basketball Hall of Fame. Courtesy of the UTEP Athletic Department.

8. Nolan Richardson had been TWC's leading scorer the year before Haskins arrived. "I hear you can't guard a telegraph poll," said his new coach. Nolan became a defensive specialist and, after graduation, a Haskins friend and Hall of Fame coach in his own right. Courtesy of the UTEP Athletic Department.

9. (*top*) Because of Rupp's aversion to the distraction of girlfriends, Tommy Kron and Dianne Berger arranged with a Lexington jeweler to sneak in at night to select her engagement ring. Courtesy of Dianne Kron.

10. (*bottom*) After beating Michigan in the Mideast Regional in Iowa City, Rupp's Runts—(*left to right*) Larry Conley, Rupp, Tommy Kron, Thad Jaracz, Pat Riley, and Louie Dampier—believed they were eighty minutes away from UK's fifth NCAA Championship. Courtesy of the University of Kentucky Athletic Department.

11. (*top*) The referee ruled that Kansas star Jo Jo White had stepped out-of-bounds before he made the thirty-foot jumper that would have ended TWC's season. Watching game film, Rupp's Runts thought his foot was above the line, not on it, and that Kansas should have won. Photo by Rich Clarkson.

12. (*bottom*) Jerry Armstrong helped to slow down Utah star Jerry Chambers in the semifinal game of the NCAA Tournament. Legendary coach Henry Iba said TWC wouldn't have made it to the championship game without his defense. Photo by Rich Clarkson.

13. After blocking Pat Riley's first shot, David Lattin followed Haskins's pregame instructions, "flushing" the ball over Pat, drawing a foul, and establishing inside dominance. Photo by Rich Clarkson.

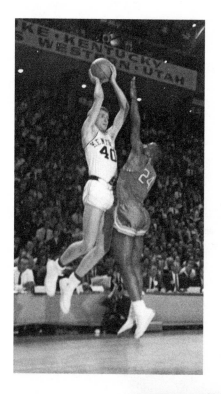

14. (*top*) On Kentucky's first posses-sion, six-foot-three Larry Conley couldn't believe his luck. "I had a five-six guy [Willie Worsley] guard-ing me. It shouldn't have worked, but it did." Photo by Rich Clarkson. 15. (*bottom*) An injured knee made it impossible for Harry Flournoy to keep up with Pat Riley, so he took himself out of the game, leav-ing Texas Western without its best rebounder for thirty-four minutes. Photo by Rich Clarkson.

16. Ten seconds after stealing the ball from Tommy Kron, Bobby Joe Hill picked Louie Dampier's pocket, hushing the crowd by displaying a level of quickness Kentucky hadn't seen all season. Photo by Rich Clarkson.

17. (*top*) "You stupid sons-abitches!" shouted Rupp, after the steals and a David Lattin dunk put Kentucky on the short end of a 16–11 score. Kentucky would never regain the lead. Photo by Rich Clarkson.

18. (*bottom*) Bubbling with confidence, Bobby Joe Hill told Haskins, "I can steal it from him anytime you want me to." "Just lay off," said Haskins. "You've got him gun-shy now." Photo by Rich Clarkson.

19. One of two Miners (with Harry Flournoy) recruited sight unseen out of Gary, Indiana, Orsten Artis had a silky-smooth jump shot. He was the only player who could beat Don Haskins in a free-throw contest. Photo by Rich Clarkson.

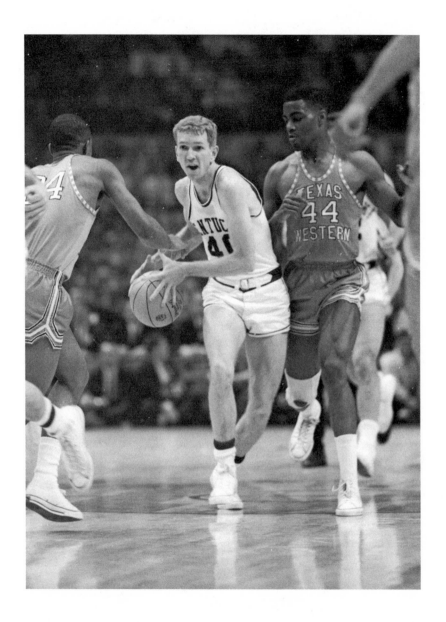

20. "The key to Kentucky," wrote Frank Deford in *SI* near the end of the season, "is Conley, a frail and unusually perceptive young man who is a rarity, a play-making forward." Photo by Rich Clarkson.

21. Haskins, who always covered his eyes during free throws, missed seeing the Miners go twenty-eight for thirty-four at the foul stripe against Kentucky, including one stretch where they made twenty-six of twenty-seven. Photo by Rich Clarkson.

22. (*top*) Out of the game on fouls, Thad Jaracz (55) still believed. "Our confidence was unbelievable," he said. "We thought we were going to win the game until we got beat." Photo by Rich Clarkson.

23. (*bottom*) Don Haskins had a bear hug for team leader Bobby Joe Hill in the victory celebration following the Texas Western win. Photo by Rich Clarkson.

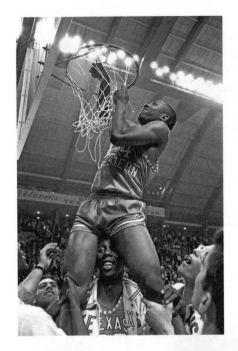

24. (*top*) Balanced on Nevil Shed's head, little Willie Worsley took down the nets loop by loop while teammates Jerry Armstrong and Dick Myers held him steady. Photo by Rich Clarkson.

25. (*bottom*) As Nevil Shed walked off the court with his arm around Harry Flournoy, he spotted his parents in the crowd and pointed at them to say, *Thanks for everything*. Photo by Rich Clarkson.

26. A backup guard in the Rupp's Runts season, Bob Tallent was kicked off the team the following year for arguing with Coach Rupp. He went on to set single-season scoring records at George Washington University that still stand. Courtesy of George Washington University.

27. Front row (*left to right*): Bobby Joe Hill, Orsten Artis, Togo Railey, and Willie Worsley. Second row: David Palacio, Dick Myers, Harry Flournoy, and Louis Baudoin. Third row: Nevil Shed, Jerry Armstrong, Willie Cager, David Lattin, and Coach Don Haskins. Courtesy of the UTEP Athletic Department.

28. Front row (*left to right*): Adolph Rupp, Gene Stewart, Pat Riley, Louie Dampier, Bob Tallent, Steve Clevenger, Jim LeMaster, and Harry Lancaster. Top row: Tom Porter, Gary Gamble, Tom Kron, Cliff Berger, Larry Lentz, Brand Bounds, Thad Jaracz, Larry Conley, and Mike "Slim" Harreld. Courtesy of the University of Kentucky Athletic Department.

not suspicion. Rupp started calling Tommy and Larry the Katzenjam-mer Kids, a reference to comic-strip brothers Hans and Fritz who were always pulling pranks, always rebelling against authority, and always getting spanked at the end of the panel.

This time the Katzenjammer Kids got back in from their dates with-out Harry's interception and were on time for breakfast the following morning, a bit blurry-eyed but on time.

After breakfast the team flew from Gainesville 350 miles north for a Monday-night encounter with the University of Georgia. In those days, as now, the Georgia Bulldogs were known as a football power that also, rumor had it, played some basketball. Ken Rosemond had known bas-ketball glory as a member of McGuire's 1957 national champion North Carolina Tar Heels, but now, ten games into his career as Georgia's head coach, he was finding out what it was like to move through life unno-ticed. On Monday night people noticed.

With Stegeman Coliseum exceeding the fire marshal's designated capacity of 10,500 by at least 1,000, Rosemond's Bulldogs played the Wildcats to a draw. Not once, but twice. Their tenacious defense shut down Rupp's vaunted fast break. Their in-your-face offense kept pound-ing the ball inside, kept rebounding, kept matching Kentucky shot for shot. And now, in the final minutes of the game, both Thad and Pat were in foul trouble.

"There was never a mistake about [Pat's] fouls," said Larry. "If a guy went in for a lay-up and beat him, [Pat] would hammer him and knock him into the third row and then help the guy up and say, 'Are you okay?' Pat didn't have any cheap fouls." With Thad it was different. If he was having trouble guarding his man, he would reach out and grab him. Larry would say, "You think you might move your feet just a little bit?" Thad's response: "I can't keep up with the sonofabitch." "He was bad about that," Larry recalled. "Oh, my God!"

When Thad was whistled for his fifth foul three minutes into the sec-ond overtime, Bulldog fans sensed an upset. Cliff Berger, who'd watched most of the game from the bench, checked into the Kentucky lineup with something of a target on his back. A late-game substitute, six feet eight, hasn't played a lot. "It wasn't exactly Hack-a-Shaq," he recalled some fifty years later, "but basically, that's what happened." After Kron made a twelve-foot jumper to put Kentucky up by two, the Bulldogs targeted the new guy with a hard foul, hoping to get the ball back.

On the season Cliff Berger's free-throw percentage hovered in the mid-70s, but lately he'd been struggling. So much so that, at the morning shootaround, senior cocaptain Kron came over to observe as the sophomore backup center went through his foul-shot routine: bounce the ball three times while concentrating on the front of the rim, then into his shooting motion, making some, missing some. Kron had a suggestion. Because Berger had a deadly turnaround jumper from fifteen to seventeen feet—even with a defender's hand in his face—why not use the same approach at the free-throw line? "Instead of staring at the rim," Kron instructed, "concentrate on the ball. Bounce it three times, look up, see the rim, shoot."

GOOOO DAWGS! Sick 'em. WOOF, WOOF, WOOF! screamed Bulldog fans, bringing their traditional football cheer indoors for this most improbable occasion. Oblivious of the crowd waving their arms frantically on the stage behind the glass backboard, Berger toed the line, focusing on his new routine. When the referee handed him the ball, he bounced it three times. As he came up into his shooting motion, he eyed the rim for the first time. The ball was up and . . . in. Second shot, same routine, same result.

Georgia was almost out of options when guard Dick McIntosh made a shot from the corner to renew Bulldog hopes. Now Kentucky was playing keep-away. When the ball went to Berger in the low post, the Hack was on again. Six seconds on the clock. Wildcats up by two. Just maybe.

The sound of the crowd was deafening as Berger stepped to the line, focused on his routine. Bounce the ball three times. Begin shooting motion. Look at the rim. Two shots. Two points.

When the game was over Dampier had his usual twenty-three, Riley and Jaracz fourteen apiece, but it was Cliff Berger who saved the day, and the win streak. In the second OT, thanks to his free throws, Kentucky finally got the advantage, winning a 69–65 thriller. In his book Harry Lancaster wrote of a time when Rupp said, "Beating Georgia is like kissing your sister." Not this time.

On the flight back to Lexington, with a spent team trying to get some sleep on the seats behind him, Adolph was content. Looking down as they passed over the flickering lights of rural Kentucky, he leaned across the aisle. "Slim, I think we got them so shook up tonight, they just can't go to sleep."

21

Togo Time

Togo Railey glanced at the clock, triggering the reaction from the hometown crowd he knew to expect: *To-Go. To-Go.* At the other end of the bench, Coach Haskins seemed not to hear. With less than three minutes to play against New Mexico State, in their third straight cakewalk after the finals break, the Miners were ahead by a comfortable twenty points. It was definitely *Togo Time*. He looked at the clock again, then up at the stands. The chant grew louder: *To-Go. To-Go.* Still no reaction from Haskins. Now, in a slow-motion movement, "I reached down and unzipped one pant leg," said Togo. "By the time I did my striptease and got out of my warm-ups, I knew I was going to get to play a little bit." With the crowd now going wild, Haskins smiled. *He was my human victory cigar*, Haskins would say, a reference to Boston Celtic coach Red Auerbach, who lit a cigar when a Celtic victory was ensured. When Togo got the nod, the Miner faithful went wild. With fourteen games left in the championship season, it would be Togo's final appearance.

Albert T. "Togo" Railey was a military brat whose dad was stationed at El Paso's Fort Bliss. Togo attended Austin High School, where he was a good-enough basketball player to be part of a platoon tasked with guarding Nolan Richardson when Austin squared off against Bowie High School. "We shut you down, big guy," Togo tells Richardson whenever they've met over the years. Well, almost. Richardson averaged twenty-eight points a game that season. Against Austin (and Togo) he scored a mere twenty-seven.

Togo earned a spot, and a good deal of playing time, as a walk-on freshman in Haskins's second season at Texas Western and continued as a nonscholarship player his sophomore year. After Togo sat out the next year Haskins asked him to rejoin the team for what turned out to be the championship season. "With a scholarship?" Togo asked. "We'll take care of you," said Haskins.

With another year of eligibility Togo Railey stayed on scholarship the following season and actually became a starter. For one game. "Togo," said Haskins as the team was about to take the floor for a home game against Mississippi State, "you're starting."

"Everybody was shocked," said Togo. "Mostly me." It took the home-town crowd more than a minute to realize what was happening, but when they did a very nervous player was greeted with a chorus of "*To-Go, To-Go, To-Go*." After playing the point for some four minutes, he was back in his accustomed place at the end of the bench. But ever after, when asked about his playing career, Togo Railey gives a straight-faced answer: *I started*. "I did. For that one game. I was so proud."

Years later Railey asked a serious question. "Coach, I want to know why you kept me around all those years." "Oh, Togo," Haskins responded. "I was trying to make an All-American out of you."

22

Clyde and the Commodores

After dodging a bullet to keep their winning streak alive, it was about to get serious for Kentucky. Vanderbilt was coming to town, and Rupp was even more nervous than usual. Nervous because their All-American center Clyde Lee, all six feet ten of him, was back for his senior year and on track to repeat as SEC player of the year. Lee had dominated the boards at both ends of the floor last season, leading the Commodores to the conference championship. More important to Adolph was a pair of Kentucky losses that needed avenging. Last year he had John Adams, who matched Lee's size if not his athletic gifts. This year, as Adolph kept stressing in a continuous loop in practices and the film room, the designated avenger was Thad Jaracz. Thad, all six feet five of him, had held his own against the big men he'd faced so far, but Lee was different. "This guy's for real," said Rupp. "If you don't put a body on him, he'll steal your hat, ass, and raincoat."

It was a matchup between second-ranked Kentucky and third-ranked Vanderbilt, and it was a game that lived up to the hype. Lee proved his All-American bona fides with a solid thirty-point, eleven-rebound performance. It wasn't enough. The Wildcats won the battle of the boards 50–40 and mounted the most balanced scoring attack of the season. Louie Dampier and Pat Riley led Kentucky with twenty-eight and twenty-four points, with Tommy Kron and Thad Jaracz adding sixteen and fifteen. Larry Conley had eleven. Those five players accounted for all but two of Kentucky's points. Cliff Berger added a pair of free throws to bring the final score to 96–83.

It was all a matter of conditioning and those god-awful Joe B. Hall wind sprints. Other teams hung in there for a half or three quarters, but in the waning minutes . . . "Then it was just a matter of, all right, who's in the best shape?" said Conley. "Let's decide it now. And that was going to be us."

After the Vandy game the Wildcats moved beyond sports columns to the pages of *Time*. An article titled "The Baron's Runts" told of sixteen straight wins and had Rupp on track for an unprecedented fifth national championship. The magazine's cover story was about Secretary of State Dean Rusk forecasting another win, this one by American forces in Vietnam. A body count ratio of ten to one in the United States' favor made victory all but inevitable. Maybe, just maybe, there was a "light at the end of the tunnel," as Johnson administration officials kept saying. On the other hand, one day when Coach Rupp was reading the *Wall Street Journal* while waiting to board an airplane, something he always seemed to be doing whenever he had to wait even a few minutes, he shook his head sadly. "We killed forty of them and they killed three of us, and so we won? I don't think they've got that right. I think if you talked to Ho Chi Minh, he'd say they won." What President Johnson, Rusk, and Defense Secretary Robert McNamara didn't seem to understand, he said, is "they're fighting for their country."

There was another Kentucky story in that week's *Time*. Kentucky governor Edward Breathitt had just signed a civil rights bill that "opens to Negroes all public facilities except barbershops, beauty shops and private clubs." The story said the governor had "reason to be proud" because it was the first civil rights bill in any state south of Ohio.

23

They Could Be Very Good

"What do you think, Eddie?" asked a local reporter after one of the early-season games in El Paso. "Is it going to be a good team?" Eddie Mullens looked around the group gathered at the Pancake Cottage a block away from Memorial Gym and nodded. "I do. I think they could be very good." Now, fifteen games into the season, he still thought so, but the Texas Western Miners still hadn't faced any serious competition. Tonight they would.

Colorado State University had won the Western Athletic Conference Championship in 1965, losing a squeaker to Oklahoma City in the opening round of the NCAA Tournament. With high-scoring guard Lonnie Wright back in Fort Collins for his senior year, the Rams were on their way to another WAC Championship and a second straight trip to what, a decade later, Hall of Fame coach Al McGuire would call the Big Dance.

There wasn't much dancing tonight. It was hard-core, bust-your-butt basketball, with neither team able to gain much of an advantage. With twelve seconds to go and the game knotted at 66, Bobby Joe Hill brought the ball across the midcourt line. Lonnie Wright, a gifted athlete who went on to play professionally both football and basketball, was playing him loose for good reason. Hill had been displaying his uncanny ability to weave through a thicket of Rams all night long. Then it was lay-up city, or, when the weak-side defender moved in to help, Bobby Joe dumped the ball off to Lattin or Flournoy for easy baskets. This time, to the surprise of nearly everyone in the gym, Bobby Joe hit the brakes, jumped into the air, and let fly from close to thirty feet. Swoosh! The buzzer sounded. The ball cut cleanly through the net. The team kept on running to the locker room. For the first time all season, *Sports Illus-*

trated noticed. "Texas Western remained unbeaten, but just by a gasp. After waltzing by New Mexico State 104–78, the Miners visited Colorado State at Fort Collins and were on the ropes 66–66 with 12 seconds left. But TW's Bobby Joe Hill threw in a 25 foot running jumper and the Miners had their 16th victory, 68–66."

The following week, the Miners had notched an impressive nine-point road win against the University of Arizona in Tucson and engineered a miraculous come-from-behind victory over the University of New Mexico. They arrived in Albuquerque ranked seventh in the national polls but started the game looking like the ranking was a colossal mistake.

"*Seven no more! Seven no more! Seven no more!*" came the chant from Lobo fans as New Mexico ran up a twenty-point first-half lead against a Miners team that was sputtering like a Model T with a faulty carburetor. Usually, when a Haskins-coached team was out of sync offensively, it made up for it on the defensive end. Not tonight. Tonight they were up against six-foot-nine Mel Daniels, whom some were calling the best center in the country. Bobby Joe called him Homie when they played together at Burlington Junior College because both grew up in the Detroit suburbs, playing against each other in high school and with each other on AAU teams. With the Lobos up by twenty in the first half, Daniels was well on his way to summertime bragging rights. Bobby Joe was furious. This was real. This was personal.

"If you can't guard him, sit your ass down and I'll do it," he said, getting up in Lattin's face while Lobo fans upped the volume of their *Seven no more!* chant. Haskins, who'd called a time-out to make a few much-needed adjustments, stood off to the side and let it happen. "What about it?" Bobby Joe challenged. "You going to play or sit? Tell you one damn thing, I'm not going back to Detroit losing to him again. Got that? You got that?"

Lattin got it. In the closing minutes of the first half and on into the second, there was a noticeable difference in his play. He was up against a skilled player who dominated big men throughout his college career, but, as Lattin upped his own game, Daniels, the future Indiana Pacer and seven-time American Basketball Association all-star, lost some of his mojo and began to lose his temper.

At halftime everybody thought, *Oh, hell. Haskins is going to come in here and blow his top.* Instead, he came into the locker room with a quizzical look on his face. "You've got twenty minutes to catch them," he said. "Don't do it too fast."

"And that's when our leader took over," said Shed. Bobby Joe Hill was a laid-back, Motown-loving cool cat and the only player on the team who called the coach Don. Now, with Don looking on, his leader on the floor was becoming the team's inspirational leader as well. After ripping into Lattin again he turned to Nevil Shed. "If *you* ain't going to get out there and play better, sit your ass down, too."

"He became a true . . ." Shed paused years later, searching for words. "He became *the Man* because Mel Daniels was his Homeboy."

With neither a shot clock nor a three-point shot to help in their comeback, the Miners traded baskets with the Lobos for the first seven minutes of the second half. Texas Western was still down by twenty points when the comeback started to happen on the defensive end. Picking up their men at half court, the Miners fought through screens and went to work denying Daniels the ball. Mad at what he thought were missed calls against Lattin, Daniels picked up a couple of quick fouls himself. With time running out and the Miners within striking distance, the big man fouled out. A tie sent the game into overtime. Then, down by one, a flustered Lobo inbounded the ball directly to Shed, who took it to the hole, clinching a 67–64 win.

An hour later when the Miners emerged from the locker room, Lobo fans were still sitting there staring at the clock. None of them were chanting.

24

The Naked Truth

"Fellas, I want you to go home tonight and look at the sports page."

A dozen players and five student managers exchanged questioning looks as they gathered around Coach Adolph Rupp at midcourt, awaiting his preemptive disclaimer. Usually he said, "Don't read the newspaper" or "Don't look at that story," but today was different. "The reason you should look at the sports page tonight," Rupp continued, "is because you're going to see something you will never, ever see again. The top three teams in the country are Kentucky, Duke, and Vanderbilt. They're all from the South, all white, and you're never going to see that again." He was right.

The following season Vanderbilt would integrate the SEC by recruiting Nashville native Perry Wallace, but after his little homily Rupp's focus was this year's Vandy and a game that just might determine the championship of the all-white conference. In those days to get your ticket punched for the Big Dance, you had to win your conference championship. Kentucky had beaten the Commodores in Lexington seventeen days earlier by a comfortable thirteen points, but Vanderbilt had rallied since then and the rematch had the potential of being an old-fashioned donnybrook.

On the Kentucky campus the pregame meals were always in the same dining hall: same room, tables, chairs, and, more important, lack of interruption. On the road, while they tried to avoid the hustle and bustle of the more popular public eating places, they sometimes had to settle for a hotel restaurant. They sought out tables away from the door where they had the best chance of dining (if you could call it that) under the radar. Usually, that worked out pretty well. Sometimes it didn't. And when it didn't Coach Rupp made Basket Case seem like Tranquility Base.

There were only a few scattered diners in the restaurant when the team sat down for their five o'clock pregame meal that perfectly replicated the usual Lexington fare: well-done steaks with the delectable taste of burned cardboard and Sahara dried toast with no butter in sight. Regular. Routine. As ordered. But then it all went south. There were no Vandy students to disrupt concentration, no horns or cowbells. Instead, the interruption came from a carload of UK alums who had made the two-hundred-mile journey from Lexington to support the team. If they had been the regular run of fans, there might have been a way to head them off at the door, but these were *friends of Adolph.* The coach, like the head monk in a monastery interrupted at prayer time by visiting dignitaries, gave a little nod of recognition and a pasted-on smile. True friends should have noticed, but these guys were so psyched to have stumbled onto the objects of their adulation, they missed the signals. Instead, they went from player to player, patting them on the back and offering words of encouragement.

Aghast, Adolph jumped to his feet and headed for the elevator. "Slim," he said, tapping his student manager on the shoulder, "come on up to the room. I want to talk to you." In the restaurant he was dressed, as always on game day, in one of his identical brown suits. When Slim arrived at Rupp's room the coach was buck naked. Fresh from the shower he stood there, toweling off his Pillsbury Doughboy physique without a trace of modesty.

"I got too nervous," he said. "Sweating up a storm." While he dressed—boxer shorts, sleeveless undershirt, white shirt, brown suit, and tie—he talked about that night's Vanderbilt challenge, their strengths and weaknesses, with the kind of specificity he used when breaking down game film. By the time he was fully dressed, the shower and monologue had produced their calming effect. He sat down in an overstuffed chair and started musing about the miraculous season and prospects for next year. "I should have red-shirted Clevenger," he said, referring to Steve Clevenger, a six-foot sophomore guard who'd seen only limited playing time. "Should have kept him on the bench and red-shirted him. That was stupid of me."

That evening, still smarting from the loss in Lexington two weeks

ago, Vanderbilt coach Roy Skinner was determined to win the battle
of the boards. To that end his Commodores started the game in a tight
2-3 zone. In early going it was so tight that every time Kron or Conley
worked the ball into Jaracz down low, he found himself in a vice between
Clyde Lee and one of the forwards. Kentucky was up by eleven at halftime when Joe B. Hall made a suggestion to Harry Lancaster. Sometimes it seemed the two of them were locked in a turf war, but Harry
passed it on. "Thad, I want you to set a high screen up on top of the key
for Louie." Instead of doing battle on the inside, Thad was to become
the designated screener.

In the second half Thad didn't shoot at all. Instead, he set hard, decisive screens on the Vanderbilt guards that were impossible for them to
break through. When that put him in foul trouble, Cliff Berger became
designated screener. For Louie, it was like shooting over a garden fence—a
high and wide garden fence. When he came off a screen at full speed on
a normal play, his man was always at a disadvantage. The screens made
catching up in time to get a hand up all but impossible.

With Kron and Conley playing setup, Dampier slammed on the breaks
behind Thad's screen, rose up, and shot. The ball came off his right
hand with perfect rotation, making an arch that couldn't have been more
perfect if it were drawn with a protractor, swishing through the net in
a gentle whisper.

Bob Tallent, who played against Louie every day in practice and was a
student of the art, put it simply: "He had a soft touch." A Louie Dampier
miss was so soft that "the rebound never came out more than three or
four feet." On this night Louie went eighteen for twenty-nine, scorch-
ing the nets for a career-high forty-two points.

When Vanderbilt switched to a trapping, pressing man-to-man, Riley
found himself being guarded by a big forward who couldn't match his
quickness. Scoring on fast breaks and jumpers from the corner, he ended
up with twenty-eight. Thad scored only four points, while Berger had
eleven points and eleven rebounds. When the game was over both had
Christmas-morning grins. The stat sheet didn't have a place for screens,
but everybody knew Thad and Cliff were responsible for at least half of
Louie's points and for holding Clyde Lee to twenty-three. Coach Hall

wasn't much of a grinner, but the strategy was his. In the rebound department it was UK 51, Vandy 38.

Commodore fans watched in silence as their team's twenty-six-game
home-court win streak came to an end, 105–90. What happened next
was something that almost never happened. While the coaches and
players were shaking hands on the court in front of them, Vanderbilt
fans rose to their feet to give Rupp and his charges a standing ovation.

On the day after the Vandy win, there was a knock on the half-open
door of Adolph Rupp's office. "What can I do for you, Windsor?" said
Rupp, greeting Kentucky's All-Conference tight end with a welcoming handshake. "Well, Coach," said Bob Windsor, "I saw you all play
last night, and I think I can help." Rupp guffawed, slapping his hands
on the desk. "We're number one in the country, Windsor. Why do you
think you can help me?" Windsor shrugged. He'd played high school
basketball and, at six feet four, certainly had the height to fit right in.
"Why don't you give me a try?" At practice that afternoon, Rupp said,
"Windsor. Guard number 42." *Oh, my God. Pat Riley.* Windsor was up
for a challenge but prepared for a letdown when Rupp came up to him
after a long, hard scrimmage. "Windsor, you're on the team," he said.
"Nobody's held him to twenty points in a long time."

The Sporting News headlined its story on the Vanderbilt game "They
Came to Bury Rupp's Wildcats, but Mourners Stayed to Hail Revival."
John Carrico wrote,

> Around the turn of the century, Mark Twain retorted crustily to a pre-
> mature announcement of his demise: "The reports of my death have
> been grossly exaggerated." Adolph Rupp . . . might well echo those
> words in rebuttal to those who hinted last season that last rights were
> in order for the Baron of the Bluegrass. . . . "One of the best acts since
> Lazarus," quipped one irreverent Wildcat backer.
>
> Vanderbilt assistant coach Don Knodel, who has surveyed the Cats
> frequently, thinks [Thad] Jaracz, a brawny 6-5, 230 pounder may be
> the touchstone of success. "He gives them a lot more movement than
> John Adams did a year ago." . . . Another coach was sure that teamwork
> was the key to the reversal of fortune. Senior forward Larry Conley

and senior guard Tommy Kron were scoring stars in high school, but they have taken a back seat on offense to juniors Pat Riley and Louie Dampier. Asked if he missed the thrill of being a top gun, [Conley] answered, "Heck no . . . I think passing is what I do best. Really, I don't care as long as I can look up at the scoreboard after the game and we're ahead."

As their undefeated string stretched to eighteen with decisive wins over Vandy, Georgia, and Florida, Rupp's Runts arrived at Auburn ranked number one in the country. The Tigers they played in Lexington two weeks before played more like pussycats, losing by thirty-seven points, but Coach Rupp wanted everybody to understand the potential of what he called the "Auburn Shuffle." The shuffle was really a weave, with players in constant motion, cutting off multiple picks until somebody got an open shot. "You let them get that going," said Rupp, "and it's damn near impossible to stop."

Unfortunately, the film available for review was of the pussycats, not the Tigers. For most of the first half a full-court press had kept them shuffling at Kentucky's end of the court. "We've got to do that again," said Adolph, "but this time, fellas, we've got to have some defensive intensity, by God."

As the win streak mounted UK alums increasingly started showing up for road games, and with Kentucky grads attending the Alabama-Auburn Vet School, there was a built-in fan base. There were more than a hundred former UK students crowded into the World War II Quonset hut where Auburn played its basketball, an actual cheering section for Big Blue. One vet-school student and ardent Kentucky fan who couldn't get a ticket climbed a fifteen-foot drainpipe and watched the game through a window at the end of the building. Inside the gym it was so packed that referees had to move people over to make room for players to inbound the ball on the sidelines.

Auburn was ready for the press this time, but not for Kentucky's offense that kept them down by ten to fifteen points throughout the game. Thad Jaracz was guarding their best man, six-foot-six Lee DeFore. With less than two minutes to go DeFore outmaneuvered Thad on the wing and drove in for a dunk. Coach Rupp fumed. On the next Auburn possession Thad anticipated another drive and went for a fake. DeFore stepped back and scored on a fifteen-foot jumper. This time Adolph came off the bench screaming, "Shit, Jaracz!" The Wildcats were still up by eleven points, and everybody in the gym knew they were going to win. That was when Thad found himself open at the top of the key. Usually, when a big man is wide open twenty feet from the basket, there's a reason. "No, goddamnit!" yelled Adolph as Thad's shot cut cleanly through the net. After the game was safely in the win column, Thad explained his thinking. "My man had just made two baskets. I had to make the old man forget."

Two days later, when Kentucky arrived in Tuscaloosa to take on Alabama, people were talking about the article in the February 14 issue of *Sports Illustrated* that raised the question, "Is this Rupp's best team ever?" "The big showdown [the win over Vandy] turned out to be a big letdown," according to *si*'s "Basketball's Week." "Vanderbilt tried everything against the precise Wildcats—a zone defense, man to man, full-court and half-court presses—to no avail. Kentucky players just ran when they wanted to, set up flawless patterns when it suited them and shot like demons."

The article told of Riley's twenty-eight points and quoted Rupp saying Dampier (who had forty-two) was "the best shooter I've ever seen in college basketball." Then came the question about whether this teams was Rupp's best. The coach demurred, saying only that "it's as quick a team as I've had." But Vandy's coach, Roy Skinner, was effusive, calling it "the finest team [he'd] seen," adding, "I believe it can go all the way to the national championship."

25

Working Hard and Hardly Working

The comeback against New Mexico was as close to a near-death experience as there is in basketball. Texas Western had stared into the abyss and miraculously escaped with their win streak intact. With Arizona State coming to El Paso two days later, there was little time for reflection, but the Miners were starting to believe they were a team of destiny. In a long and typically arduous practice, their coach sought to disabuse them of that notion. Haskins picked the game apart with the precision of an Internal Revenue Service auditor in the presence of indisputable fraud. As usual, his complaints weren't as much about specific failures of execution as they were about effort.

Early in the season, when the competition was weak, the Miners would play full-out for a while, build up their lead, and then coast. "My guys could play so good on defense it was ridiculous," Haskins wrote. "Eventually we would have this huge lead and they'd stop trying." Against New Mexico it was the other way around. They did their coasting early, turning it on in the second half to pull out the victory.

Before every game Haskins liked to have his charges relax, stretching out on the benches or towels on the floor. Lights were low in what was supposed to be a deadly serious contemplation of the game ahead. On this night the players could hear Haskins, assistant coach Moe Iba, and trainer Ross Moore talking in an adjacent room. Otherwise, all was quiet. Then they started to hear a gurgling, snorkeling noise. The sound came from Flip, who was stretched out on a bench with one leg in the air. As Togo pumped his leg up and down, Flip spit out streams of water. It was Vaudeville slapstick, but it broke the tension and got everybody loose.

Coach Haskins didn't respond to the muffled laughter, but a few minutes later, when he came into the locker room, his pregame talk was about being too loose. "I want you to run out onto the floor tonight, not jog, but run. Got it?" His players nodded, but Haskins wasn't finished. "When I was a freshman at Oklahoma A&M, the football players used to shave the freshmen's hair off," he continued. "And I wasn't getting my head shaved. So I went and found the biggest football player I could find, and I kicked the hell out of him. And I'm letting you all know, if any of you feel salty—that you can't follow my orders because you're eighteen and zero—I'm willing to oblige you. Now run out on the floor."

The statement would have been laughable coming from Rupp, but even though Haskins had downed a few beers since his playing days and had a midsection barely contained under an ill-fitting sports coat, he was six feet three and 240 pounds and looked like he probably could *oblige*.

His team ran. They ran out onto the floor, and they played the Sun Devils with an intensity totally missing in the first half of the Albuquerque game. On this night the intensity held, but the outcome was in doubt until the final possession. It was one of many games when Orsten Artis came up with crucial shots. "When the pressure was on, you could count on him," said Harry Flournoy. "When he shot it, you might as well go back down the floor because he was going to make it. There was something about Orsten's makeup. He never got riled. He never got upset. He was level. No matter what, he was level."

In the final minutes, when it looked like Arizona State might be pulling away, Artis hit a pair of baseline jumpers that brought the Miners back to even. Then with the score tied and overtime all but inevitable, Artis got a pass from Bobby Joe, faked right, drove left, stopped, and popped from twenty feet. Silky smooth. Perfect arch. Bottom of the net with barely a ripple. Game over. Final score 69–67.

"This was easily the most talented team I had ever coached," Haskins would write, "but they were a pain in the ass when it came to practice." Practices leading up to the next game—Texas–Pan American—were no exception. It was a team thing, but his main concerns were about David Lattin and Bobby Joe Hill. Hill, wrote Haskins, "would rather take a punch in the face than practice hard." With Lattin the problem was motivation. "Coach, the dude, black guy or white?" he'd ask about

WORKING HARD AND HARDLY WORKING   145

the center he would be facing in the next game. When the answer was "white," Lattin would say, "Aw, man." To him, white centers didn't offer enough of a challenge.

The dude in question for Texas–Pan American was six-foot-eleven Otto Moore, an African American player who would go on to a twelve-year career in the NBA. Moore was enough motivation for Lattin, but it was another game where team effort came in spurts. It was another game where his Miners played just well enough to pull off a victory, 65–61.

Even Haskins now believed his team could navigate the final four games of the regular season and arrive at the NCAA Tournament undefeated. The next game was against West Texas State, a team they'd beaten by nineteen points at the end of January. This was an away game, but another easy win, 78–64.

After a seventeen-point home win against Colorado State, it was on to Las Cruces and New Mexico State. With the dust of the high school gym only a memory, the Miners beat the Aggies by seventeen. Their final game was three days later against Seattle University, a team they'd beaten easily two months ago. Even though Haskins was always harping on them about their intermittent lack of effort, there was every reason to believe they would enter the tournament, along with Kentucky, as the only undefeated basketball teams in the country. On the other hand, Haskins wrote, "We were so over confident. I knew we were fixin' to get our ass blistered in some game. I just didn't know when."

26

Tennessee Two-Step

In a scheduling quirk, Kentucky's next two games were against the University of Tennessee, which allowed Coach Rupp to give the Volunteers twelve days of undivided attention. Several years later this football school would vault into national basketball prominence with the Bernie and Ernie Show, featuring a couple of New York recruits, Bernard King and Ernie Grunfeld. The 1966 team didn't have the skill Bernie and Ernie would bring to Knoxville, but they did have Coach Ray Mears, one of the best basketball minds in the country.

To compare the Mears and Rupp styles of basketball is like comparing quicksilver to molasses or the tortoise to the hare. While Rupp teams ran with a capital *R*, Mears seemed to view the fast break as an aberration. Rupp was all about getting the ball down the court as fast as humanly possible. If there had been a shot clock in those days, the buzzer would have atrophied from underutilization. Mears, on the other hand, brought the ball up slowly and ran a methodical half-court offense that ate up clock time, keeping the score down and the possibility of a Tennessee victory up.

It wasn't hard to analyze the Mears approach, but preparing the Runts to defend against it was like teaching thoroughbreds the two-step. Fortunately, Rupp had a secret weapon in the person of Brad Bounds. A junior from Bluffton, Indiana, Brad was a decent-size kid—six feet five—and an okay athlete. But while he lacked both speed and quickness, he was a great practice player. With the Blue Team running Mears's Tennessee offense of set plays, picks, and cuts, Bounds was on a romp. Again and again, he circled around, brushing his man off pick after pick until he got an opening. Then it was shoot, swish, and smile.

Adolph wasn't smiling. As Bounds eviscerated the White Team defense, Rupp became more and more agitated. Finally, he'd seen enough. "Oh, goddamn it, Bounds, you should have gone to Tennessee." Bounds, who'd been recruited by Coach Mears, chuckled to himself. As a sophomore he thought he deserved more playing time. By now he'd come to realize his lack of foot speed didn't fit Rupp's offensive scheme. But he *could* shoot the ball. He was one of those guys who came off the bench when Kentucky was up by twenty with the crowd yelling "We want Bounds" and hit three in a row before the clock ran out.

In the first of two games against Tennessee, the practice with Bounds paid off. Coach Mears had obviously used his lead-up practices to prepare the Volunteers to defend against the run-and-gun style, but the Wildcats were better athletes and, clearly, the better team. In its season review, the *Kentuckian* described the offense this way: "Rupp stationed Riley in one corner and brought Dampier to the other, moving Conley out to a back court position. With Conley and Kron hitting first Riley and then Dampier, the two got 28 and 29 points."

In the second half, when Tennessee seemed to be finding its way back into the game, Coach Rupp had a sudden inspiration. "LeMaster, get Clevenger and Tallent and go warm up."

"I looked at him like he's the craziest guy I'd ever seen," says Jim LeMaster. Rupp never substituted more than one player at a time, and rarely this early in a game. "It just surprised me to death." It took him a minute to process.

"Damn it, LeMaster, I said get Clevenger and Tallent and go warm up."

The three guards went back under the stands and passed the basketball around for a few minutes, wondering what in the world was going to happen. The answer was . . . nothing. "Coach, we're ready," said LeMaster when they returned to the bench. "Okay," said Rupp. "Sit down. We'll see."

While they were warming up, Tennessee switched defenses, completely ignoring Conley and Kron. Tommy responded by hitting a pair of twenty-footers, and Larry slipped inside for an uncontested lay-up. Kentucky pulled back into a comfortable lead again. Jim LeMaster, Steve Clevenger, and Bobby Tallent never got in the game but had front-row seats to what *Sports Illustrated* called "the slickest basketball unit in the country."

"The key to Kentucky," wrote *si*'s Frank Deford, "is Conley, a frail and unusually perceptive young man who is a rarity, a playmaking forward." With Larry passing up open shots and garnering six assists, it prompted Mears to declare him the most "unselfish player and as fine a college passer as he has seen." As for Riley, "He wears contact lenses on the court, horned rims off the court, and might be accused of being Clark Kent, except that he could never fit into a phone booth to change his clothes." The title of the article was "Bravo for the Baron." It was Rupp's picture on the cover of the magazine, and it was "a new mellow Adolph Rupp" who led his team "into the hazardous role of favorite for an unprecedented fifth National collegiate basketball championship." In those days there was only a little talk about the *Sports Illustrated* cover jinx.

As if to disprove the "mellow" part, Rupp doubled down on sarcasm in the week between Tennessee games. In the *si* article, Deford quoted the old Rupp as blasting Kron: "Someday I'm going to write a book on how not to play basketball, and I'm going to devote the first two hundred pages to you." Now his target was Larry. "Why? Why? Why would you do a thing like that?" he shouted after Conley threw a pass behind Riley in a scrimmage. "I want you to go back to the dorm tonight and write me a three-page paper explaining why you'd ever do a stupid thing like that." It was Adolph being Adolph. But even if Rupp hadn't turned mellow, Deford was right about two things. He was "a man of consummate pride," and he was obsessively pursuing "the only challenge left, trying to top himself."

When the Runts started showing up near the top of national polls, the local newspaper decided its readers needed pictures of the players in unguarded moments away from the basketball court. While they were walking across campus, stopping by the library, or chatting with classmates, a photographer would poke his camera out from behind a tree, bush, or garbage can and snap away. *Candid Camera* was one of the popular programs on television that year, but players named this not-so-candid shutterbug for a radio program of their childhood: *The Shadow*.

(Who knows what evil lurks in the hearts of men? The Shadow knows.) Click! Flash! He'd taken another picture. One day Conley walked into the locker room with a comically perplexed look on his face. "I'm afraid to open my locker. The Shadow might be in there."

On the Sunday between the Tennessee games, the printed version of the Shadow's work hit the newsstands. There was Pat Riley in his horn-rim glasses looking pensive, Kron in the classroom looking studious, and Conley on the dance floor looking . . . His back was to the camera, so you couldn't really tell, but the girl smiling up at him looked thrilled. Along with the pictures were stories about each player with those little tidbits of information usually reserved for movie-star profiles in the magazine *Photoplay*. Readers learned:

That Larry Conley thinks that "people are the most interesting thing in the world" but sometimes likes being alone. "There's a pond, it's about 15 miles from Lexington, and I go out there and throw rocks into it and think about things."

That Louie Dampier loves to eat liver, and "now I never get it any-place." He had to settle for playing center fielder on the Wild-cats' baseball team because "Coach Rupp . . . wasn't about to risk the sensitive hands of the deadeye at the often bone-cracking position of catcher."

That Thad Jaracz plays the guitar and sings folk songs with room-mate and teammate Bobby Tallent ("It helps us relax") and reads Aristotle and Plato: "Once you get into them, you are sur-prised. They've got a lot to say."

That Tommy Kron has dinner with his parents and girlfriend after home games and comes from an athletic family that believes in the value of competition: "I give talks on it to church groups around here."

That Pat Riley once wanted to be an Olympic ice skater or swim-mer, that he wants to "travel while I'm still young, and have some fun and gain some experiences," and that he has trouble studying on the road: "Whenever I crack a book all I can see is, 'NCAA Championship—College Park, Md.'"

Magazine readers that morning learned that Kron was looking ahead: "Athletics teaches you how to win and lose, and how to bounce back after you do lose. If you've learned to lose and come back in school, playing sports, the shock of losing isn't so great later in life. . . . It teaches a person to be competitive."

"Discipline is the big lesson you learn from coach Rupp," said Dampier. "That and learning how to cope with pressure. He puts the pressure on the team at all times in practice so you'll be able to take it in the game."

Jaracz said it was those preseason running drills that taught him to dig deeper. "There were times I thought there was no way in the world I could run any more. Somehow, when I was tired like that, I found the strength to run a little more." His lesson learned: "It seems in life there's always a little something extra you hold back. Tap that, and you're in."

And what of their postcollege lives? Conley planned a career in dentistry, Kron in business, Jaracz in law. Both Dampier and Riley were planning to teach and coach basketball. "I'll want to get my master's degree first," said Riley. "That can mean the difference between getting $6,000 or $9,000 a year wherever you teach."

It wasn't in the article, but Slim had thought of a similar career path and was having second thoughts, especially after being named UK's outstanding accounting student. The honor that came with a five-hundred-dollar check from one of the Big Eight accounting firms was reported on the back page of the student newspaper, but Conley saw it. "Hey, man, congratulations," he said one day after practice. "Five hundred dollars?" "Damn," said Riley, letting out his breath slowly. "That's more money than I've ever had."

It was one of Rupp's articles of faith that you never (make that NEVER) looked beyond your next opponent, but his next opponent was the one he just beat, so the focus of the team might have been past Tennessee to the tournament beyond. On the other hand, as Adolph continued to stress, if Tennessee could pull an upset, it was still possible Kentucky could lose the final game against Tulane and end up tied with Vanderbilt, two conference losses each. That would set up a playoff game and open the way for Vandy to dash dreams of a fifth NCAA Championship.

Bounds again played a featured role in practices with the Kentucky defense against Mears's half court getting better every day. By the time the team got to Knoxville in early March, their number-one ranking in the polls made them quite the media darlings. On a Friday evening before a Saturday-afternoon game, they were booked into a downtown restaurant. Slim shared a table with Jaracz and Conley when a photographer from the *Knoxville Banner* showed up and started clicking away. Because they both had played exceptional games in beating the Volunteers in Lexington, Slim may not have been the big attraction, but he was the one Coach Rupp singled out for comment. Irritated by the distraction and because he wasn't in total control of the situation, he called out, "Slim, when you're through posing for pictures I've got some things I need you to do." There was more grief the following morning when that picture was featured on the *Banner*'s sports page, possibly because there was no picture of Coach Rupp.

By game time that afternoon everybody had bought into Adolph's truly frightening scenario. Lose against Tennessee, and the Wildcats just might spin their way down from the exalted heights of basketball's world—just possibly Rupp's best team ever—to the depths of degradation and despair. There had been tension for the Illinois game early in the season, tension while warming up for the Vanderbilt game a month ago, but nothing like this. You could see it in the team, but especially in the coaches. Rupp, who always talked himself into game-time frenzy, was clenching and reclenching his fists. Harry, usually the calmer of the two, was doing the same. It was another example of Conley's line: "When Adolph exhales, Harry inhales."

The clock was ticking down to the start of the game when the public address announcer said the words that sent tensions wafting off in the breeze like dandelion fluff in a windstorm. "The University of Vanderbilt has just lost to Mississippi State University, 92–90." Thank you, Babe McCarthy. Adolph smiled. Harry smiled. Conley and Kron exchanged high fives. The announcement made it official: Rupp's Runts were SEC champions and on their way to the NCAA Tournament.

The team was gathered around Coach Rupp for final instructions when the Tennessee band struck up "Rocky Top" for about the thirtieth time. Their cheerleaders burst through an enormous orange oval at the far end of the court followed by Volunteer players. "Now all we need is Ray Mears and his orange jacket," said Slim. As if on cue Coach Mears stepped through the oval wearing an orange blazer. Even Rupp allowed himself a smile. The team was relaxed and ready. While a sea of orange sang and resang the chorus of good ol' "Rocky Top," Jaracz leaned over to Slim. "I won't be able to take the ball out-of-bounds. These Tennessee girls are so good lookin', I might just grab one of them."

"All right!" said Rupp, as the new SEC champions clasped hands. "Now let's go out there and play like we earned it."

They didn't.

What had been do-or-die just minutes before had become not exactly irrelevant, but no longer imperative. Win or lose, the Wildcats were SEC champions. Win or lose, they were on their way to the Big Dance. Everybody still wanted what Adolph always wanted, another win. But somehow the twenty-three straight victories had evaporated.

The only bright spot of the afternoon was the defense Tommy Kron clamped on Tennessee's six-foot-four guard Ron Widby. Widby was a really good athlete—he lettered in both basketball and football, was drafted by the Chicago Bulls of the NBA, and went on to punt for the Green Bay Packers—but he couldn't drive with the basketball. Before the game Harry said, "Tommy, you get in Widby's jock strap and don't get out till the game is over." By the end of the game Widby must have thought they'd gotten married. Tommy just rode him.

That was the good news. The bad news was Mears's slow-down game. Kentucky had handled it before, but this time it took them completely out of rhythm. Howard Bayne, their big man who missed the game in Lexington, was back pounding the boards as the Volunteers outrebounded the Wildcats 43–31, one of only five times that happened all season. Down by twelve in the second half, Kentucky rallied to within four in a stretch run but ended up on the short end of a 72–69 score.

Flying into Lexington that evening, the team was met at the airport by a crowd of more than five thousand fans cheering and chanting "Go Big Blue!" You would have thought they just won the national championship instead of faltering in their moment of triumph. Airport personnel had rolled out the blue carpet the way they always did when the team came back from a road trip. The mayor was there handing the coach a ball of twine. "Here, Coach, let's start a new string." The crowd cheered; a group of students started singing the fight song. Rupp nodded. "All right," he said. "We'll do our best."

Some were calling it a Good Loss. "Kentucky possibly had the monkey off its back" was the way *Sports Illustrated* described it. It was a sentiment Adolph Rupp could never share. "A good loss," he scoffed. "That's when the other guy loses, not Kentucky."

27

Seattle Surprise

"We're number one!" shouted David Lattin, beaming his "Big Daddy D" smile. "Damn straight," said Willie Worsley, jumping up and down and hugging everybody in sight. "We did it," said Jerry Armstrong, wrapping Bobby Joe Hill in a bear hug that lifted the little guard off the floor. Nevil Shed and Willie Cager, the New York tandem who arrived in El Paso together three years ago, shook their heads at the wonderment of it all. Those cats back in the Bronx, those guys who were always ragging on them—always saying, *What's that little jerkwater school you're going to? TWC? What's that stand for, Teeny-Weeny College?*—now they would know. Come Monday, *Sports Illustrated* would spread the word: the Texas Western Miners are the only undefeated team in all of college basketball. Damn!

Nobody on the team actually bought the magazine—too expensive—but every Monday two or three of them went down to the local Minute Market to check it out. Always it was the same, Kentucky, Kentucky, Kentucky. Always there was some article about Rupp's team being "the slickest basketball unit in the country" and, just maybe, his best team ever. Texas Western was moving up in the national rankings, but as long as Kentucky remained unbeaten the Wildcats were *favored to win an unprecedented fifth national collegiate basketball championship*, and the Miners weren't even part of the conversation. Now all that had changed. The Kentucky loss meant Texas Western College would be on top, where they belonged.

The Miners were relaxed and confident. One reporter described their pregame routine—Bobby Joe's behind-the-back passes and multiple dunks by Lattin, Flournoy, Shed, and especially five-foot-six Willie Worsley—as a "junior Harlem Globe Trotters act." They had beaten Seattle in El Paso two months earlier by a comfortable twelve points and were on something of a roll. The Chieftains were led by their all–West Coast power forward Tom Workman. A tenacious (some said psychotic) rebounder, the six-seven Workman was destined for a career in the NBA. On the other hand, Lattin and Flournoy contained him before, so why not tonight? Besides, after the news from Knoxville, the Miners felt invincible.

They weren't.

When a high-flying team has a flat night, there are always excuses. A guy with the bass drum right behind the bench kept pounding away all game long. The basketball court was on top of an ice rink left in place for a hockey game the following night. "It was cold, man," said Willie Cager, who led the team in scoring with eighteen points. "Colder than a witch's tit." But basically, it all came down to this: "We went in and stunk up the place," said Lattin.

All night long they were missing lay-ups. Worse, for a Haskins team, they were missing foul shots. Lattin, who missed a pair in the first quarter, made a resolution. "I said to myself, 'I'm not going to miss any more free throws.'"

Late in the game Bobby Joe was undercut by a Seattle player when he drove to the basket. It was an obvious foul to everyone but the referee, whose whistle was silent. Even though the call went their way, Chieftains fans seemed to be booing. But what sounded like "Boo, Boo" was actually "Louu, Louu." They were calling out the referee's name. "Damnedest thing I ever saw," wrote Haskins. "Ol' Lou took care of them pretty good. We didn't get a damned call all night."

With twenty seconds left on the clock, Texas Western pulled even and seemed on the verge of the kind of late-game heroics they would become known for in the postseason tournament to come. Not this night. Instead, Tom Workman bulled his way past Lattin for a buzzer-beating lay-up, putting him one point above his season average with twenty-three. Seattle won, 74–72.

While the Seattle Chieftains carried Coach Lionell Purcell off the court in triumph, the Bear was in a rage. "Are you blind?" he shouted, chewing on Louu-Louu as he chased the referee off the court. "Is that whistle of yours a decoration, or do you know how to use it? Damn, man, that was charging."

The dream of a number-one ranking was no more, but, to a man, the Miners believe the loss put things in perspective. "We were kind of cocky," said Willie Worsley. "We thought we could just walk onto the court and win . . . play three quarters of a game and get away with it." About the loss he said, "It was a blessing in disguise, absolutely." Haskins agreed, calling it "a good loss," the kind of wake-up call the team needed.

That was later. Right after he'd dealt with the referee, the Bear was in full grizzly mode. "Do you know what just happened?" he growled, looking around the locker room at his dejected players. Years later, friends described him as having *this crust of an exterior but being a softie on the inside . . . like Jell-O.* There must have been a little Jell-O when Haskins looked across the room and saw six-foot-eight Nevil Shed crying. "Okay, you've lost one game," said Haskins. "You can go out there, win the next five, and win it all." A few minutes later, it was the crust that showed. "You had a chance to be the only unbeaten team in the country," he said in disgust. "Number one in all of basketball. So what did you do . . . ?" He turned away and then turned back. "You guys are on curfew," he growled. "In your rooms by eleven."

It was their first curfew of the season, but some of the players were experiencing a strange, almost inexplicable, feeling of relief. They'd been wondering when it was going to happen, and now, thanks to Seattle, Tom Workman, and bad calls by Louu-Louu, the weight of the unbeaten streak had lifted. Curfew? They needed to blow off steam.

Shed was waiting in the hotel lobby, ready to sneak out to join some teammates, when Haskins came through the door, obviously on his way to check rooms. While the Bear headed for the elevator, Shed sprinted to the back stairs. Taking them three at a time, he made it to the fourth floor, breathing almost normally thanks to a season of conditioning. As he hustled into his room he heard the *Bing* of the elevator down the hall. Jumping into bed fully clothed, he pulled the covers up and waited.

"Where the hell is Hill?" asked Haskins, barging into the room.

"I think he might be down in Flournoy's room."

Haskins seemed suspicious. He walked over and stood beside the bed, looking down at Shed, who had the covers pulled up to his chin, fully expecting the coach to see through his charade. Instead, the Bear walked toward the door and then turned as he had when he announced the curfew. "Why is it that you're still in bed, that you're the only one here?"

"Coach, can't you understand? We lost the game . . . I just couldn't . . ."

Haskins came back across the room and patted Shed on his blanket-covered shoulder. "Son, you *will* play tomorrow."

The following morning a dozen tired basketball players loaded onto a charter for the 1,800-mile flight from Seattle to Wichita, Kansas, to start the NCAA Tournament with a play-in game against Oklahoma City University. (In those days the nine conference champions automatically made it into the tournament, while twelve other teams played preliminary games to move on to what would come to be called the Sweet Sixteen.) Haskins, sitting in his usual seat at the front of the plane, was angry—angry about the way the team played, angry about the curfew violations, and just possibly angry about stories in the morning *Seattle Times*. There was no mention of race, but the writer seemed to delight in the outcome of the game way beyond normal support for the hometown team. *Texas Western is a fraud. Their win streak was against nonentities. We knew they would be found out sooner or later.*

Sports information director Eddie Mullens and Moe Iba had an assignment. "Coach says no sleeping!" said Mullens as he walked the aisle during the flight east, shaking the shoulders of players whose heads were nodding like churchgoers lulled by the droning of a particularly boring preacher. Bobby Joe's solution was a whispered conversation with seatmate Jerry Armstrong. Moe, forsaking his usual role as soother between Haskins and the Miners, put finger to lips. When B.J. gave him an *Aw, come on* look, Iba shook his head sternly. Haskins was angry, his orders specific: "No sleeping. No talking. Period!"

The pregame meal in Wichita was fried chicken, but everything else about the lead-up to the Oklahoma City game was strange. After the team was taped, dressed, and ready, they waited for Haskins. He didn't show. Instead, Moe Iba came into the locker room with the starting lineup. There was no pep talk, no instructions, no preliminaries of any kind, just the lineup that, for the first time all season, did not include

Bobby Joe Hill. Harry Flournoy, David Lattin, both Willies, and Orsten Artis had all violated curfew, but their coach had concluded (correctly) that Bobby Joe was the ring leader.

The Oklahoma City Chiefs were a classic fast-break team, and they came out of the starting gate like Man o' War at the Derby, surging to an early ten-point lead with their run-and-gun offense. The Bear was acting as if he couldn't care less, but with eight minutes to go in the half, with the Miners behind by ten, he finally put B.J. into the game, igniting their comeback. At halftime neither Haskins nor Iba came into the locker room, but trainer Ross Moore did. His message was simple: "You've come too far for this. If you don't want to win it for Coach Haskins, win it for yourselves."

They did.

In the second half, with Bobby Joe leading the way, the Miners shut down the Chiefs' fast break and, basket by basket, asserted their superiority, winning by fifteen points, 89–74.

"Don was mad during the game," said Iba, "but he didn't carry it over to the next day."

Back in El Paso the team had the relative luxury of four full days to prepare for the high-flying Cincinnati Bearcats at the Midwest Regional in Lubbock. Now they were preparing for a team they'd actually read about. Now even Bobby Joe Hill gave practices his game-time intensity.

28

The Mountain Man and Cazzie

Two days after Tennessee spoiled Kentucky's perfect season, Tulane University came to town. It was the final game of the regular season for both teams and Tulane's last game before leaving the conference. Two days before Adolph was raising the specter of a Green Wave tsunami sweeping away SEC Championship hopes. Now, they *were* the champs, the Wave but a babbling brook offering the opportunity to wash away the Tennessee Torpor in a fun run for twelve thousand adoring fans.

Tulane was a far better team than season opener Hardin-Simmons, but Rupp's game plan was the same. After the starters racked up a 52-36 halftime lead, he emptied the bench. Players who sat and watched all season long as their teammates rolled over one opponent after another had a chance to show their stuff. That fact might have gone unnoticed at another school, but UK fans—sophisticated connoisseurs of the game— understood: a Rupp's Runts kind of season requires the skills and dedication of practice players as well.

"It takes a village, I guess, if you're going to be successful," said Thad Jaracz, looking back. "We had seven or eight other guys who could play basketball anyplace in the country, and they're sitting there knowing they're not going to get in the game probably. That didn't stop them from coming back on Monday and giving it to you just as hard as they could. I said this a lot: some of the hardest games we had that year were the Thursday-afternoon scrimmages. That's one of the things that team doesn't get enough credit for is the other guys that were involved."

On this day the other guys got the credit. Every one of them played, including four who had ridden the bench in twenty-three straight games since December 1. It was a romp that produced virtually the same score as the Tulane game the year before—103-74—and had the Big Blue Nation in a roar as if this were a must-win situation. As the clock ticked off the final seconds of a remarkable regular season, a chant started in the seats at the top of Memorial Coliseum and spread through the crowd: *We're number one! We're number one! We're number one!*

The chanting was so loud you couldn't hear the final buzzer, and it got even louder when the cheerleaders rolled out an eight-foot cake with blue-and-white frosting in the shape of an enormous number one. The names of all the players were written on the cake, obviously by the one person in Kentucky who was not a fan of UK basketball. Pat Riley was listed as James P. Riley. Smiling broadly, university president John Oswald, a forty-nine-year-old former World War II PT boat captain who often looked mournful in official photos, stood at the microphone, waiting. "On behalf of the entire university family, faculty, students, alumni, and staff, I congratulate you," he said when the roar finally subsided. "Not only for being number one in the nation, but also as magnificent ambassadors wherever you have gone this winter."

The chanting started again when Adolph Rupp was introduced as coach of the year, an honor voted by the Basketball Writers Association. "It's easy to be coach of the year," he said, with a modesty freshly minted for the occasion, "with a bunch of boys like these who do what you tell them."

Rupp was all smiles when cheerleaders presented his wife, Esther, with two dozen roses and when they were given a brand-new twenty-five-inch color television set. His smile turned to a mock frown when the student serving as master of ceremonies suggested he might use it to watch the NCAA Tournament. "I hope we won't watch it on television," he said, igniting another round of chanting.

There wasn't much time to bask in the afterglow of the celebration. Three years before, when Kentucky backed into the NCAA Tournament because SEC champions Mississippi State decided not to participate because they would have to play against teams with black players, Rupp had a problem motivating his team. "Okay, you've got to realize an opportunity here," he said. "If you hadn't played like you did, you could be walking with your honey in the BO-tanical Garden." With the Runts motivation wasn't a problem.

They were slated for the Mideast Regional in Iowa City, along with Dayton, Michigan, and Western Kentucky. Game one had them playing Dayton and their seven-foot monster man, Henry Finkel. There were four days to turn Rupp's pre-Christmas theoretical into the *Xs* and *Os* of a workable defense, four days to prepare Thad to defend a man who would tower over him like a Paul Bunyan or the Beanstalk Giant. What he needed to help him prepare was a Brad Bounds with height or a reasonably mobile stepladder.

He had neither. What he had was an Adolph Rupp kind of intensity and determination. Earlier in the year, when it became obvious who the starters would be and how little opportunity there would be for anyone else, players like Cliff Berger, Jim LeMaster, Gary Gamble, and Bobby Tallent had to adjust their thinking. "A lot of nights I felt very down," says Tallent. "But the team was so good, it was great to be a part of it. It's pretty nice to be ranked number one in the country, and the guys who were ahead of me, they were such great guys. We were very close, all of us."

Practices that week were among the best of the season, and the feeling of confidence was palpable. It had been a heady feeling when they first topped the polls. Now they were comfortable with their ranking, comfortable but not complacent. To a man the team believed they were the best in the country. It wasn't exactly a legacy situation, but four other Kentucky teams had won NCAA Championships. Why not the Runts? Dayton's Henry Finkel was a mountain they were ready to conquer. Or so they thought.

Slim was bent over at midcourt in the Iowa Field House gathering up basketballs at the end of a morning shootaround when he glimpsed a presence out of the corner of his eye. "I turned and looked up and up and up some more. My God, I've got myself in the middle of a monster movie." There beside him, stretching toward the ceiling and wide enough to totally block his field of vision was the Thing, the Blob, or maybe Frankenstein's Monster. He'd been reading about how Finkel was twice drafted by NBA teams, but nothing he'd read prepared him for the man himself. From his size-20 Converse All-Stars to his flat-top haircut with slicked-back ducktail sides, he was gigantic. Adolph had been talking about how Finkel could be contained, but his massive size and pockmarked face that had fought a losing war against acne were intimidating. "At that moment I thought, 'He's going to kill us.'"

He very nearly did.

Flyers coach Don Donoher had Finkel moving back and forth under the basket and four outstanding sophomores who knew how to get him the ball. He wasn't very mobile, but he was so big mobility hardly entered the equation. "He was killing us," said Larry Conley. "All they'd do is drop the ball into the post, and all he'd do is turn around and drop it into the basket," his Finkel-Dinks. Add to that a nice little left-handed hook shot off the backboard that was nearly impossible to stop.

With Kentucky playing him man-to-man, Thad looked like Finkel's little brother, allowed into a pickup game to even the sides. He was in perfect defensive position, but he might as well have been waving at airplanes.

"Push him, damn it, push him!" shouted Rupp, leaping off the bench, his face red with frustration, every time Finkel got the ball. "Goddamn it, Thad, you've got to be a man out there. You gotta push him."

At halftime Dayton was up by two. Henry Finkel already had twenty points and seemed on his way to one of his storied forty- or fifty-point nights.

In the second half Rupp called time-out to tell Thad the same thing again. "Son, you gotta push him. Gentle taps won't get the job done. Goddamn it, you got to push him."

Thad shook his head and said quietly, "Coach, I'm pushin', but he ain't movin'."

Coach Rupp looked stunned. Nobody talked during a Kentucky time-out except Adolph and Harry. Thad wasn't trying to talk back, but he was exactly right. You could push on Stone Mountain, but it wouldn't help. What did help was a change in tactics. "Why don't we try our one-three-one?" said Harry when Rupp calmed down enough to listen. "Let's see what they'll do."

What Dayton did was move Finkel out to the foul line, in the process reducing his effectiveness by more than half, turning him into just another player. For the first time all night when they came into the front court, their monster man wasn't under the basket. For the first time all night, when Dayton shot, both Thad and Pat Riley were between Finkel and the basket. Now every time Finkel got the ball, he was surrounded, his path to the basket blocked. The change in defense upset their momentum. They started missing shots they'd been making, and Thad started getting rebounds, limiting them to one shot per possession.

Like most teams all season, Dayton figured to neutralize Kentucky's speed and quickness on the defensive end by playing what amounted to a matchup zone. Like most teams all season, it didn't work. Against the Flyers' zone, Conley flashed to the middle, and once he had the ball the rest was basketball magic. Larry wasn't a razzle-dazzle passer like Boston Celtic great Bob Cousy, but he achieved the same results. "Sometimes when you start a game . . . you look up and there's recognition," says Larry. "I knew they had it that night. Louie was dead-on. Pat was dead-on. You'd just say, 'Backseat for me tonight. I'll do all the other things I need to do to help us win this game. The scoring part of it is taken care of.' I knew. I just knew."

When Louie or Pat or Thad got into a position to score, the ball was there. "Larry would fire passes, buddy," said Bob Tallent. "And if you're not ready for it, he'd hit you right between the eyes." That night his sharp, crisp passes found Louie Dampier for thirty-four, Pat Riley for twenty-nine, and Thad Jaracz for seventeen.

In the end Henry Finkel got his thirty-six, but the mountain had been conquered. Final score, Kentucky 86, Dayton 79. (The following year a Finkel-less Flyers team went all the way to the national championship game, where they lost to UCLA and a big man who matched Finkel's height and had a kind of mobility no big man had ever before displayed. It was Lew Alcindor, soon to be Kareem Abdul-Jabbar.)

With Dayton in the rearview mirror and twenty-four hours to prepare for the University of Michigan, it would have been natural for Coach Rupp to be concentrating on a game plan to stop their three-time All-American, six-foot-five Cazzie Russell. Runners-up to last year's national champion, UCLA, Michigan was a concern, but Rupp was obsessing over the possibility the Wolverines might lose. The very thought of having to play against their opponents, the Western Kentucky Hilltoppers, had Rupp nearly paralyzed with fear.

"Sweet Jesus!" Adolph sputtered, looking up at the television set where the Toppers' Clem Haskins had just made a driving lay-up.

Rupp's players watched the game with him while eating their post-game meal in a private dining room back at the Holiday Inn. Watching and rolling their eyes as he grimaced over every Western basket and groaned over every Michigan miscue.

It was a puzzling exhibition unless you understood Adolph. In his thirty-six years at the University of Kentucky, Rupp had never scheduled a game with another Kentucky school. First, because he wanted his Wild-cats to be *Kentucky's Team*. His second reason was even more important: there would be no possible upside to such a game. Win, and he was sup-posed to. Lose, and it would upset his carefully crafted dynastic order.

There might have been another factor. Three of the Hilltoppers' start-ing five, Haskins and the Smith brothers (Greg and Dwight), were black Kentuckians Rupp did not recruit. In his view there wasn't a Jackie Rob-inson among them, and he wanted his first African American recruit to be a breakout star like Robinson, who broke Major League Baseball's color barrier back in 1947.

Rupp was in the locker room winding down from the Dayton win dur-ing the first half as Western's six-foot-six center, Steve Cunningham, matched Cazzie Russell point for point, helping the Toppers to a 47–41 halftime lead. Now as Adolph cut into his sirloin steak, Michigan finally pulled ahead. It was a narrow lead, but holding as two superb teams traded baskets down the stretch. "No, damn it!" Adolph grumbled when Western scored. When Michigan countered he said, "Yes!"

And then it happened. With thirty-six seconds to go, Cazzie caught a pass at the top of the key, slipped, and fell, losing control of the ball. Clem Haskins scooped it up for Western, passing it to Cunningham for a fifteen-foot jumper, giving Western Kentucky a 79–78 lead. Rupp groaned, shaking his head in dismay.

Back at the Iowa Field House, Slim was watching the game with Harry Lancaster when Western guard Wayne Chapman stepped into the pass-ing lane near midcourt, stealing a Cazzie Russell pass for the defensive play of his career.

Before he transferred from Kentucky Chapman played on Harry's

freshman team with Riley and Dampier and was just as talented, offensively. Defensively? Not so much. In those days Wayne's idea of guarding his man was waving at him as he drove by on his way to the basket.
Harry was on him every day in practice, but nothing changed. One game,
with Chapman's parents sitting right behind Kentucky's bench under
the defensive basket, his man got the ball and a Wayne Wave, rolling in
for an uncontested lay-up. "Goddamn you, Chapman!" yelled Harry, his
voice echoing in a nearly empty coliseum as if he'd been connected to
the public address system, "I'm going to kill you, you sonofabitch." The
senior Chapmans were not happy. Wayne endured Harry's fury for the
rest of the season, and then, not surprisingly, he transferred.

Now Chapman's defense had given the Toppers a chance to put the
game away. In desperation a Michigan player fouled Chapman, sending
him to the free-throw line for a one-and-one. Make both, and Western
Kentucky is up by three with sixteen seconds to go.

"I bet he's going to miss," said Slim.

While Chapman moved to the free-throw line, Slim told Harry about
a similar situation in a high school tournament game when Chapman
missed the front end of a one-and-one, costing his team the victory over
Owensboro High.

With thirteen thousand in Iowa Field House plus all of Kentucky watching on television, Chapman toed the free-throw line, bounced the ball
three times, and stiff-armed a shot that barely hit the front rim.

"He was probably thinking about high school," said Harry.

Greg Smith, Western's six-foot-five forward, skied over Russell and
the rest to grab the rebound. Cazzie immediately tied him up.

Jump ball!

Smith was a leaper; Cazzie was not. Advantage Smith. Lining up opposite Smith at the free-throw line, Cazzie stepped back once and then
again, clearing his throat and acting as if he was about to make the leap
of his life.

The referee's toss in a jump-ball situation is seldom perfect, but this
one was so bad it could have been the opening argument in the case for
virtually eliminating the jump ball from the game. Instead of going up
between the players, the ball sailed over Cazzie's head. Smith soared to

the ball, tapping it to Chapman. His momentum carried him into Cazzie, who dramatized the contact by staggering backward. For a moment it seemed it would be *Referee Error, Play On*, that Chapman's missed free throw wouldn't matter after all. But the referee was blowing his whistle. Foul on Smith.

Fifty years later the call is still remembered by Hilltopper faithful as *the worst in the history of the game*. There's a link on the school's website where you can watch it in a continuous loop and reach your own conclusion, but the only opinion that mattered that night was the referee's.

Back in the Holiday Inn Adolph stood in front of the television set, clenching and reclenching his fists.

Cazzie Russell was on the free-throw line, shooting one-and-one. Make the first, and the game is tied. Make both, and the University of Michigan is up one with time running out. A career 85 percent free-throw shooter who was eight for ten this night, Cazzie went through his preshot routine while Western fans held their collective breath. Adolph seemed to be holding his breath, too.

Like all great foul shooters, Cazzie's routine at the free-throw line never varied. It was all a matter of technique and repetition. Before the referee handed him the ball, he shook the tension out of his hands and arms. Ball in hand, he bounced it twice and went into a rocking motion, his legs and arms moving in fluid synchronization—*One thousand one, one thousand two*. Instead of following the flight of the ball, his eyes remained fixed on the glare on the front of the rim through his release and until the ball entered his field of vision.

Swish! Game tied.

Russell shook his arms again, then toed the line for his second, all-important, shot. This time the ball hit the front of the rim—*Ball, don't you dare come out of there*. Obeying his silent command, it took a friendly bounce forward, kissed the glass, and fell through the net.

Michigan 80, Western Kentucky 79.

Adolph let his breath out slowly. Nobody was expecting him to break into a chorus of the "Hail to the Victors Valiant," but he was obviously relieved.

There was still a chance for the Hilltoppers. They inbounded the ball to

Clem Haskins, who'd scored fifteen points on the night and had earned the nickname "Clem the Gem" during a stellar college career. Haskins dribbled the ball to the right of the key, putting up a jumper from seventeen feet. The ball hit the rim and bounded away as the buzzer sounded, ending the game.

"God, that's great," Adolph sighed, letting the stern lines of his soft, round face relax into what passed for him as a smile.

At a team meeting the following morning, Coach Rupp was a little less celebratory. "I don't know if we can beat these guys," he said, looking around at a roomful of confident players.

His concern, perhaps a bit late in coming, was real. The University of Michigan had three big, strong players—John Clawson, Oliver Darden, and six-foot-eleven Craig Dill (all of whom would play in the NBA)—and his team was the Runts. Coach Rupp's biggest concern was a future NBA star whose free throws had saved his Wildcats from having to play a nightmare game against Western Kentucky. "We just don't have anybody who can guard Cazzie Russell," he said matter-of-factly. "I don't know what we're going to do. Harry, do you have any ideas?"

Truth be told, nobody had come up with any ideas about how to stop Cazzie Russell since his days at Chicago's Carver High School. He was a prototypical big two-guard who didn't overwhelm you with his speed, but, like his role model, Oscar Robertson, he knew how to use his body. Robertson, a three-time All American at the University of Cincinnati who was cutting a wide swath in the NBA, was a better leaper. But like the Big O, Cazzie was a defender's nightmare. Put a big man on him, and Cazzie was too quick. Try to match his quickness with a smaller guard, and Cazzie would post him up. Like Oscar, he could use his hip, back a smaller man down, take two quick dribbles, stop, jump, and release. Like Oscar, Cazzie had the peripheral vision to see a double-team coming and react with a spot-on pass to the open man.

Since arriving in Ann Arbor he'd led the Wolverines to three Big Ten Championships, two Final Fours, and last year's game for the national championship against UCLA. This year's Wolverines weren't as strong, but Cazzie was cruising along at thirty-plus points per game and was everybody's choice for player of the year.

"Coach, I can guard him," said Tommy Kron, jumping to his feet.

"I was hoping you'd say that," said Rupp, obviously proud of a player he'd given the most grief during practices all season. That book Adolph was going to write on how not to play basketball, with the first two hundred pages about Tommy? Totally forgotten.

"Hell, yeah, I can guard him. I'm as big as he is. He can't post me up. I'm just as quick, maybe quicker."

Tommy was an honest six feet five, had a wingspan of a Condor, and, importantly, could flat move. Nobody was going to shut Cazzie Russell down, not this game or twelve years' worth of games in the NBA, but Tommy was psyched to try.

In his usual pregame stew Coach Rupp watched as the University of Michigan team warmed up in front of him, his focus on Cazzie Russell. Russell moved from spot to spot in an arc some seventeen feet from the basket, hitting jumper after jumper with a casual, loose-jointed, almost hypnotic rhythm. Rupp had seen the scouting reports and the film, but that was as if through a glass darkly; this was face-to-face.

Like a scientist peering through a microscope at some exotic new life form, Coach Rupp was searching for a better understanding, any telltale tendency that might give Kentucky an advantage. Then, suddenly, surprisingly, the specimen under close observation was looking directly back at him.

The three o'clock position on Russell's jump-shooting arc was directly in front of where Rupp was sitting on the Kentucky bench, and the Michigan All-American was walking toward him with a friendly smile, his hand extended.

"Mr. Rupp," he said, as Adolph struggled to his feet, "I'm Cazzie Russell. I just wanted to shake your hand."

Like Rupp, Russell had an almost preternatural competitive drive. "I was Dr. Jekyll and Mr. Hyde," he would recall nearly five decades later. "I liked you after you left the floor, but if you had a different-color uniform on, you were my opponent, my enemy." He had prayed about his decision to choose Michigan over Cincinnati and would go into the Christian ministry after his basketball career. Mr. Hyde would make his appearance, but now he was in his Dr. Jekyll mode. "I'd heard so much about

the Baron, I'm going to go over and see what he's all about." There were
no cameras to record the moment when the best player in the country
met the best coach in the history of the game. "I did it out of respect,"
says Cazzie. "His record spoke for itself. Numbers don't lie."

At tip-off Coach Dave Strack's Big Ten champions seemed sluggish,
as if they'd left it all on the court, both physically and emotionally, the
night before. Michigan had a height advantage at nearly every position,
but when the ball went up the Wildcats did what they'd been doing all
season: they blocked out. Never mind that Wolverine captain Oliver
Darden, a three-year starter along with Russell, was six feet seven. Never
mind that James Meyers was six feet nine. They had second-row seats
behind a couple of basketball Runts, Conley and Riley, two guys who
were only six feet three. Pat was a leaper with an instinct for the basketball, and Larry knew how to back his man out of rebounding range.
In addition to blocking out, the Wildcats were moving the basketball,
finding the open man.

It was the kind of unselfish basketball they'd been playing all season,
but Michigan's defense seemed to be based entirely on what they'd seen
last night. Against Dayton Larry Conley and Tommy Kron had scored
a combined total of four points: three for Tommy, one lone free throw
for Larry. Because Louie and Pat combined for sixty-three, it was only
natural to concentrate on them—natural but wrong.

Before the season Larry and Tommy had made a pact. They would
do whatever it took for the team to win. On most nights that meant
sacrificing their own scoring. On this night, in the early going, what
the team needed them to do was move without the ball, get feeds out
of double-teams from Pat and Louie, and hit their shots. Both Larry and
Tommy ended up with fourteen points on 50 percent shooting that forced
Michigan out of their trapping defense into a man-to-man. The result
was another balanced scoring night for Kentucky, with all five starters
scoring in double figures, led by Riley's twenty-nine.

Meanwhile, the storied Maize and Blue offense was sputtering. Living up to his promise, Kron was holding Cazzie in check, if not exactly
shutting him down. But the Michigan team that had averaged an aston-
ishing ninety-five points per game during the regular season on 49 per-

cent shooting—making it college basketball's statistical champions—was having trouble penetrating a withering defense. The Wildcats were up by ten at the break, 42–32, against a team that had earned the phrase in its fight song, "The Champions of the West."

Nobody was expecting praise from Coach Rupp. His team had done what it was supposed to do with another half of basketball to be played. Everyone in the locker room knew Rupp would deliver some version of his *counting your chickens* speech.

"It's a forty-minute game," said Adolph, looking around to make sure everyone got the point. "Forty minutes. That means we've got twenty to go. And, fellas, the University of Michigan didn't get to be Big Ten champions by playing like they have so far tonight. They'll be back, and you better be ready."

Rupp couldn't find anything on the stat sheet to complain about, so he repeated his litany: block out, rebound, find the open man, and run them into the ground. "Twenty minutes, fellas. Twenty minutes."

Adolph was right about the Wolverines and their comeback. When a coach like Dave Strack has engineered three straight Big Ten Championships and back-to-back Final Four appearances, you had to figure he would have a fix for their first-half woes. It wasn't anything dramatic, but it was effective. Little by little they were climbing back into the game. Six-foot-four John Clawson and Meyers hadn't found their shooting touch, but they were competing on the boards, and Cazzie was starting to look more like the All-American he was.

In twenty minutes of basketball, he showed an array of hook shots, jumpers, and moves to the basket that made him the consensus player of the year. Tommy Kron held Russell's shooting to 40 instead of his usual 50 percent, but Cazzie made nine straight free throws to go with ten field goals for a total of twenty-nine points. It was two below his season average—in the end, not enough.

Midway through the half Michigan took the lead, and for the next five minutes they went back and forth, with Pat Riley matching Cazzie point for point for his own twenty-nine and Louie and Thad chipping in for fifteen and twelve. After a bad first half Michigan was overpowering inside, with Oliver Darden setting the pace. Darden was four inches taller than Larry and half again as wide. Once, when Conley tried to snatch a rebound away from Darden, it became a tug-of-war. "He took the ball and me," said Larry. "I'm still holding onto the ball, flying through the air—whoosh."

Despite their size and strength, the Wildcats had the advantage in both quickness and speed. "They were big," said Larry, "but they weren't really as quick as we were. We took full advantage of that. Whenever I got the ball I would bust it down the floor. Or if I had the ball one-on-one and got by my man and somebody came to help, I'd drop the ball off to one of our guys. I think that's where we got them. None of their guys were very quick." And once again, it was a matter of conditioning. In the final six or seven minutes, it started to happen. Gradually, Kentucky was pulling away. The Wildcats were going to the Final Four.

It was something Slim had been dreaming about since Kentucky went all the way back in 1951. The All-American part didn't work out, but the dream of helping Kentucky win another national championship remained. Suddenly, surprisingly, the little boy who danced around the room shouting, "We did it! We did it!" way back then bubbled up again. Right there in front of Kentucky's bench in the Iowa Field House, in front of thirteen thousand basketball fans, Slim started dancing a little jig. Because half of them were celebrating too, it really didn't matter except for one thing: a television camera. When he saw the CBS Eye pointing in his direction, it hit him like a blast of Arctic air, freezing him in middance. What would Adolph think? What would Harry do? He sat down before they noticed.

For the players, the coaches, and one subdued student manager, the celebration that followed was a low-key affair. Cocaptains Conley and Kron accepted the NCAA Mideast Regional Championship trophy, while cameras flashed, capturing the moment for tomorrow morning's newspapers. The Wildcats were surrounded by excited fans who thought the win should be celebrated by cutting down the nets. "We don't allow that," said a large man with a dark suit and an even darker disposition.

One man, even a large man with an authoritarian personality, wasn't likely to stop a scrum of Kentucky fans on a quest, but security personnel moved in and the Big Blue Nation moved on. The nets they really wanted were nine hundred miles and two wins away, in Cole Field House on the campus of the University of Maryland.

By the time the team left the locker room an hour later, none of them were thinking about nets. Their focus was on the East Regional in Raleigh, North Carolina, where Syracuse University was playing Duke. Kentucky would play the winner. The Orangemen had crashed the NCAA party for only the second time in school history, behind All-American guard Dave Bing and his scrappy running mate, Jim Boeheim. They weren't supposed to be much of a challenge, but this was the NCAA. Upsets were what the tournament was all about, and Syracuse was hanging in there.

In the hallway outside the locker room, four middle-aged guys wearing Kentucky caps, sweatshirts, and thousand-watt smiles were waiting. The lead guy approached Coach Rupp with his hand outstretched. The congratulatory handshake Adolph expected turned out to be a pair of nets. The foursome had waited in the shadows until houselights dimmed and security guards departed before performing their extraction.

Even before the plane taxied to a stop the following afternoon, the team could see and hear the clamoring crowd awaiting their arrival at Blue Grass Field. There were some twenty thousand members of the Big Blue Nation with handmade signs and heartfelt cheers: *We're number one! We're number one! We're number one!*

It had been eight long years since his Wildcats last headed to the Final Four, and Rupp was clearly savoring the adulation, but reluctant to embrace it fully. "I've got to go to New York [to receive his Coach of the Year Award]," said Rupp as the plane taxied to a stop. "Get some sleep. We can have an even bigger celebration next week."

29

Time and Overtime

Lubbock's dome-shaped Municipal Coliseum, host of the Midwest Regional bracket, had been a turning point for Rupp's Runts back in December with a win against Texas Tech, and now it was about to provide a reaffirmation for the Texas Western Miners. The Oklahoma City game had turned into a pretty good outing for a while, but the Chiefs were a run-of-the-mill team. Cincinnati was anything but. The Bearcats had been in the national spotlight ever since Oscar Robertson arrived from Crispus Attucks High School in Indianapolis in 1957. The three-time All-American led them to a three-year 79-9 record, including two NCAA Final Fours. By now the Big O was well into his Hall of Fame professional career, but his legacy lived on. Just as Bad News Barnes "showed kids around the country that Texas Western was a place where great players played," Robertson did the same for Cincinnati. As Haskins said, "Nothing attracts great recruits like great players."

As Oscar traveled the country he would sometimes drop in on promising high school athletes for a little one-on-one recruiting. He was a persuasive influence. The scary thing, for Texas Western players looking back, is how close Oscar came to recruiting Cazzie Russell. When the Cincinnati Royals (Robertson's NBA team) were in Chicago to play the Bulls, "Oscar came to my high school," said Cazzie Russell. The student body might have been more impressed if the Beatles or Cassius Clay had suddenly appeared, but Robertson's star power was definitely in that league. There he was, the Big O, eating lunch in the Carver High School cafeteria with one of their own. "He increased my popularity with the ladies," said Cazzie, still reveling in the memory more than five decades later. "When they saw me talking to Oscar Robertson, they thought, this guy must be someone."

While Cazzie ultimately resisted Oscar's magnetism, the Oscar Effect helped to bring Cincinnati back-to-back NCAA Championships in the two years after he graduated, followed by a fifth-straight Final Four, something no other team has ever done with the exception of UCLA under John Wooden that would make it seven straight on their way to winning ten national championships. The Bearcat team that faced off against the Miners lacked a superstar in the mold of an Oscar or Cazzie, but their starting lineup had both speed and height (a six-foot-five average), and four of the five were scoring in double figures.

Moe Iba had taken to the telephone earlier in the week in search of Cincinnati game film but came up empty. So Haskins did what he always did when he didn't have film, which was most of the time. Instead of worrying about Cincy's game, he would make them play his. It worked, but just barely.

From the starting tip-off the Missouri Valley Conference champions lived up to their impressive 21-6 record. With six-six forward Don Rolfes, who transferred from Kentucky to Cincinnati after his sophomore year when he got married—a Rupp no-no—leading the way, the Bearcats and the Miners traded basket for basket for forty minutes, with neither team gaining the advantage. There had been times when Haskins was disturbed with his team "for not putting out for forty minutes," said Iba. "There were times when they wouldn't play as hard until they were in trouble."

Not tonight.

With feeds from Bobby Joe Hill, David Lattin was having the kind of scoring night he used to have back at Houston's Worthing High School. Again and again, he got the ball down low, faked right and then left, before making a quick step to the basket, flushing it over a Bearcat defender. Usually, that was Ron Krick, Cincy's six-foot-eight center who had a two-inch height advantage on Lattin but lacked the poundage to compete with the revved-up Big Daddy D, who ended the evening with a season-high twenty-nine points and eight rebounds.

The game was getting a little rough midway through the second half, and, down by seven, Hill showed the kind of leadership that made him the Miners' indispensable man. "He gathered the guys together and yelled at them," wrote Haskins. "He could do a lot more with 'em than I could." Whatever B.J. said proved the motivation needed to play the Bear's defense the way he'd taught them. Before Cincy would score again the Miners were up by seven.

As Haskins told the story, Bearcat forward Rolfes, "a big old white boy, knocked the crap out of Jerry Armstrong [another white boy] when Armstrong wasn't looking." That was when Nevil Shed stepped in. Before that "he kept elbowing me," said Shed, and Haskins said, "Aw, come on, to hell and damn, you just get on down the court." Now Rolfes "had a handful of my shorts, so I clocked him." The referee blew the whistle. The Shadow was out of the game, and Haskins went ballistic.

"You're done!" he shouted. "You're finished!" Not just *finished*—off-the-team, scholarship-revoked finished. "I was so mad at him," wrote Haskins, "not because he had done it, but because he had done it at a critical juncture of the game."

Cincy fought back in the final minutes, with Rolfe making a lay-up to knot the score at 69. With ten seconds left in regulation, Willie Cager went to the free-throw line with a chance to put the game away. It was not to be, but in overtime he was a man possessed. Cager followed a driving lay-up with a hook shot and a pair of free throws, scoring six of the Miners' nine points and giving them a 78-76 win. The stage was set for the regional championship game against Jo Jo White and the Kansas Jayhawks.

In the locker room after the game, while his teammates were celebrating, the Shadow did his best to live up to his nickname, staying on the outer edge of activities for fear the Bear would remember his pronouncement. He remembered. When it was time to board the bus back to the hotel, Haskins made sure Shed was left behind. A half hour later, after answering questions from reporters, Mullens found him wandering around near the locker room and gave him a ride.

"I'm scared to death," said Shed as they pulled away from the coliseum.

"Aw, come on," said Mullens reassuringly. "You know the coach. He'll get over it."

"I'm not scared of the coach," said Shed, shaking his head. "I'm scared about my mother."

He had reason to be afraid.

Haskins was expecting an appeal for clemency when he talked to Shed's mother on the phone, but as he wrote in his book, she was madder at her son than he was. "Coach, make that boy walk home. Make him walk back to New York. Don't even give him a ride to the bus station."

"I decided then and there to keep him on the team," wrote Haskins. "I figured I was saving him from the whipping of his life."

Not knowing about the coach's decision, Shed stayed as far away from him at the pregame meal as possible. "I was miserable," he recalls. "I thought he was going to send me home."

In the locker room before the Kansas game, Shed put on his uniform, still doing his best to escape the coach's attention. It worked until it didn't. He was bringing up the rear as the Miners headed to the floor for their pregame warm-up.

"Shed."

He stopped cold. Somehow he had managed to get through the day without Haskins noticing him. Now his worst fear was about to be realized.

The Bear's glower morphed into a bemused half smile. "The next time you decide to be Cassius Clay, you make sure you knock him down so he doesn't get up."

Saved from banishment, Shed knew he was still in the doghouse when Haskins announced a starting lineup that did not include him. He found a place at the opposite end of the bench, hoping to ride out the storm.

"Shed," said Haskins, "where the hell are you going? Get yourself back here." He took his seat next to the coach, figuring the proximity might be the coach's vindictive punishment.

Enter Walt Wesley.

A six-foot-eleven, 225-pound center, Wesley had helped lead his Jayhawks through a 23-8 season with occasional glimpses of big-man dominance the University of Kansas had come to expect from the likes of Clyde Lovellette and Wilt Chamberlain. At the start of the second semester, Wesley was joined by Joseph Henry "Jo Jo" White, and magic started to happen. Seven straight wins brought them the Big Eight Championship and catapulted them into fourth place in the national rankings. Near the end of the game Wesley and White would execute the play that became the most controversial in KU history, but before that it was Wesley versus Lattin.

Big Daddy D had twenty pounds on the slender Wesley, but the Jayhawk All-American had an altitude advantage of five inches. While Bobby Joe was going head-to-head with Jo Jo, scoring twenty-two to White's nineteen points, the big men slammed and jammed down under. David Lattin muscled his way to seventeen rebounds on the night, but his aggressiveness on the boards put him in foul trouble. Midway through the first half, Nevil heard the magic words. "Shed. Get in there for Lattin."

Back in action, the Shadow was rejuvenated, scoring twelve points, pulling down five rebounds, and, more important, keeping Walt Wesley to his season average of twenty-one points per game.

Pregame betting odds favored fourth-ranked KU to advance to the Final Four over the third-ranked Miners, but as the game got down to what, in those pre–shot clock days, could have been the final possession, Texas Western was up by three.

"Time-out," said Haskins, using his rolled-up program to flash the T sign to Bobby Joe.

On the sideline Haskins mapped out a play designed more to run clock than score points. As they broke huddle he had one more instruction that proved prescient. "If they steal the ball, don't foul. Got that?" He looked around at his players, Bobby Joe, Orsten Artis, David, Nevil, and Willie Cager. "Got that? We're up by three. If they steal and score, we're still up by one, and we've got the ball with time running out."

With fifteen seconds to go it happened. Jo Jo White gambled and came up with the steal, driving in for a lay-up. Willie Cager, coming down the lane, thought he had a clean block. The referee disagreed. Jo Jo made the lay-up plus one.

All he had to do was miss that one free throw, and the game was over, but All-Americans like White are not in the habit of missing uncontested shots, especially from the foul stripe with the game on the line. The ball cut cleanly through the net, knotting the score 69–69.

Overtime, the Miners' second in as many nights.

The OT was a cat-and-mouse affair, with both teams playing keep-away, with only four points scored, two by the Jayhawks' Walt Wesley, two by the Miners' David Lattin. With the clock winding down again, Jo Jo White came off a Wesley pick near the left sideline and put up a jump shot from thirty feet.

"When Jo Jo shot that sucker, it was going so slow, I could read the serial number on the basketball," Shed recalls. When it rippled the net, he thought, "The dream is over. To lose on a buzzer beater like that has to be one of the most excruciating pains anyone could have. Oh, man . . ."

"Well, it was a good run," said Willie Worsley, sitting on the bench next to Harry Flournoy, who had just fouled out. "Yeah, it was," Harry responded.

"It hurt more than Seattle," Worsley recalls. "There, win or lose, play again. We were a basketball family. All of a sudden that ends."

At the other end of the bench, Texas Western reserve Dick Myers was celebrating. Instead of following the shot, he watched referee Rudy Marich waving *No!* Marich pointed to the sideline, ruling Jo Jo had stepped out-of-bounds.

When the ball went in the Kansas crowd erupted, and so did Myers for the opposite reason. "Because I am from Kansas . . . that was even sweeter. Absolutely."

After the game and for decades to come, Jayhawk faithful criticized the call, some even questioning whether referee Marich made it because of his home state (Texas) bias. An investment banker when not refereeing basketball games, Rudy Marich lived in Greeley, Colorado.

Whether Jo Jo's foot was on the line, Haskins would tell friends, didn't really matter because the ball was still in White's hand when time ran out. A photograph of the referee pointing at the out-of-bounds line also shows one lone fan in the middle of the crowd. He, too, is pointing. Apparently at the clock.

At the end of the scorer's table, Eddie Mullens was close enough to the Jayhawk bench to lip-read Coach Ted Owens's question to Jo Jo. *Were you out-of-bounds?* White nodded.

From despair to jubilation in a matter of seconds and then to resolve: "Once he waved it off, we knew no matter what it takes, we're going to win this game," said Harry Flournoy. "We might have played five overtimes; we're going to win."

Jerry Armstrong wasn't so sure. "To be honest with you, I was just praying: Oh, please, God, give us the strength and the power to overcome."

"One more time!" shouted Shed. "One more time, man!"

In the second overtime (their third in twenty-four hours), Shed made a pair of free throws down the stretch, getting him out of Haskins's doghouse and helping his team to an 81–80 victory. The Texas Western Miners were on their way to College Park, Maryland, for the school's first appearance among the elite at basketball's holy of holies, the Final Four.

There had been a crowd when the Miners returned from their Oklahoma City win, but the one that greeted them at El Paso Municipal Airport the following morning made the other one seem as tame as a Sunday-school picnic. A city where some had questioned the makeup of the team now embraced it without reservation. Thousands of cheering fans followed them from the gate to baggage claim to the waiting bus, taking pictures, shouting encouragement, waving hand-lettered signs that never applied to a Texas basketball team before or since: *We're number one!*

30

Larry Conley's Ass

On the screen in front of the room Duke was beating Michigan in an overtime game played earlier in the season, but what seemed to bother Coach Rupp as his team watched film of the game was Mike Lewis. Duke's six-foot-seven sophomore center was a defensive specialist who always scored in the teens, always hauled down his share of rebounds. The Runts wouldn't learn until later why Rupp's reaction to him was so visceral. They were paying more attention to Duke's All-Americans, Jack Marin and Bob Verga.

The six-foot-six Marin matched Cazzie Russell with thirty points that night and seemed to be able to score from anywhere on the floor. But it was Verga who attracted the most attention. With Duke down by fourteen at halftime, Verga exploded with twenty second-half points, including nine of their final eleven. Louie Dampier was the best pure shooter Kentucky players had ever seen, but, from evidence on film, Verga had to be in that conversation. He helped engineer what Coach Vic Bubas called "the greatest comeback any Duke team has ever staged." Everybody knew Duke was the team Adolph wanted in the Final Four, but their play against Michigan underlined the challenge they represented.

All season long there had been talk about how the Blue Devils were *really* the best team in the country. Early in the season Duke won decisive back-to-back games against defending national champions UCLA, causing Coach John Wooden to say, "When you get whipped, you just get whipped." And now on film they were slicing and dicing Cazzie's Wolverines, a team that started the season number two in the polls. Playing Syracuse would have been, as Adolph once said about Georgia, "like kissing your sister." Against Duke Rupp (and his Runts) had something to prove.

Kentucky hadn't played Duke since its Sugar Bowl matchup in New Orleans three years earlier, when the then second-ranked Wildcats played the eighth-ranked Dukies in a barn burner. In those days the Wildcats were Cotton Nash and four other guys. He'd already scored thirty points that night, and, with the game tied and only seconds to go, everybody in the Loyola Field House knew Adolph Rupp was drawing up a play for Cotton to take the final shot. On the inbound pass Nash was surrounded. The ball went to Terry Mobley, who was open near the free-throw line. It was catch-and-shoot, with Mobley hitting the game winner at the buzzer.

Suddenly, uncharacteristically, Coach Rupp rushed onto the floor. "Remember, Harrodsburg," he said, using his name for Mobley, who comes from Harrodsburg, Kentucky, "between you and me and the gatepost, we knew Duke thought Nash would get the ball, so we outsmarted them and told you to take the last shot." The following morning New Orleans woke up to snow-covered streets for the first time in twenty years and the story of the game in the *Times-Picayune* under the headline "Rupp Surprised Duke—Calls on Mobley to Take Last Shot."

There were multiple surprises this time around, none of them positive. Thad Jaracz had a cold, Pat Riley had athlete's feet so bad it was hard to get his shoes on, and Larry Conley had the flu. At a press conference Rupp said, "I'm taking a bunch of sick boys to the championship finals."

Thad's cold ran its course. Pat could play hurt, but Larry's flu was a problem. Doc Jackson "stuck me in the ass five times with that needle," said Larry. Those were the five that *took*. Several other times, as Larry tells the story, Jackson would stick him and say, "Oh, I got it in the wrong place." Jackson's official title was team doctor. To Larry he was "the most incompetent physician ever." "I'm going to tell you my ass was black and blue on both sides. I sometimes [thought] I can get over this flu if I can just get my ass to feeling better." The Wildcats wouldn't learn until game time on Friday that Duke was having its own medical problem.

Despite Conley's ass things were going well. After taking Monday off to recuperate from the Michigan game, the team had Tuesday and Wednesday to prepare for a Duke team that, according to *SI*, could play it fast or slow. "Wake Forest ran and lost [to Duke] 103–73. North Carolina walked—well, almost—and lost 21–20." A Mike Lewis free throw with four seconds left gave Duke the win.

From film and scouting reports it was easy to see why the Blue Devils were ranked number two; actually, there were five reasons. Like Kentucky, the Dukies had five starters who were excellent basketball players. Heightwise they more than matched the Runts. A pair of six-foot-six forwards—Jack Marin and Bob Riedy—against Larry's and Pat's six feet three each. Center Mike Lewis was a sophomore like Thad, but two inches taller. Because of Tommy Kron Kentucky had a height advantage at guard, but Steve Vacendak had been named ACC player of the year, and Bob Verga was everybody's All-American. Like Dampier, he was quick. Like Dampier, he was a deadly outside shooter. Rupp knew their offense and was prepared to defend against it. He knew their defense and was prepared to attack it. His team was ready.

Along with the basketball side of things, there was the all-consuming job of helping Coach Rupp deal with the overwhelming demand for tickets and autographs. Ever since his Wildcats moved to number one in the national polls, there had been a surge of requests for Rupp's signature. It was a problem Adolph hadn't faced over the past few years, but now, every time he arrived in his office, there were mailbags full of balls, shirts, and caps awaiting his signature. Adolph loved the requests but hated the process until one day he had an inspiration. "Slim," he said, turning to his student manager, "how's your penmanship?"

It wasn't bad. As the requests for autographs mounted in that Final Four week, Slim's Adolph F. Rupp got better and better. No handwriting expert would have been fooled, but fans were fans, thrilled that the Baron of the Bluegrass responded to their request, never doubting he did it with his own hand.

Tickets were another matter entirely. While the supply of Rupp's autographs was theoretically endless, the number of tickets allocated to the University of Kentucky was finite. The Final Four was a pretty big deal for fans of college basketball across the country. For the Big Blue Nation it was the Holy Grail. Every once in a while, during a break in practice, Adolph would call Slim over and send him to tell athletic director Bernie Shively another name he'd just thought of that must be included among the Chosen.

The team had been flying good old reliable Purdue Airline charters all season long with no real problems except for one time when the DC-3's right engine started spewing oil as the team sped down the runway at Lexington's Blue Grass Field. The pilot slammed on the breaks and pulled to a stop just short of the end of the runway. Takeoff aborted.

"Oh, God," said Adolph. "I thought we were a goner."

This time the team flew commercial, so what could possibly go wrong? Flying high over cotton-candy cloud fields, they were free to concentrate on the challenge ahead. After a smooth hour-and-a-half flight, they were coming in low and slow along the Potomac River, the Capitol and Washington Monument on the left, Arlington Cemetery and the Pentagon on the right, with no sign of the airport. Nobody had explained what pilots call the "River Visual" approach to DC's National Airport.

Seeing the iconic landmarks of the nation's capital was a first-time experience for most of the players. As the plane flew lower and slower, some of them were thinking their first view of the landmarks might turn out to be their last. All they could see below and in front of them was water. Where the hell is the runway? White-knuckled and wide-eyed, Bobby Tallent was thinking, "My God, we're not going to make it," just seconds before rubber met tarmac to a chorus of cheers.

The bus skirted downtown Washington, heading north to Silver Spring, Maryland, and the Sheraton Hotel. Thirty minutes after check-in it was back on the bus for a twenty-minute drive to College Park and the University of Maryland. Midafternoon traffic was light, stoplights mostly green, smooth and easy.

Cole Field House, with a seating capacity of 14,500, was swarming with reporters when the team arrived for its pregame shootaround. Reporters had already watched three of the Final Four teams and were anxious to see this Rupp's Runt outfit that nearly everyone thought would win it all. They would have to wait. Other coaches conducted open practices. Not Adolph. With the single exception of the shootaround the day of the annual Notre Dame game in Louisville's Freedom Hall, Rupp practices were closed. End of discussion. Reporters were not happy.

The following day was a case study in Rupp's game-day routine. There was the usual Benedictine silence as the team ate steak, potatoes, peas, and dessert in the Sheraton's private dining room at noon. There was an afternoon of quiet in their rooms. Everything was going as it usually did before any run-of-the-mill road game until they got back together for their pregame meal. The dining room, a study in monochromatic bland tan just hours before, was transformed. Kentucky cheerleaders, untutored in Adolph's game-day rituals and wanting to give their Wildcats an appropriate sendoff, had decorated one wall with an enormous sign: BEAT DUKE! On the table in the middle of the room was a large wooden paddle inscribed with the words *Beat the Devil Out of Duke!*

"Here's what you do tonight," said Slim, grabbing the paddle and hitting a chair repeatedly. His antics might not have played with another audience, but the Runts laughed as if he were Bill Cosby doing Fat Albert.

Just then Harry arrived, pushing silence before him. "The trouble with you is you don't know when to shut the fuck up." If there had been a crack in the wall, Slim would have crawled into it.

Slim counted the players as they filed onto the bus for their ride to Cole Field House. *All present and accounted for.* In addition to the team, the coaches, the trainer, and Doc Jackson, the passengers included athletic director Bernie Shively, university president John Oswald, and their wives. It was the first time all season they had women on the team bus, but it was only a short trip, so what problem could they possibly encounter?

Stoplights.

On Thursday afternoon there wasn't much traffic, lights were mostly green, and the bus made the ten-mile trip through the connecting suburbs of Silver Spring and College Park in less than twenty minutes. Now it was Friday afternoon, rush hour, and there wasn't any rushing to be had. Every last federal employee had come pouring out of downtown DC, hitting the road at the exact same time. On another Friday some of them might have car-pooled or even called in sick, but not today. Today, each drove their own car, each headed north through (you guessed it) Silver Spring or College Park.

As if that wasn't bad enough, some nefarious miscreant—probably a Duke fan—had tripled the number of stoplights along the route and jiggered them to give preference to north–south travelers. The bus was heading east.

"Goddamn stoplights," said Adolph, under his breath as the bus came to a sudden, lurching stop behind a half dozen cars. He fumed for the next thirty seconds and then boiled over when the driver, the soul of caution, failed to make it through the intersection before having to stop again.

"Jesus H. Christ," said Rupp. "Get the goddamn lead out, driver. We've got a fucking game to play."

The driver had no reaction, but now his pugnacious passenger was on his feet, standing in the aisle beside him. A second of hesitation between green light and acceleration was filled with another string of expletives directed at the driver, the light, the traffic, and the situation that had college basketball's coach of the year stuck in traffic, nearing a state of apoplexy.

This time the driver glanced sideways as if to say, *Who the hell are you?* Some were reminded of the story about the time Adolph wrote a check for a country ham at a rural Kentucky grocery store. "Do you know who that is?" he asked as he signed his name with a flourish. "I hope it's you," said the grocer, unimpressed.

With each stoplight Rupp let out a new torrent of obscenities. When none of them succeeded in making an impression on the driver, Adolph started pacing the aisle, his head down, ranting his way past the athletic director, past the college president, past their genteel ladies. Before the bus pulled out of the parking lot, the ladies were engaged in friendly banter about some faculty tea. Now they sat with white-gloved hands folded on fat laps, their faces frozen, their eyes staring straight ahead.

Slim was horrified. It wasn't the language. He'd grown up with a father who'd commanded an artillery battery in World War II and could have conducted graduate seminars in scatological expression. What horrified him was the makeup of Rupp's captive audience.

The ladies might have heard some of Rupp's vocabulary in isolation, but never in the combinations that came spewing forth as he paced the aisle. "Jesus, the goddamned, fucking lights. Shit, damn sonsabitches. How the hell are we going to make it to the fucking field house with these jerk-off cocksuckers poking along like a daisy chain bound for a church social?"

Adolph always fussed, cussed, and complained about any stoplight anywhere. "Well, just run the goddamn light, George," he said one night when Larry Conley's dad was driving him back to the hotel after a game in Tuscaloosa. Another time George glanced both ways to make sure no one was near and fired through a red light. "George, by God, what are you doing?" shouted Rupp. Safely through the intersection, he settled back in his seat, "By God, George, you did it."

This driver wouldn't do it. As Rupp approached the front of the bus again, the driver—*steady as she goes*—heeded the yellow caution light and braked to a stop, reigniting Adolph's fury.

"Shitfire, man, drive the fucking bus. Jesus, you've got balls the size of goddamn peanuts."

With multiple lights, monumental traffic, an unresponsive driver, and the Duke Blue Devils to compound his anxiety, Rupp's mouth was like the pressure valve on a steam engine, a Mount Vesuvius spewing forth molten language over a defenseless vehicular Pompeii.

31

The Runnin' Utes

All season long, the Runnin' Utes of the University of Utah got about the same level of attention as Texas Western before the NCAA Tournament. In the West Regional the spotlight wasn't on the team and its easy wins over Pacific and Oregon State, but on their star, Jerome Purcell "Jerry" Chambers. The six-foot-five forward had averaged just under twenty-four points per game on the season but came out of the blocks against Pacific with forty and blistered Oregon State the following night with thirty-three.

That was the bad news. The good news for Texas Western was that the Runnin' Utes' power forward, George Fisher, had broken his leg in the Western Athletic Conference Championship game against New Mexico and would be watching the Final Four from the sidelines.

For Texas Western there was new life after the Kansas squeaker, but a muted celebration. Haskins believed, and his team now believed with him, the Miners were eighty minutes away from a national championship; Utah first, then either Duke or Kentucky. In four days of practice following their demanding regional games, the Bear never let up. He had seen minor flaws in team defense against Cincinnati and Kansas that needed fixing.

Again there was no game film, but this time Haskins had personally eyeballed his opponent. As he wrote in his book, before the season, he'd called Utah coach Jack Gardner, asking if he could drop in on practice (a fairly common occurrence among college coaches) when he was in Salt Lake City for the Texas Western–Utah football game. With no idea the Utes and Miners might possibly meet in the NCAA Tournament the following spring, Haskins was interested in seeing Gardner's vaunted fast break, and Gardner was welcoming.

Giving his team a rare Saturday off, Haskins flew to Salt Lake City with the football team and watched, fascinated, as Gardner ran his charges through his five-on-two fast-break drill. "The Mr. Iba in me saw this drill and got to thinkin' about flippin' it around," wrote Haskins. "Instead of coming back with a five-on-two fast break drill, I came back with a two-on-five defensive drill. . . . What we did was work on stoppin' the ball, always getting somebody to guard the basket." It was a drill the Miners ran throughout the season and one reason they were so successful against teams that employed the fast break.

The other emphasis as the Miners prepared for their journey east was foul shots. As they had done throughout the season, every time someone was fouled in practice, he shot a free throw. Despite the Bear's free-throw addiction, his team had shot only 70 percent during the season. For most teams a free-throw-shooting average of 70 percent is *a consummation devoutly to be wished*. For a Haskins team it was a B-minus. Nobody said the words, but they didn't have to. Everybody knew the coach's mantra: "The free-throw line is where games are won and where games are lost."

Before and after practices the players shot free throws, going through their preshot routines before every shot, just as they did in regular game situations. Nevil Shed and Willie Worsley were still practicing their foul shots on a side basket with a rim reducer that left no room for error. If the arc of the shot wasn't perfect, there was no friendly bounce. To make the Haskins-required ten in a row before hitting the shower required perfect form and absolute precision.

On Thursday morning of Final Four week, the Miners, their coaches, the Texas Western band, and team boosters boarded a plane at El Paso Municipal Airport for the three-hour flight to Baltimore. Usually, in March that trip would be a plunge into a comparative deep freeze. This time the weather in the nation's capital was unseasonably warm. This time instead of the hulking DC-3 that hopscotched its way across the country to Illinois in late December, they flew an American Airlines charter.

In that week's *Sports Illustrated*, Frank Deford's tournament preview looked beyond the Utah game to a possible matchup between Texas Western and either Duke or Kentucky: "All seven Texas Western regulars are Negroes, hardly a startling fact nowadays, but one that becomes noteworthy because of the likely meeting with Kentucky or Duke. Both teams are all white. It is unfortunate—but it is a fact—that some ethnics, both white and negro, are already referring to the prospective national final as not just a game but a contest for racial honors."

Haskins's focus was on another black player. "If we didn't figure out a way to stop [Chambers]," he wrote, "then we were never going to get to play 'for racial honors' or whatever the hell *Sports Illustrated* was talking about."

Early in the game David Lattin guarded Chambers, and it wasn't working. Big Daddy D could do a lot of things on a basketball court, but keeping up with Jerry on this night wasn't one of them. Within the first few minutes of the game he'd picked up three fouls with no noticeable impact on Chambers's offensive output beyond providing him the opportunity to find his range, undeterred, from the free-throw line. After a quick time-out it was Shed's turn.

The Shadow had worked his defensive magic on quicker players in past games, but Chambers's moves had Shed jumping at ball fakes, while the Utes' star blew past him. After Chambers scored three quick baskets on wide-open ten- to twelve-foot jumpers, Shed finally tracked him down, blocking a lay-up. The satisfaction of the accomplishment was short-lived. Chambers got the rebound and put it back in before Shed could recover.

"I was just out of sync," said Shed, looking back. "God, I wish I could have had another chance to play that guy. I knew I was quick enough to do what I was taught to do, but I didn't do it that night."

Jerry Armstrong had been watching Chambers's fakes from his position on the bench and thought he saw a pattern. Chambers, who was on his way to a twenty-four-point half, would bring the ball up in front of him where a defender might be able to get a hand in and disrupt his timing. "I think I can shut him down," Armstrong said to no one in particular. With four minutes left in the half, Haskins had the same thought. "Armstrong. In for Shed."

Sizewise, Jerry Armstrong was an inch shorter than the other Jerry, and Chambers was probably half a step quicker. The first time down the floor he used his quickness to backdoor Armstrong. Taking a bounce pass from Ute guard Rich Tate, Chambers drove in for a two-handed dunk. When the ball bounced off the back rim to Flournoy, Armstrong turned to Chambers as they ran up the floor together. "Hey . . . that's the last one you get."

It was.

There were no more back doors, no attempted dunks, and Chambers was working harder for his shots. When he tried the fake-right, fake-left, and back-right pattern Armstrong spotted from the bench, Jerry C found Jerry A waiting. Armstrong didn't shut him down. Nobody had done that all season. But he did slow him down, fighting over screens the way he had done in practices against Lattin, Shed, and Flournoy. Twice in the final minutes of the game, Armstrong got a hand in, deflecting the ball, leading to lay-ups by Orsten Artis, who ended the game with twenty-two points. They were the turning point. In the end Texas Western won by 7.

Chambers had scored a game-high 38 points and the following night would go on to set a four-game NCAA Tournament record of 143 points and be named Final Four MVP. At the rate he was going when the other Jerry entered the game, his point total could have been a lot more and the game might have had a very different outcome.

After the game, as his teammates gathered around with congratulations, Jerry Armstrong was wilted. "I think the emotion and adrenaline got to me," he said. "I was one tired puppy."

What Armstrong didn't know as he walked off the court that evening—what nobody in Cole Field House knew, perhaps even including Don Haskins—was that he had just played his final college basketball game. At a team reunion twenty years later, Armstrong recalls, Haskins was second-guessing his decision to play only blacks. "He said, 'Jerry, I owe you an apology.' I said, 'What for?' He said, 'Because you should have played in that championship game.'"

"I wanted to play, and I felt like I could have helped," said Jerry as the fiftieth anniversary of the championship season approached. But then, "It all worked out great. So, in the end, it was all right."

In his book Haskins wrote, "We won by 85 to 78, but only because of Armstrong. Maybe Jerry Armstrong is the white guy who should get the credit for integrating college basketball. It sure as hell wasn't me guarding Jerry Chambers."

A proud man, Jerry Armstrong has saved a copy of *Sports Illustrated* because of what Haskins's old coach Hank Iba said. "It quoted Mr. Iba saying, we wouldn't have been in that championship game if it hadn't been for me. That was a great tribute that I'll always cherish."

32

The Real Championship Game

After most games David Lattin enjoyed a long, leisurely shower, letting the water wash over game-weary muscles with its soothing, penetrating heat. This night was different. On this night, while his teammates were laughing and splashing, he was in a hurry. Utah was history, and on the floor where the Miners had just won their semifinal victory the teams ranked numbers one and two in the country were taking their warm-ups. Everyone was saying Duke-Kentucky would be the Real Championship Game. But whoever won would have to prove themselves against his Miners, and Lattin wanted to see what he'd be up against.

There was the usual congratulatory bedlam around him in the locker room while Lattin was getting dressed, but it was as if he were in a separate dimension with his own dark thoughts. In foul trouble from the earliest minutes of the Utah game—with the referees "calling it like a girls' game," "Baby Fouls," Shed called them—he'd spent most of the second half on the bench watching and wondering. On this night, as Jerry Armstrong finally brought an end to the Chambers challenge, the usually positive Big Daddy D had nagging doubts. *What if being the best team doesn't mean we'll win the championship? What about tomorrow's game? What if the white referees won't let us win?*

Hurrying up to the floor, his hair still wet from the shower, Lattin stood in the tunnel near the court and looked out onto the floor. *Son-of-a-gun*, he thought. *I didn't know that.* Despite the fact that both teams had received a lot of *SI* ink over the past couple of months, he'd never read anything about their racial makeup. Both teams were lily-white, not a single brother among them. He tried to think if his team had seen that anytime earlier in the season and decided the answer was no, not once.

The other thing he noticed was size. All season long he'd been giving up three to five inches to opposing centers in every game. Neither of these teams had any kind of length. *Marin: Right. Duke's All-American. Read about him. More of an outside threat. Mike Lewis? Hmmm. Six-seven. Broad shoulders. Might be a banger.* But as the game got under way, he saw that neither team was going to the hoop. *Two teams of jump shooters. Great jump shooters, but jump shooters.* Even though sportswriters were calling the Kentucky team Rupp's Runts, the Wildcats were surprising. *Only one who has any height at all, and he's on the bench. Their center, the guy with the strange last name. Maybe six-five. They're not trying to get him the ball.* Yet everything Lattin had read gave the nod to the Wildcats. *Not good to get overconfident*, he thought. Then, *How in the world can they compete?* He was about to find out.

When Kentucky first took the floor, it looked like the Big Blue Nation had moved to Maryland's Cole Field House en masse. It was the same sea of blue they were used to seeing at Memorial Coliseum back in Lexington. Half the blue was Kentucky, and there were *Beat Duke* signs sprinkled throughout the Kentucky stands like the one decorating the dining room back at the Sheraton. The other half belonged to Duke. It would be another couple of decades before their fans would be dubbed the Cameron Crazies, but they were already known for humorous pranks and cleverly funny sayings. For the Final Four they'd come up with a takeoff on the Avis Rent-a-Car slogan: *We're number two. We try harder.*

"This is a terrific field," Rupp told hometown reporters. "I don't think the three top-ranked teams in the polls have ever made it to the finals together. The team that wins the NCAA championship this year is going to have to play almost perfect basketball to do it." Everyone knew it was Duke the Baron was focused on. They spent part of the season in the top spot before late-season losses bumped them out and Kentucky in. This was the Runts' chance to prove their ranking was legit.

"I'm not getting much sleep thinking about this thing," Rupp told reporters. "Our scouts tell me Duke has a tremendous team with height, speed and good shooting."

As the Blue Devils went through their warm-up in front of him, Adolph looked stricken. They were taller than they appeared on film, a lot taller.

Partly, it was because the film was shot from a high angle, which has a way of shrinking even the tallest player. Partly, it was because, player for player, the Wolverines matched Duke in height. The Runts didn't. Not even close.

On film and on paper the three-inch height advantage their forwards had didn't seem all that intimidating. In person it did. On the other hand, the *We try harder* sign was wrong. Unlike Haskins's Miners, Rupp's Runts had overcome their lack of height because they played with precision and energy all game, every game.

Adolph knew there was no quit in his team. What he didn't know—what nobody knew—was how Conley's flu would factor into the equation. Down at the other end of the floor Larry was going through the motions in his warm-up routine, looking like the wind-down cycle of a windup toy.

As game time approached Rupp ran down the defensive assignments one last time. When he came to Mike Lewis, he paused. Lewis had scored a season-average fourteen in the Michigan game they'd seen on film that afternoon and pulled down a mind-boggling twenty-one rebounds in an early-season win over last year's national champions, UCLA. What more was there to say?

"I recruited this boy," said Rupp. "He just took a plane and flew right over Lexington on his way to go down to Durham to that damn ACC *school*." Adolph spat out ACC as if it stood for Association of Communist Conspirators instead of the Atlantic Coast Conference.

Hearing the story some fifty years later, Mike Lewis recalled the phone call that came one evening during his senior year in high school. Southern accent, Kansas twang. *It's for you*, said Helen Lewis, handing the phone to her son. *He says he's Adolph Rupp, I think.* "There may have been one or two mothers in the state of Montana who knew who he was," says Mike, "but my mother wasn't one of them." Mike knew. "I almost had a heart attack. Oh, my God, I can't believe it." The conversation lasted only a few minutes, as Mike told the winningest coach in America, "I don't want to make a trip to Kentucky and waste your money and time because I have no intention of going to school that far away from home." Though Rupp would never believe it, Mike says, "I was being truthful at the time."

That was before Mike's high school coach sent film to Duke coach Vic Bubas, before Bubas sat down with Mike's parents in their Mazola, Montana, home. "He talked to my parents, and that was all it took," says Mike. "He was a master salesman." Mike had nothing against Rupp and his basketball program, but once he saw Duke's campus he was sold. For Rupp, as he prepared his Wildcats to face the Duke Blue Devils that night, the rejection was personal.

As Coach Rupp delivered his standard "What this means to the university and the state of Kentucky speech," Slim gave Larry a questioning look. *You okay?* Larry gave a little shrug. *We'll see.*

That question seemed to be answered as Larry found an opening in the Duke defense and went to the basket for a driving lay-up and the first basket of the game. Pat Riley hit one from the corner. Thad Jaracz launched one of his patented wrong-foot hook shots, and the Wildcats were sailing along to an 18-11 lead eight minutes in. Larry hit a midrange jumper several minutes later, but he seemed to be running out of steam.

"Conley's wilting," Harry told Adolph. "Better get him out of there."

With Larry on the bench—replaced by Bobby Tallent—it was up to Tommy Kron to guard Duke All-American Jack Marin. Tommy had the height and quickness to guard the six-foot-six Marin; what he didn't have was experience guarding a forward with such an instinctive ability to move without the ball and find gaps in the defense. Two times in a row Marin went backdoor on Kron for easy lay-ups. In six minutes Duke scored nineteen points to Kentucky's eight and took a 30–26 lead.

"That's it!" said Adolph, his face flushed with anxiety. He turned to Larry, sitting next to him in his warm-up jacket with a towel around his neck. "I don't give a shit how sick you are, you're going back in."

Defensively, it made a difference; offensively, not so much. This wasn't the Larry Conley fans had been watching all season. The point forward whose passing triggered so much of the offense lacked his usual zip. It wasn't the kind of thing most people would notice, but passes that usually found Riley and Dampier in rhythm arrived a half beat late. "I think this flu bug has hurt my passing the most," Larry said after the game. One assist in twenty-eight minutes was not a typical Larry Conley performance.

That might have put his team at a serious disadvantage, but Duke guard Bob Verga was even sicker than Larry. Stricken with strep throat and a bronchial infection after a team-leading ten-for-thirteen shooting night against Syracuse last Saturday, Verga was wheezing as if his next breath might be his last. Louie took advantage. Face-to-face with the Duke All-American for the first time, Dampier gave a little head fake, Verga lunged, and Louie drove past him, hit the brakes, and buried an open fifteen-footer. What promised to be the matchup of the evening with two cat-quick guards going at it head-to-head turned out to be a one-sided affair. Dampier got his twenty-three points on eleven-for-twenty shooting. Bob Verga, who averaged eighteen points on the season, was a weak-kneed two for seven and spent most of the evening watching from the Duke bench.

Still, Duke was up by a point at halftime, 42–41. Adolph was fulminating. "This isn't Kentucky basketball," he said, reaching for a Kleenex from the box Slim was holding at the ready. "Jesus, Kron." He blew his nose loudly. "You ever see a backdoor before? You let that sonofabitch go by you like a fucking freight train . . . twice." He looked around the locker room for another target. Thad cleared his throat, and he was it. "Shit, Thad, do you think you could move your feet? Just once? That Montana kid [he was talking about Mike Lewis] is playing you like a one-string banjo. Move your feet, son. You can't just reach out and grab him."

In the second half Kentucky regained the lead, gave it up, and got it back again. At one point a ten-foot jumper by Marin and a stick-back by Mike Lewis put Duke up by four. Thirty seconds later Riley got out in front on a pass from Larry and scored an easy lay-up, and Louie came off a Kron screen at the top of the key for one of his signature jump shots and then returned the favor, setting Tommy up for an eighteen-footer, putting Kentucky up by two. Altogether there were six ties in the second half, with neither team able to hold a lead.

With four minutes on the game clock and the score tied at seventy-one, Larry made a pair of free throws, and Riley got another fast-break basket after a Dampier steal. With Thad Jaracz on the bench with five fouls, Cliff Berger entered the game and was fouled twice in less than two minutes. Both times the routine he'd been using since his Tommy Kron tutorial on the morning of the double-overtime Georgia game back in January came through. Bounce the ball three times, spot the rim, smooth stroke, swish! Four in a row to keep the Wildcat momentum going.

Kentucky's lead was back down to two with less than a minute to go when Mike Lewis rolled to the basket, coming straight down the middle for an uncontested lay-up. Adolph's Montana nemesis had already scored a season-high twenty-one points and sent Thad to the bench with five fouls. Now he looked like he was going to dunk the ball until he made a last-second decision to lay it off the backboard. The ball hit the glass, hit the rim, and then bounced away.

Larry Conley gave up four inches and thirty pounds to Lewis, but despite his weakened condition he used his body to create space, grab the rebound, and head up court. At the top of the key he hesitated for a split second while the Dukies scattered, looking for their men. Nobody found Larry. He faked left, saw his opening, and drove right to the basket with a burst of speed that surprised five Duke defenders and the man with the ball. Final score: 83-79.

Way before Conley scored his game-clinching lay-up, David Lattin had the answer to his pregame question about how Kentucky competes. Despite their lack of size he was "amazed at how well they played together." *Awesome*, he thought. *Very quick. Knew exactly what they were doing.* They were constantly moving and then, "All of a sudden somebody would get open. Boom! They were really a great team." Lattin had long since reached the same conclusion about Haskins's Miners. Making his way toward the team bus, "I knew I was going to be able to do whatever I needed to do to help the team win."

At halftime of the Duke-Kentucky game Haskins and Iba ran into sports information director Eddie Mullens in the hospitality room. "So . . . what do you think?" asked Haskins. "Hell, we can beat either one of them," Mullens responded. "For God's sake, don't say anything like that to the players," Haskins sputtered, looking around quickly to make sure they hadn't been overheard. Mullens nodded, then added, "Coach, they can see."

33

The Smart Money

Like nearly every other newspaper in the country, the Saturday-morning *Washington Post* treated Kentucky's win over Duke as if they'd won the championship, calling it "the perfect end to a long season." There was a story about Texas Western beating Utah in the other semifinal game, but Kentucky was the headline, its expected win against the El Paso team a mere formality. And why not? They had just won a hard-fought game against the mighty Duke Blue Devils, the number-two team in the country. Besides, Larry seemed to be on the mend.

A sick-versus-sicker sidebar—Larry Conley versus Bob Verga—concluded with Rupp, "college basketball's coach of the year," complaining good-naturedly about having to pay $5.98 for a vaporizer to help Larry recuperate and, typical Adolph, pooh-poohing modern medicine. "These antibiotics are great for pharmacists, but we just packed Larry in goose grease. What I mean is good old Vaseline Jelly."

Most of the Runts were still sleeping when Slim got a call from Harry Lancaster. He'd been checking around and found a film of Texas Western's win over Kansas in the Midwest Regional down in Lubbock. Harry handed him the keys to a rental car and a map of the DC metro area and sent him on his way.

Slim had always been pretty good with directions back in Kentucky, but this was the big city. The map showed a labyrinth of highways, streets, and avenues that looked like a vast, unfathomable maze, the kind that could keep even the cleverest rat confused for weeks. The Sheraton hotel was on the north side of the warren of roads. His destination, the Holiday Inn in Arlington, was southwest. There was probably some way to navigate around the city and avoid downtown traffic. Probably, but the

Potomac River snaked in from the northwest, and there was only one bridge that seemed to get him to where he was going. So with the map spread out on the seat beside him, he headed straight south, through the neighborhoods of Brightwood, Petworth, and Columbia Heights, into the heart of the city.

It was a warm, sunny day, the kind that would have the White House, Capitol, and Tidal Basin swarming with sightseers, but there was no touristing for him. The world (Adolph and Harry) was waiting. Somewhere along the way he missed a turn, and, before he knew it, he was heading west along Constitution Avenue. From the map he knew he was paralleling the Mall with the Lincoln and Jefferson Memorials, but he was still surprised when he realized what he was seeing in fleeting glimpses through the trees. *Oh, my God, the Washington Monument. That's really it.* He thought of the line from the eulogy for President Washington he'd learned in Miss Mason's second grade: *First in war, first in peace, first in the hearts of his countrymen.* Second grade was the year his dad's Foo Foo dust helped Kentucky win the national championship. It seemed like an omen.

As he threaded film into the sixteen-millimeter projector after lunch, Slim thought back to the first film session of the Rupp's Runts season. Then, they were looking at Hardin-Simmons, a Division III school they played as kind of a warm-up for the season to come. Then he got a good laugh for his *If you guys can't beat this piece of crap, we're in for a long season.* Now the long season was practically over and, especially after the dressing-down he got from Harry last night because of his antics with the *Beat the Devil Out of Duke* paddle, he was determined to keep his mouth shut.

Rupp's Runts were about to watch film of another Texas team, only this one had gone through the season with a 27-1 record, identical to theirs. They were the last team standing between them and a fifth national championship. They had to be taken seriously.

"I told them they were in for a battle," said Joe B. Hall, who scouted the Texas Western–Utah game. "This team was much better than they were billed. They beat a good Utah team, and they beat them soundly. Texas Western's quickness was a problem. It was kind of a mismatch in that . . . their guards were quicker than either Dampier or Kron. Their defense out front was not only sound, but they gambled defensively. That Bobby Joe Hill was a ball-hawking madman."

And then there was the question of size. Kentucky had been out-matched sizewise all season long, and Coach Hall said these guys were very powerful on the boards, especially their six-foot-six center. "There has to be help inside when [David] Lattin got the ball." They were in for a big challenge.

On the other hand, the Duke game was behind them, and everybody in the room believed the reporters had it right, that the odds against lowly Texas Western beating mighty Kentucky were overwhelming. "I know young people," said Hall. "That has an effect. There was the feel-ing the Duke game was for the championship, that they'd already won."

As the black-and-white film projected onto the screen at the front of the Sheraton dining room, the team knew next to nothing about Texas Western, and most of them couldn't have found El Paso on a map. Hall said they were "a sound basketball team," but nobody had followed them through the season. They hadn't played anybody Kentucky played. There was no basis for comparison. And the film turned out to have a mixed message.

Texas Western–Kansas was a really good game against evenly matched teams that ended in a double-overtime victory for Texas Western. You could see Bobby Joe Hill's quickness. You could see Lattin's strength down low, but everyone knew about the desperation shot by Kansas guard Jo Jo White, and that became the focus. With time running out in the first overtime he launched a twenty-five-footer from the left side-line over the outstretched hand of a leaping Bobby Joe Hill. The shot swished through the basket. Kansas was on its way to the Final Four . . . for about five seconds. The referee was pointing. Jo Jo had stepped on the out-of-bounds line. Or had he?

"Let's see that again, Slim."

In rewind the ball reversed its course, swishing up through the net with a flutter, arching through the air and into Jo Jo White's right hand. As he brought the ball back to chest level, they could see the referee pointing at the sideline. Everybody in the room was watching Jo Jo's left foot. It was behind the right with the heel of his white Converse All-Star basketball shoe hovering above the sideline. *Above it*, not *on* it.

Being a smart-ass had put Slim in momentary focus in the Hardin-Simmons film session. Now, with his mouth shut, he was again the center of attention.

"Again, Slim. Run it again."

He did, again and again and again. The referee was in good position to make the call. He was watching the play unfold in front of him in real time. Still, in Kentucky's mind, there was no disputing the replay evidence. The call was wrong; Kentucky's opponent in tonight's game should be the University of Kansas Jayhawks.

They would have been better off focusing on the Miners' speed and quickness, their dominance on the boards, the fact that they'd played the number-four team in the country to a draw. They would have been better off girding their loins (and minds) for the battle Coach Hall warned them about. Because of the film, it was impossible to shake the feeling: Texas Western doesn't deserve to be here.

Willie Worsley didn't usually read the morning papers, but the *Washington Post* on this sunny Saturday morning was pretty hard to ignore. *A fitting end to a perfect season?* What the hell was that? The *Washington Daily News* was even worse. The headline on the story read, "Miners Run into 'the Machine': Kentucky 'Runts' a Fearsome Unit." After labeling the Duke-Kentucky game, "for all intents and purposes, THE title game," it went on to describe the Miners' game with Utah as "a stinkeroo." As for the championship game, "On the basis of last night's games alone, Texas Western should be no trouble for the disciplined Kentucky offense. A pressing Wildcat defense might also cause a panic. Rebounding seems to be the Miners' lone advantage. . . . The Kentucky players didn't have to say that, already in this long season, they've subdued many a punishing board team. . . . If the Miners upset the Wildcats, they'd better be ready to take a saliva test."

The smart money had Kentucky as a six-point favorite, with some saying they just might run the Miners off the floor. At least the *Baltimore Sun* thought the championship game might be worth playing. It quoted broadcaster Hot Rod Hundley as saying Texas Western "can do every-thing with a basketball except sign it." The story went on to say, "The Miners, who don't worry much about defense but try to pour the ball through the hoop as much as possible, will present quite a challenge to Kentucky. The running, gunning Texas quintet can do more things with the basketball than a monkey on a 50-foot jungle wire."

There was no mention of race in the *Sun* story, but that monkey-on-a-wire bit played into the stereotype. Because Texas Western had black players, a reporter who'd seen them play exactly once, knew an immu-table truth: like all black players they could run-and-gun, but like all black players they were lazy. Defense took hard work, and, let's face it, black basketball players are just too lazy for that.

"They disrespect us even though we're ranked number three," said Worsley. "That got to us more than anything else. Absolutely! No doubt about it."

There are differing versions of what happened that day, some of them influenced by time and some by "reality" as depicted in the movie *Glory Road*. Texas Western memories unite in dismissing the scene where Haskins got his whole team together and told them he had decided to play only blacks in the championship game. No way. Didn't happen. Everybody agrees, that was Hollywood being Hollywood. There is less agreement about what actually happened.

According to Harry Flournoy, Coach Haskins gathered his seven Afri-can American players in the room Harry shared with cocaptain Orsten Artis and told them the same thing. *I'm only going to play you seven play-ers. Don't tell the others, but I've made the decision. I'm only going to play the guys in this room.* "That's what he said. And what he said he'd do, that's what he did."

"You know me better than that," Haskins told SID and lifelong friend Eddie Mullens. "No way I'd ever say anything like that." Perhaps, but Moe Iba isn't so sure. Five decades later, when asked if Haskins would have made the blacks-only decision without discussing it with him, Iba responded, "I don't know if he would or not," adding, "If the players said he said it, then he said it, and maybe I wasn't there."

On the other hand, as Haskins wrote in his book, he did use "race as a motivating factor. During one of my meetings with the team on the afternoon of the day of the championship game, I mentioned to the players I had heard some rumors that Rupp had said that he 'ain't losin' to a team of black players.' I was trying to fire their asses up." (While many "knew about" the Rupp quote, nobody ever claimed to have actually heard him say it.)

"Haskins was a con artist," said Lattin, one of several Texas Western players who doubt Rupp actually made the statement. "I was playing a national championship game. I didn't need anything to motivate me."

It was the rest-in-your-room phase of game-day preparation, but Slim was too keyed up for rest and didn't have enough concentration for study. Then he saw the message light flashing on the telephone, friends of Adolph saying there ought to be a team party to celebrate tonight's victory. With their two hundred dollars he set off to buy some beer.

With two cases each of Budweiser and his dad's favorite, Bush Bavarian, he called the front desk and ordered four buckets of ice. With the beer icing down in the bathtub, he called the dining room and told them what he was up to. How much for sandwiches, chips, dips, the whole shebang, for a party of twenty, make that thirty? The lady on the phone said something about hors d'oeuvres and asked if he wanted caviar. He didn't know from hors d'oeuvres (when he'd seen it in print he thought it was pronounced *horse doo-vers*), but he knew about caviar. Why not? He still had a lot of money, and how many times in life do you have something as big as a national championship to celebrate?

While the hotel staff was bringing in tables and setting things up in his room for the big postgame celebration, Slim hung out with Conley and Kron, his two best friends on the team, watching a rerun of *The Twilight Zone*. With time to kill while Duke and Utah were suiting up for the consolation game, it was a welcome diversion.

The story was about a small town that has all its food radiated. Eat it and you'll die, said a government official. So for two or three weeks townsfolk survive on noncontaminated food shipped in from the other side of the mountain. There is barely enough to go around, so people are hungry until this Mr. Macho guy comes along. A type-A personality,

204 THE SMART MONEY

he is the very definition of *hail fellow well met*, a Falstaff oozing charm and charisma from every pore. The government is wrong, he says. The food is okay to eat. The townspeople are convinced, except for one nerdy guy—think Woody Allen—who keeps insisting the danger is real. In the scene before the final commercial, people are crowded around a table, happily gorging themselves on the kind of potluck dinner they used to have in the basement of the Buena Vista Baptist Church back in Owensboro.

During the commercial Larry was stretched out on the bed, his head resting on a couple of pillows, looking pretty much the way he always looked on game-day afternoons. He had played on pure adrenaline against Duke, but twenty-two hours is barely enough recovery time for a player in the bloom of health. Larry wasn't.

At 100 percent Larry Conley was not only the triggerman on offense but also the heart of Kentucky's defense. He was so good in the one-three-one zone that Tommy Kron, playing out front, always tried to channel the ball to Conley's side—to the offense's left—because he was so good at anticipating, deflecting passes, and trapping. "He was such a core to the total team effort," said Joe B. Hall. "To remove him would have been like taking one wheel off your car." But if he played at only 60 or 70 percent . . . ? "Rupp felt he needed whatever [Larry] could give."

The final scenes of *The Twilight Zone* showed the nerdy guy walking along the main street of the town. At first it was just him, looking around. The music has an eerie, foreboding quality. Then . . . bodies, the recognizable remains of the townspeople who rejected his warning. Finally, there is Mr. Macho lying there beside them.

Slim counted the players onto the bus that evening the way he always did. The difference this time was that *Sports Illustrated* reporter Frank Deford watched him do it. *Why the extra suit?* he asked, looking at the freshly dry-cleaned suit in a clear plastic bag Slim was holding in his noncounting hand. His answer: "Tradition!" He wasn't thinking about Zero Mostel's song from *Fiddler on the Roof* that was getting a lot of play on the radio in those days. The tradition he hoped to become part of was the one where student managers of national championship teams get thrown into the shower. After that the celebration would continue, and he wanted to be, in the words of another Broadway musical, "spruced up and looking in [his] prime."

Fifty years later it is still an article of faith among many Wildcat fans that Adolph never (make that *NEVER*) would have permitted total access to a non-Kentucky reporter, especially one representing a national magazine like *Sports Illustrated*.

He did.

With justification Coach Rupp believed himself to be the best basketball coach in the history of the game. Deford, in an *SI* article after the first Tennessee game, had stroked Rupp's ego. It was Deford who called Rupp "a man of consummate pride and well-earned privilege ... [who] continues to pursue the only challenge left—trying to top himself. And that is some tough act to follow." Deford was the one who called Rupp's Wildcats "the slickest basketball unit in the country." It was Deford who wrote about Rupp the teacher: "It seems that Rupp, who has never been encumbered by modesty, used to teach a basketball course at UK, and he would always give all his students straight A's. Rupp's reasoning was simply that no one could learn basketball from Adolph Rupp and not get an A. The reasoning is as sound today, although this bunch of Wildcats would deserve their A's. Teacher should get an A, too."

Coach Rupp expected to win his fifth national championship that night. Deford, a twenty-seven-year-old Princeton graduate, had written basketball for *SI* since 1962 and was the logical person to capture Adolph's crowning achievement for the ages. At six-foot-four Deford looked like he might be a player himself. He was with Kentucky on the bus, with them in their pregame locker room, and, yes, with them at halftime.

This time, with only Deford and UK football coach Charlie Bradshaw along for the ride, the bus accomplished the ten-mile trip from Silver Spring to College Park in light traffic, with few lights and no Adolph outbursts. They were on their way to the championship game, something they had been dreaming about since Rupp's little pre-Christmas talk back in Lubbock. Only now they were wide awake. Their dream was coming true.

Everything was different. When they arrived for yesterday's game, it was late afternoon. Now it was night, and the lights of Cole Field

House gave off an ethereal, otherworldly glow. The muffled sounds of the consolation game between last night's losers, Duke and Utah, grew louder, throbbing with anticipation, as they approached the locker room. The feeling was surreal, a combination of weird and wonderful, like a weightless dream where you are light as a feather, gliding along above it all, swooping, soaring, exhilarating. It didn't last.

When the Texas Western team arrived, their white bus driver seemed bemused. "Why are you guys even playing this game?" he asked David Lattin. "You don't actually think you can beat Kentucky and Adolph Rupp. Why waste your time?" Lattin didn't respond.

34

And Then There Was David

The Texas Western players who knew how much Harry Flournoy was hurting from his dive to the floor for a loose ball near the end of the Utah game might have expected a change in tonight's starting lineup. None of them expected the change Haskins made. *We're going to start Orsten and Bobby Joe, David and Harry.* He paused. *And Willie, you're starting tonight.* Little Willie Worsley patted his fellow New Yorker on the shoulder. If the Shadow wasn't starting, it had to be six-foot-five Willie Cager. Haskins shook his head. Last night, watching Larry Conley play the point-forward role in the Kentucky offense, Haskins made a calculation. With Lattin and Flournoy pounding the boards against one of the shortest teams his Miners had faced all season, he could go without Nevil Shed's height. What he needed to disrupt the flow of Kentucky's game was quick. It would be five-six Willie Worsley guarding six-three Conley. Quick on quick.

The three-guard offense set Texas Western up for something it had never done before. All season long, said Iba, "When we shot the ball we would drop two guards back defensively and rebound three." On this night, out of concern for Kentucky's fast break, Lattin and Flournoy would crash the boards, while three guards dropped back. "We thought we could defend them on the half court. The thing we didn't want to do was give up transition baskets."

Earlier, Harry had told Haskins, "I can make it, Coach." All day long he'd been saying to himself, *I'm going to play; I have to play*, but now he was having second thoughts. The pain in his right knee had kept him up all night, and now, as he put weight on the leg, he wondered. This was a game for all the marbles, for the national championship. He wanted to play, but should he?

While Harry gingerly tested his leg, Bobby Joe was stretched out on a bench at the other end of the locker room, his eyes closed, a toothpick in his mouth. Eddie Mullens, making a tour of the room, chuckled under his breath. In twenty minutes the little guard would be on the biggest stage in college basketball, and now he was copping some z's. When Mullens stopped beside him B.J. opened one eye and gave a little grin. "What's happenin', Judge?"

One thing happening was Haskins becoming increasingly agitated. As he looked around at his players he thought his little motivational ploy of the afternoon was a bust. Instead of being fired up as he wrote a few final words of instruction on the blackboard, they seemed almost lackadaisical, especially Bobby Joe. The only sign of life from his so-called team leader was an ever-so-slight movement of that damn toothpick, holding his mouth slightly ajar.

"I was so angry I couldn't think straight," Haskins wrote. "I picked up an eraser and beamed him with it," sending chalk flying all over the locker room. "I hope you get your ass kicked!" Haskins screamed. "I am so damn sick and tired of this crap!"

Later, Kentucky players would comment on the intensity they saw in the Miners' eyes. "Intensity, my ass," wrote Haskins. "This was the loosest team I ever had." Still hoping to get them hyped, he gave last-minute instructions.

"Listen, David, when you get the ball I want you to flush it. I don't care if you run over somebody or travel, run into them, charge, I don't care what you do. Just dunk the ball as hard as you can, got it?"

David Lattin nodded. He'd been intimidating opposing players with slam dunks since his freshman year in high school back in Houston and was looking forward to doing it against Kentucky. Bobby Joe might be cooling it, but Lattin was psyched and ready.

Haskins had instructions for Hill, too. He wanted his little guard to be more cautious than usual. "Do *not* try to steal the ball from Louis Dampier," he said. "He's too good a ball handler, too damn quick." Bobby Joe tilted his head to one side, quizzically. There was no toothpick now, but it was the same casual grin. "Coach, how many times do you want me to take it from him?" Haskins shook his head. *Incorrigible!*

"THIS IS IT," said Coach Rupp as his team gathered around him. "Back in Lubbock I told you . . . you could be national champions." He paused, looking from face to face—Larry, Pat, Louie, Tommy, Thad, Cliff Berger, Bobby Tallent, and the others—with as close to a smile as he ever had at game time. "Tonight's the night to turn my prediction into reality."

"Let's do it," said Kron, with the others joining in. Hands came together. "*Team!*"

Rupp gave a satisfied nod. "Who's captain tonight?"

"It's Pat's birthday tomorrow," said Larry.

"All right, then, let's have a birthday present for him."

As the top seed in the tournament, the University of Kentucky wore white uniforms with blue numbers, while Texas Western College had orange uniforms with white numbers. But the Miners team that trotted out to the middle of the floor at tip-off time in front of the capacity crowd of 14,500 was different from the one they started against Utah the previous night.

In the preseason a reporter asked Rupp, "If you had to choose between big and quick, which would it be?" "Well, Bob," said Adolph, "big *and* quick, but if I had to choose, I'd take quick." That was the decision Don Haskins made, too. A three-guard lineup of six-foot-one Orsten Artis and five-foot-ten Bobby Joe Hill would leave Worsley guarding who, Larry? He was sick, but not that sick. The Miners were a strictly man-to-man team, but maybe they'd decided the only way to compete was to play a zone. By cutting down their size advantage, they added to their quick. A lot.

The Miners still had six-foot-five Harry Flournoy and David "Big Daddy" Lattin, who was listed at six feet six but looked like his picture should be in the dictionary next to the word *intimidation*. Kentucky had played against *Big* all season, but this guy not only was tall but had shoulders that would make most football players seem a bit puny. And as Kentucky was about to discover, he could play.

What Wildcat players didn't see, or at least didn't really notice, was color. They beat a Michigan team with four black players to make it to the

Final Four, and none of them had seen Deford's *Sports Illustrated* tournament preview raising the question of race and *a contest for racial honors*.

For the players involved it was just a game. "As for the race aspects," said Thad Jaracz, Kentucky's sophomore center, "I don't think they were there. It was a wonderful opportunity to do something very few people got to do. That's what our focus was on." "I don't remember thinking of it as a white team," said Willie Worsley. "That part never crossed our minds," said Orsten Artis. "We didn't think of them as black players," said Larry Conley. "We thought of them as players." "When the basketball goes up on the boards, I don't have time to see whether the guy's black or white," said David Lattin. "I just go after the ball. We're just out there trying to win. They were trying to beat us, and we were trying to beat them."

The atmospherics as the teams came onto the court were surreal. Partly, that was because this was a game neither team had expected to be playing when the season started back in December. For the Miners there was also the nature of the crowd. Their supporters seemed to be lost in a vast sea of white: white players, white referees, white cheerleaders, a white crowd. And then there were the Confederate flags, or were there? In the Hollywood version of the game, you see fleeting glimpses of the flag. In reality? Memories differ. The white players didn't see them. Some of the black players did. "It was a little intimidating," said Harry Flournoy. "You're on the Mason-Dixon line, and then there are the flags."

One writer who saw film of the game decades after the fact wrote, "Kentucky fans wave a confederate flag as the Wildcats' five white players line up for the opening tap." He not only saw flags others fail to see in the black-and-white CBS film, but, somehow, was able to discern that those waving the flags were Kentucky fans and not just generic racists who, back in the mid-1960s, were very much a part of the fabric of a racially divided country.

If there were racial taunts from the Cole Field House crowd that night, nobody noticed. Coach Haskins had insulated his team from that kind of distraction early in the season with a simple rule: *If I don't turn around, you don't turn around.* "We saw it all," said Harry Flournoy. "You had to see it, but your mind is trained just to take care of the business at hand, to concentrate on what's going on between those black lines, so that's what we did."

It was Pat Riley against David Lattin for the opening tip. Both had been *Parade* High School All-Americans three years before, averaging an identical twenty-nine points a game. Riley prevailed as he had for most of the season, this time by quick-jumping the referee's toss, tipping the ball on the way up. So two seconds into the game, Texas Western got the ball out-of-bounds on the side. For the next couple of minutes, it was a Lattin-Riley face-off at both ends of the court. Lattin was called for a foul while blocking a Riley shot (Pat made one of two). A minute later, on the Miners' second possession, Lattin got a lob pass from Bobby Joe Hill, took one step inside, and slammed it home over Riley. Lattin, following Haskins's instruction, flushed it hard, drawing a Riley foul.

Lattin was all business as he stepped to the free-throw line. The dunk had been muscle-powered intensity. Now, while the teams lined up for his free throw, he shook his arms to relax, bounced the ball three times, and shot. TW 3, UK 1.

True to form, the Miners were playing man-to-man, and Larry Conley made a surprising discovery. "I had a five-six guy guarding me," he marveled. "It shouldn't have worked, but it did." A Wildcat fast break—Dampier to Riley to Conley for a lay-up—tied the score at three. It would be Kentucky's only fast break of the game. After back-to-back jumpers by Riley and Dampier and Louie's free throw, the Wildcats pulled even, but neither team found their shooting touch and the score was tied at nine after nine minutes of play.

"*This has certainly been a slow-starting game*," said Kentucky play-by-play man Claude Sullivan on WINN Radio in Louisville. "*Fans are in a hush wondering when the two teams will go at each other.*"

After a time-out Nevil Shed made a free throw that gave Texas Western a lead they would never relinquish.

As Tommy Kron brought the ball up the left sideline, Bobby Joe Hill moved to center stage in a most spectacular manner. Kentucky knew he was quick, but they'd seen nothing in the Utah game or on film like what was about to happen.

Kron was dribbling some thirty feet from the basket. When Texas

Western guard Orsten Artis moved up to meet him, Kron turned back toward the middle, switching from a left- to a right-handed dribble. Bobby Joe flashed across from the head of the key, picked Tommy's pocket in middribble, and streaked toward the opposite end in one of the quickest moves ever seen on a basketball court. It was the kind of defensive freelancing that would have bought B.J. bench time earlier in the season. Not only had he left his man, but the man he left was All-American Louie Dampier, a lights-out shooter, one of the best in all of basketball.

"Jesus H. Christ!" Adolph sputtered.

On the very next play—ten seconds later on the clock—Hill was guarding Dampier one-on-one near the right sideline about twenty-five feet from the basket. Louie turned his back to Hill, switching to a left-handed dribble. Bobby Joe came around from behind, snatched the ball cleanly, and streaked in for his second straight left-handed lay-up. The crowd that came expecting to see a Texas Western beat-down let out its collective breath in an audible "Ooo."

"*Say, now, this looks pretty bad,*" said Sullivan. Earlier he told radio listeners on the Standard Oil Sports Network back in Kentucky, "*The Washington press has pretty much conceded that Texas Western cannot stand up to Kentucky.*" Now he said, "*Kentucky has just gone flat-footed. Kentucky has lost that bounce and zip. The Miners have got a little zip going.*"

Less than a minute later David Lattin got the ball, took one step, and slammed home another dunk.

"You stupid sonsabitches!" shouted Adolph, signaling for a time-out as he got to his feet in a red-faced rage. "Thad, goddamn it, you've got to step in there and take the charge." Texas Western was up 16–11.

"*Fans are sitting in stunned silence,*" Sullivan told his radio audience. "*The University of Kentucky scored only eleven points in eleven minutes. Unbelievable. Just unbelievable.*"

Larry walked over to where Kron was sitting on the bench. "What are you guys doing out there?" It wasn't a rhetorical question. "I never saw either steal," Larry said. "Never saw either one of them. I was coming up the floor to get into my position. I turned around and looked back, and the ball's going the other way. And I go, 'What the hell happened there?'" Larry ran to midcourt as Bobby Joe made his first lay-up. "So I turn around, coming back to get in position again, ... and I look back and he's going back with the ball the other way," again. Some five decades later Larry would say about the steals, "I haven't seen them yet."

In the Texas Western huddle Bobby Joe was brimming with confidence. "I can steal it from him anytime you want me to," he said. Haskins shook his head. His tie was still on, as it would continue to be throughout the game, but so was his game-face intensity. The steals had worked . . . twice, but he wanted team defense where each player took responsibility for his own man. "No, just lay off. You've got him gun-shy now."

There were no more Bobby Joe steals, but the Miners' inside strength continued to manifest itself, despite the fact that Harry Flournoy, the Miners' number-one rebounder, had taken himself out of the game. The injury didn't affect his rebounding, but he was guarding Pat Riley. It took only a few times up and down the floor, and he knew: he couldn't make the lateral moves to stay between the Kentucky forward and the basket. It wasn't a difficult decision. *If I couldn't protect the baseline like I wanted to, I had no business being out there.* He had two points, two rebounds, and out. For the next thirty-four minutes Texas Western would play with only six players, replacing Harry with either Nevil Shed or Willie Cager.

With just under five minutes left in the half, Willie Worsley hit a twenty-footer from the right corner, and Thad Jaracz answered, breaking by Lattin for a left-handed lay-up. Thad's first basket of the game brought the Wildcats to within six points until Willie Cager left him behind with a spin move from the free-throw line, flashing down the middle for a two-handed dunk, putting the Texas Western lead back to eight. Harry Flournoy, watching from the bench, smiled. Cager had a determination and a work ethic that were rare. "You can't tell him he can't do something because that's what he's going to do. He came in and just stepped up. He played the best I'd ever seen him play." Several times during time-outs, Willie Worsley came over to Harry. "Flo, you've got to get back in there, man." Harry shook his head. Selfishly, he wanted to play, but the way Shed and Cager were playing, he knew the team was better off without him.

For Kentucky the change of momentum was shocking. They kept running their one-three-one defense, but Bobby Joe wiggle-wormed his way through, slithering past Larry on the left or Louie on the right as if he were coated with some of Larry's goose grease. They couldn't trap him. They couldn't double-team him. He controlled the basketball. To Deford he looked like "the best broken field runner since Red Grange [a 1920s running back known as the Galloping Ghost]."

"*Hill took on the entire left side of Kentucky's defense and went right through it*," said Sullivan. "*Put it right in.*"

The *Baltimore Sun*'s "monkey-on-a-wire" guy saw a Texas Western team that was exactly the opposite from the "*don't worry about defense*" team he described. The Miners walked the ball up the floor and ran a disciplined, patterned offense, often passing the ball five, six, seven times before attacking the basket. On one possession Texas Western passed the ball twenty times before finding Lattin for another of his slam dunks. Their emphasis was the same as it had been all season, on defense, the kind of defense Haskins had learned well from his college coach, Hank Iba, and passed on to his players.

"We were more white-oriented than any of the other teams in the Final Four," Willie Worsley told reporter Frank Fitzpatrick. "We played the most intelligent, the most boring, the most disciplined game of them all."

The discipline showed. Texas Western could run when Haskins wanted them to run, but that wasn't his game. They were Lattin's speedy Porsche throttled back to fifty-five miles an hour, making it a much shorter game than the Wildcats were used to playing. In ten of Kentucky's twenty-eight games they'd scored in the eighties and four times in the nineties; six times they topped a hundred. They had been held under seventy points only three times: once in their double-overtime win against Georgia, once in their loss to Tennessee, and now, in their twenty-ninth game of the season, by the Texas Western Miners.

Even with Conley at less than full speed, the Wildcats wanted to run, but that was all but impossible. Before the start of the season Rupp had predicted a "fast, experienced, good-shooting team," saying that ball handling would "solve [our] rebounding problem." That had been his team's modus operandi for most of the season, but what the writer wrote in the preseason was finally coming true: "You've got to have the ball to play with it." They didn't and couldn't.

Twice in the first half the Miners got their lead up to eight points. Defensively, the Worsley-Conley matchup was starting to make sense. Larry had the advantage on the boards, but he was facing one of Texas Western's strongest defenders. And when Conley beat Worsley, there were two TW defenders standing there waiting for him. In those days there wasn't much talk of defensive rotation, what is now called help defense, but Haskins's team had it perfected. "You could beat somebody," said Larry, "but even if you beat them, here comes another guy from another angle that's going to stop you from getting to the basket." The Wildcats, known for their speed and quickness, had met their match. It was better team quickness than they'd seen all season, and it took them out of their offense. Plays were starting farther from the basket. Passes were longer. Seven and Go Backdoor, good for easy baskets all season long, was rendered inoperative.

"Very quick," Larry said, repeating himself for emphasis. "They were very quick."

Still down by eight with 3:26 to go in the half, Tommy Kron made a twenty-foot jumper from the top of the key, starting a Kentucky-style surge. Dampier and Riley hit from the outside, and Conley found Jaracz cutting across the lane for another lay-up.

"*Four straight field goals, and Kentucky has battled its way back from eight points down to within three*," said Sullivan, with a hint of relief in his voice.

Halftime score, Texas Western 34, Kentucky 31. It was the battle Coach Hall had predicted.

The game was still close, but being behind at halftime was something they'd experienced only against Dayton and Duke, and this was a team they were supposed to be running off the court. Adolph was irate, mad, and sad along with livid, furious, and fuming.

"What the hell's going on out there?" he shouted, glaring at his team. "You sonsabitches are playing like these are the goddamned Celtics. Kron, Dampier, you let that little Hill kid . . ." He sputtered to a stop, shaking his head as if Bobby Joe's steals were replaying in his mind. "Candy from a baby."

Heads were down as Coach Rupp paced back and forth, gathering steam for his next assault. "Thad, you have got to step in front of that

Lattin guy. You have to sacrifice your body, son, because, whether you like it or not, you're expendable."

Rupp coughed, blew his nose, turned away. Reaching for another Kleenex he wiped his forehead. What he said next, according to Deford, was "You've got to beat those coons," then, turning back to Thad, "You've got to go after that big coon."

The incident wasn't reported in Deford's *SI* story that week, but years later he would say that "a chill went through me," that the players, embarrassed, "kind of ducked their heads."

Perhaps.

Aside from Deford, nobody who was in the room that night remembers the word *coon*, but they were listening to a cantankerous old man in full harangue, not taking notes. They concede that he might have said *coon* or *goon* or *purple people eater*, for that matter. What they remember is that he was not happy. Deford, who had only limited exposure to Rupp, said he talked that way all the time (he didn't) and that he was a "virulent racist." He wasn't.

In a halftime interview radio listeners back in Kentucky heard former All-American Alex Groza say, "I felt if Kentucky was going to win, they would have to have a real good shooting night." Groza, who won MVP honors in the Wildcats' back-to-back NCAA wins in 1948 and '49, added, "If they don't get their shooting eye back, it's going to be a long night for Kentucky."

As the second half got under way, Kentucky seemed to be finding its game, putting pressure on Texas Western guards Hill and Worsley, both of whom ended the game with six turnovers. With 17:30 left Larry Conley made a fifteen-footer to cut their lead to one. Forty seconds later Louie Dampier hit a twenty-footer from the right side of the key, again cutting the lead back to one. Almost, but not quite.

Every time Kentucky got close, it always seemed the ball ended up in the hands of Orsten Artis. "I can still see him on that baseline from about thirteen to fifteen feet," said Larry. "He was the one who was making the shots that made the difference." Artis, who played all forty minutes, along with both Hill and Worsley, was the Miners' third-leading scorer (Hill, twenty; Lattin, sixteen; Artis, fifteen), but "it always seemed like it was him." Artis was the only one on the TW team who could beat Coach Haskins at free throws, once making 125 in a row. "He could line up that jump shot," said Larry. "He was deadly."

Kentucky got it down to one again on a Thad tip-in at the 12:30 mark, but it was one of the few times in the game when he was able to score. He was facing Big Daddy Lattin on both ends of the floor, and Lattin was using his body to keep Thad away from the basket, off balance, and in foul trouble. And fouls were eating the Wildcats alive. They put Texas Western in a one-on-one situation at the four-minute mark in the first half and put them into bonus land with ten minutes to go in the second. And on this night Haskins's players were shooting foul shots almost as well as their coach, making 85 percent.

Before the game reporters had predicted that Texas Western would get in serious foul trouble because of what Bob Ingram of the *El Paso Herald-Post* described as the "scrambling, clawing game" they played against Utah. That didn't happen. While Kentucky was called for twenty-three personal fouls (both Thad and Larry fouled out), Texas Western had only twelve. David Lattin, with four, was the only Miner in anything approaching foul trouble, and he didn't get his fourth until late in the game. Of Kentucky's starting five, only Tommy Kron wasn't in trouble.

Lattin, in his book, *Slam Dunk to Glory*, said he had "only one chilling concern" about the Kentucky game: "Would the white referees let us win?" Moe Iba thought the problem might go beyond race. "The only thing we were concerned about was Kentucky—the name of Kentucky—because it was such a giant name in college basketball at the time. Were they going to let us win?"

The answer was yes. Kentucky would make six more field goals than Texas Western, but the Miners were winning at the free-throw line.

"*Texas Western is death on the free-throw line,*" said Sullivan, stating the obvious. "*They've missed only one of fifteen.*"

Their shooting streak continued. Lattin went six for six, Artis five for five, Cager six for seven, Shed one for one, Worsley four for six, and Bobby Joe Hill six for nine. True to form, Haskins covered his eyes with barely a peak while his team made a total of twenty-eight for thirty-four.

In the middle of one streak in which they made twenty-six of twenty-seven free throws, Slim pictured his dad in their living room back in Owensboro shouting his Foo Foo dust at the television set and becoming more and more exasperated. When a Willie Worsley foul shot did a complete toilet bowl, circling the rim five times before flushing through the net, Slim was pretty sure his dad had switched to his more colorful vocabulary. For Kentucky fans the discrepancy in fouls called was also disturbing. The Wildcats went to the free-throw line only thirteen times during the game, making eleven.

With Thad in foul trouble, Cliff Berger gave Kentucky twelve solid minutes off the bench, hitting two midrange jumpers, but the game was slipping away. Assistant coach Harry Lancaster, sitting beside Rupp, was doing his usual commentary. "I think we need to shake things up," he said. "Let's get Tallent in there and see what happens."

What happened was an open jumper from eighteen feet, the kind of shot where the stat-sheet guy would have his pencil halfway down to the FG (field goal) column, ready to write a 2. The ball looked good in the air, but bounded harmlessly off the front rim into Lattin's outstretched hands for one of his nine rebounds.

"Damn," said Lancaster. "I thought Red would make that one for us."

Kentucky was back within striking distance again at the eight-minute mark when they had back-to-back-to-back shots to tie the game. Dampier, Berger, and then Riley all missed.

"*Kentucky has had all the opportunity in the world to cash in,*" said Sullivan, "*but they just can't do it.*"

It had been that kind of a game for Pat. He played all forty minutes on a night when he probably should have been soaking his foot and drinking a cold one. "When you're trying to maneuver, trying to cut, trying to run," said Larry, "the worst thing you can have is something wrong with your feet. He had this inflamed toe and it was killing him, and he never said a word about it." Pat ended the night with nineteen points on eight of twenty-two shooting. "He was a much better player than that," said Larry.

Even after Willie Cager made two free throws to extend the Miners' lead to eleven points with three and a half minutes to go, the Wildcats still thought they were going to win. "Your confidence is unbelievable," said Thad Jaracz. "You just feel like whatever you're going to do, it's going to work. . . . I think we thought we were going to win the game right up until we got beat. Those kinds of things had always happened for us."

Not this time.

"*Things certainly look gloomy at the moment,*" said Sullivan. "*They have never lost a championship game. It is almost beyond belief that Kentucky would play like this in a championship game.*" And then, "*Texas Western, if trying to describe them, they are so disorganized, it's impossible to guard them.*"

What turned things around for Kentucky in game after game all season long was conditioning. Against Texas Western that was never a factor. "Had we run with them, it would have probably killed us," said Lou Baudoin. "It was half-court basketball." The pace of the game was so slow, compared to Kentucky's usual up-tempo game, it was boring and frightening at the same time.

There was nothing dramatic about the way it ended. As the clock ticked off the final seconds, six-foot-five Willie Cager dribbled the ball near midcourt, a big smile on his face. When the buzzer sounded, ending the game, he passed it to Lattin, who launched a shot from thirty-five feet that hit the rim and bounced away.

"I kick myself," said Lattin, looking back. "I had the ball in my hand. . . . I could have held onto that ball. I could have. That ball is worth a lot of money right now."

Rupp's Runts stood there watching and disbelieving as their miraculous season came to an end, not with a bang or a whimper but a buzzer. It just ended. For only the second time all season, the Kentucky Wildcats had lost. Final score: 72–65.

35

An Unreal Thing

For Tommy Kron and Larry Conley, Kentucky's senior cocaptains, this was it. Their team very nearly fell apart that Thanksgiving weekend so long ago, yet somehow it came together as few teams ever do. Somehow their coach, in the twilight of his career, had been able to cobble together, from this improbable group of undersize young men, a team for the ages.

"*Louie [Dampier] sits down right in the middle of the floor,*" Sullivan told a disbelieving Kentucky radio audience. "*Pat Riley stands, looking at the floor dejectedly.*"

Willie Worsley was stunned. *We didn't practice winning the national championship,* he thought. *We practiced everything else: lay-ups, free throws, everything else.* He stood there in the middle of the court and looked around, his mouth open. *Damn, we're national champions.*

A jubilant team of Texas Western Miners jumped up and down, hugging each other and repeating over and over, "We did it! We're national champions!"

The Miners paused in midcelebration to accept the congratulatory handshakes from the Kentucky players and to watch as their worthy opponents stepped forward to receive the second-place trophy none of them wanted to accept. It ended up in the hands of Thad Jaracz, who carried it into the locker room, put it on top of a locker, sat down, and cried.

After Texas Western received the championship trophy, the Miners lifted little Willie Worsley up on Nevil Shed's head to take down the nets. They hadn't practiced that either. With two white teammates, Flip Baudoin and Dick Myers, on either side to steady him, Willie, who didn't have scissors, laboriously took it down loop by loop.

Later, with an arm around Harry Flournoy's shoulder, Shed looked up into the crowd and saw his mother and father. She had been his biggest fan over the years and was "jumping up and down like a crazy person." His father smiled his biggest smile. A sleeping-car porter for the Pennsylvania Railroad, he had just seen his son play basketball for the first time. Shed pointed at them, saying, *Thanks for everything.*

Watching from the bench while his teammates celebrated, Big Daddy Lattin was thinking: *What I really want to do is call my mother.* Elsie Lattin was widowed when her husband died of a heart attack shortly after David's sixth birthday. In the fourteen years since, the two of them faced the world together with the help of the good people of Saint John Baptist Church on Dowling Street, where David sang in the choir. Now, because the television station in Houston had elected to play the game on tape delay the following night, she wouldn't know the outcome until he called. Lattin's other thought was *Man, this is fun. I like this. We're going to be back next year, too.*

An hour later, on the bus ride back to the Sheraton, Thad Jaracz was thinking the same thing about his Kentucky team, talking up the prospects for next season. "Louie will be back next year. Pat will be back next year. We'll be back."

"It shows how naive you are," he would say, nearly five decades later. "We didn't think it was the end of the road. It also shows how difficult this is. How you have to catch lightning in the bottle no matter how good you are. It happens every year to somebody. It happened to us that year. We were able to catch it for whatever reason. So that's the story."

Back at the hotel Slim quietly passed the word that there was a party setup in his room. Throughout the rest of the evening players, cheerleaders, and assorted friends wandered in and out, had a beer, some hors d'oeuvres, a sandwich. A couple of guys tried a little caviar on a cracker and turned up their noses. Not a Kentucky kind of thing.

After a while Slim went outside and walked around the area, feeling like the nerdy guy on *The Twilight Zone.* Night-lights cast long, eerie, almost ghostlike shadows. The street in front of the hotel, so crowded on Friday afternoon, was empty as a windswept desert. An otherworldly silence was deeper, more penetrating than anything he had ever known. In that moment he understood, really for the first time, the Simon and

Garfunkel song "The Sound of Silence," except this silence wasn't the "old friend" of the song but an ominous, menacing presence. On the other side of the parking lot were several players with their families. They were wandering aimlessly, wordlessly. They felt it too.

Around two o'clock in the morning, the hotel's desk man, a narrow, little Mr. Peepers-type guy with wire-rimmed glasses and a high-pitched voice, came to the party room to complain about the noise. It was a bad piece of timing. "Leave my guys the fuck alone!" shouted Bob Windsor, who followed Peepers through the door a beat too late to hear his official status. A rugged UK football player who'd joined the team as a practice player, Windsor had experienced the loss and a few too many beers and was in no mood to allow some outsider to harass his guys. Windsor grabbed Peepers by the scruff of the neck and threw him against the wall, arms akimbo, smashing his watch. Bob was all apologies when he understood the situation, but Peepers couldn't be pacified. He called security, security called Harry Lancaster, and Harry ordered a bed check. It was almost three in the morning. Only half the players were in their rooms.

Earlier in the evening Louie and Pat were coming back upstairs in the elevator when Coach Rupp got on. He was carrying a bottle in a brown paper bag. In his postgame news conference he'd said, "We came to play Duke. Perhaps we keyed too much [on them]. I think the pressure got to the boys. If you're going to let the pressure get to you, then it is better to go home before the game starts." It was typical Adolph with reporters: no filter between brain and mouth. Now he was more philosophical. "You boys were part of something that's world changing tonight."

During the game Mary Haskins had been thrilled and proud, confident the Miners would win and half afraid they wouldn't. *We're here. We're here*, she thought. *It's happening. It's really happening.* She still had vivid memories of her initiation to Don's coaching career, an enormous rattlesnake on the steps of their newly rented house in tiny Benjamin, Texas. "Hon," she said, "I don't know if I'm going to like this." In Benjamin Don served as principal and bus driver in addition to coaching the girls' and boys' basketball teams and the school's six-man football team. After a year in Benjamin, four in Hedley, and one in Dumas, Texas Western came calling. Now, only five years later, it was almost beyond belief. Her husband, who used to supplement the family's meager income hustling pool in Stillwater, Drumright, and Pound Creek, was coach of the national champion Texas Western Miners.

With the pep band alternating between "The Yellow Rose of Texas" and "The Eyes of Texas Are upon You," it was finally over. People all around were hugging each other, hugging Mary, and shouting, "We're number one! We're number one!" Yet it was hard to grasp. *Little Texas Western from El Paso. We'd beaten Kentucky. Kentucky! It was an unreal thing.*

It didn't seem real to her husband, either. "It was a thrill for me," he told reporters after the game. "I'm kind of a young punk, and to play a game with Mr. Rupp is quite an honor, let alone win it.

"Before the game we feared their shooting. It was the best offensive team we played, but our team defense was excellent. It was one of the finest defensive games we've played. . . . [I]t seemed like we've been able to do it like that all season when we had to." One reporter wanted to know if Haskins had done anything different to prepare for the championship game. "About the same. . . . We just came to play our game and not Kentucky's." Any special strategy? "Yes, I prayed."

When it was Mr. Rupp's turn, he said, "I thought at the half we would win. We didn't have two bad halves all season, but tonight we did. We have been fast all season. We were fast tonight. We had a good shooting team all season, but we did not shoot well tonight, nor was our ball handling good. When those two things break down, you are in trouble." Rupp didn't credit the Miners' defense for his team's breakdown, but it had been stifling. All season long Kentucky had relied on quickness, speed, and the fast break. With their running game virtually eliminated, they were forced to rely on outside shooting. With every shot contested, their field-goal percentage was only 39 percent, their lowest of the season.

Before the game Abe Lemon, the Oklahoma City University coach who knew whereof he spoke, had a word of warning. "Kentucky, you better have zippers on your pockets because [Texas Western's] going to steal everything coming at you." After the game one reporter wrote, "Bobby Joe Hill is as quick and deft as a big city pickpocket." "That hurt us," Rupp acknowledged, "hurt us real bad."

While Rupp and his team returned to their hotel in Silver Spring, the Miners moved their celebration to a nearby steak house, where a mixed-race crowd, rarely seen in mid-1960s Maryland, was served everything from steak to prime rib to Willie Cager's favorite, fried chicken. The El Paso business leaders who had flown in with the team on the charter were mostly white. Bobby Joe's friends and family from Detroit, numbering close to twenty, were mostly black. So was the contingent from the Bronx who had come to toast the Willies (Worsley and Cager) and Nevil Shed. The Shadow's single free throw of the night would receive special mention the following morning in the *New York Times*. "Nevil Shed, a New York boy, sank the free throw that put Texas Western into the lead it never relinquished."

Everyone at the steak house was talking about winning the national championship, but nobody was even thinking about the historical significance of the game until Bobby Joe's brother brought it up. *An all-white team beaten by a team that played only blacks. That's never happened before.* At that moment none of the Miners could have imagined how their win would change basketball. They couldn't have imagined that theirs would be the first college team admitted to the Naismith Memorial Basketball Hall of Fame, that their game would be replayed for a national television audience fifty years later, that of all the teams to win NCAA Championships before and since, the Texas Western Miners would become the most honored and remembered.

With the American Airlines charter due to depart for El Paso at 7:00 in the morning, Cager was intent on an after-party celebration with his girlfriend. Harry Flournoy, who passed up the party at the steak house, sat with his mother in her rental car in the parking lot at the International Hotel. For more than two hours they talked about basketball, school, his upcoming graduation, career possibilities, and life in general. Along the way she admired the Bulova watch he'd been given that bore the inscription *NCAA Basketball Champions 1966*. When the buzzer sounded ending the game, Harry had felt relief. It was over. Then, receiving the watch, he felt exhilaration, "like I got recharged. Looking over at the Kentucky side, they had watches too, but ours said *Champions*. It wasn't like a taunting feeling, but it was a good feeling. Yeah." Recalling the feeling nearly five decades later, Harry would say, "My only regret was that I didn't give my mother the watch. She asked for it, and I didn't give it to her."

Two thousand miles to the southwest, the excitement of Texas Western's win was bubbling over into the streets. It started with the sound of car horns and shouts of *We're number one!* Then, as the *El Paso Times* would describe it, "Frolic became . . . something akin to frenzy. . . . Students shrieking, giggling and waving. A car careened around the corner with the driver blowing a trumpet." There was a "victory bonfire near the college administration building," and somebody hoisted a hand-lettered flag: Miners—#1.

Seven-year-old Steve Haskins knew nothing about the celebration. Mimi and Papa let him stay up to watch the game on television, so he knew Daddy's team had won, but he wasn't thinking about that when he wandered out into the yard the following morning. He looked up at the trees. He looked at the house. Both were draped with, what? The house and the trees in their yard had been toilet-papered, the car painted Texas Western orange. But why? Confused, he hurried back inside. His nine-year-old brother often had answers for life's perplexing questions.

"Brent, why does everybody hate us?" Steve asked.

"You dummy," said Brent disdainfully. "They don't hate us. They're celebrating."

The *El Paso Times* was doing its own celebrating that Sunday morning with a front-page headline in bright orange: "Miners—National Champs!" On the sports page, another headline: "Texas Western's Fine Poise and Scurrying Defense Upsets Top-Ranked Kentucky for the National Crown." Above the fold, interrupting the flow of the page-1 story, was a three-paragraph boldfaced prediction. "One of the greatest crowds in the history of air travel in El Paso is expected to welcome home Texas Western's national basketball champions Sunday morning." The story went on to say that the welcoming committee—the El Paso Touchdown Club—was estimating between eight and ten thousand people would be there for the expected 8:45 a.m. arrival. The estimation was spot-on.

It looked like a sea of ants down below as the pilot circled the airport to give the team a bird's-eye view of the throng awaiting them. Television screens onboard showed their plane circling, the crowd waiting. For Shed the exhilaration of that moment was "the greatest part of my life." It wasn't the crowd or the anticipation of celebrations to come. "I couldn't wait to get back to New York," he said. All the taunting he'd endured over the past three years from friends in the Bronx was about to end. "TWC. Teeny-Weeny College. After that they knew. It was fun. It was fun."

An uneasy flyer, Willie Worsley had fallen asleep "defensively" soon after takeoff from Baltimore's Friendship Field. He woke with a start when tires met tarmac in El Paso. Having missed the fly-around, he was "surprised and a little frightened" when he saw the enormous crowd awaiting them. He'd been playing in front of crowds ever since leading his high school team to a city championship in New York's Madison Square Garden, but this was different. "Basketball was my world, but this . . . My heart was pumping. It was unbelievable, out of this world, overwhelming."

The team was ushered onto a flatbed truck that served as a stage where each had the chance to say a few words. Willie Cager had his say in rhyme: "From all of us to all of you / Number one was the best we could do." "To tell you the truth," said Coach Haskins, when it was his turn at the microphone, "I can't yet believe it is a reality." Turning to his team he said, "No practice this afternoon, but there will be a short chalk talk in the morning." They thought he was kidding, but knowing the Bear, they weren't quite sure.

Then, two by two, the players climbed into convertibles for the twelve-mile ride down to the Texas Western campus and more celebration and autographing everything in sight. Along the way they were escorted by motorcycle policemen and greeted by hundreds of people lining the route, raising index fingers in salute of the newly crowned number-one team in college basketball.

Several hours later, fifteen hundred miles northeast of El Paso, the plane carrying Rupp's Runts touched down at Blue Grass Field in Lexington. Some eight hundred fans were on hand to greet their Wildcats with cheers and signs that read WELCOME HOME OUR CHAMPS.

"To be honest," said Adolph Rupp, when the crowd had quieted, "we didn't play as well as we're capable. But these boys have provided us a wonderful winter of entertainment. Only one team in the nation has a better record, and that team beat us last night."

Like their counterparts in El Paso, Rupp's Runts rode into town in open convertibles flanked by a police motorcycle escort with sirens blaring. At Memorial Coliseum the Big Blue Nation, five thousand strong, greeted the team with a five-minute standing ovation. After university president John Oswald declared them "the greatest ambassadors from our university . . . we've ever had," team cocaptain Larry Conley was introduced. Reporter Billy Reed described the scene in the next day's *Lexington Herald*: "The blond senior from Ashland flushed and stood with hands jammed in pockets and head bowed while the fans roared their welcome. 'You all might as well stop that,' he said, 'because you're just making it harder for me. . . . I was real sorry we couldn't bring back the big one.' Tears came to his eyes, and a sob welled up in his throat. 'Well,' he blurted out, 'we went out there and tried.'"

One sign in the crowd captured the feeling that has been maintained in Kentucky ever since: IN OUR BOOK YOU WILL ALWAYS BE NUMBER ONE.

36

A Matter of Pride

One incident that happened the year after the Rupp's Runts' season explains a lot about Adolph Rupp, his focus, intensity, pride, and his unchallenged standing at the university and in the state of Kentucky. In the Tennessee game late in the season, Bobby Tallent made a pass to Louie Dampier that Louie didn't see. It hit him on the head and bounced out-of-bounds. Probably they both were somewhat at fault, but Rupp exploded. At Bobby.

LeMaster in for Tallent in the Kentucky lineup.

That might have been that, but Tallent was frustrated. He'd been putting up good numbers—seventeen points a game, leading in assists—on a mediocre team until a severe ankle sprain sidelined him for two games. Now he was back, but Rupp had him in and out of the game in the first half, and now this.

"How come you're taking me out?" Bobby demanded.

"Just shut the hell up and sit down," Rupp grumbled.

"I don't like being treated like this," said Bobby, taking a seat on the bench next to his roommate and best friend, Thad Jaracz. "I'm tired of being jerked around. Either play me or keep me on the bench."

"What did he say?" Rupp asked Harry. Tallent repeated what he'd said, and then: "Shut up and leave me alone.'"

Recalling the incident some five decades later, Bob said, "I challenged him, which I shouldn't have. I should have kept my damn mouth shut. That was pretty much it."

More than he knew.

"We flew home, and I didn't think anything of it," said Tallent. "A lot of words are exchanged during games . . . between some players and the coach, some heard and some not. I figured he'd make me run the stairs and berate me and whatever. Fine. It was what I deserved."

When Tallent went in to practice the next day, the team's longtime equipment manager, George Hukel, had tears in his eyes. "Bobby, Coach Rupp told me not to give you any equipment. He says you're through."

Through? Tallent was stunned.

The Big Blue Nation had been excited three years earlier when the talented Tallent boy from the hill country of eastern Kentucky signed a scholarship agreement to become a Wildcat. Coach Rupp had been watching from afar as Bobby boosted his points-per-game average at Maytown High School from twenty-two his sophomore season to twenty-eight as a junior to a mind-boggling forty points his senior year. That won him recognition as a *Parade* High School All-American as well as the honor of having Adolph Rupp himself, who'd witnessed a couple of Tallent's games in person, make the trip up over the mountains to little Maytown for the signing ceremony.

It was the biggest event in the history of Maytown. Tallent's uncle, the principal of the high school, had just one condition: *Coach, if you want to sign Bob, you have to come and speak at our banquet.* Rupp accepted.

"He drives up in his big white Cadillac," said Tallent, recalling the scene. "Little kids were running behind. He parked his car in the middle of the street in front of the cafeteria." Rupp sent his wife, Esther, back for second and third helpings of Grandma Stewart's chicken and dumplings and then gave a speech that had the overflow crowd in stitches. Their favorite part wasn't his jokes, but this: "You know Maytown is doing pretty good, one of the best players in the United States, according to *Parade* magazine. That's pretty good coming from a little town like this."

After the speech Bobby Tallent and his family went to his uncle's office, where Coach Rupp watched him sign the scholarship. "That was a big night for Maytown," said Tallent. "People in the mountains adored him more than anyone else." After what happened to their hometown hero three years later, not so much.

When word spread that Tallent was off the team, everybody took sides. The student newspaper, the *Kentucky Kernel*, wrote in its lead editorial,

"Time to hang up the brown suit." The target of the criticism, outwardly at least, remained unmoved.

In the days that followed Coach Hall became a mediator, first convincing Tallent to apologize, then going to work on his boss. "Your pride is hurt when a kid fires back at you," said Hall, looking back. "But you have to sit down and think, 'What am I doing to this kid? What opportunities am I taking away from him? How am I disrupting his life and his whole family? Can I make him see what he's done and accept his apology and teach him a lesson?' I said all that to Coach Rupp, and I told him Bobby would come in and apologize, and he said, 'You can have him do it, but I don't know if it will do any good.'"

It didn't.

When Tallent arrived at Coach Rupp's office the next day, Pat Riley was just leaving. "Be careful what you say," said Pat. "They've got a tape recorder under the desk." What Bob said, to Coach Rupp and athletic director Bernie Shively, was "I did the wrong thing. I should never have said anything to you. I'll do anything to stay on the team."

"You'll never play another game for the University of Kentucky," said Rupp. That was the end of the conversation, except for one thing. The scholarship Bobby Tallent had signed with such fanfare three years before was withdrawn.

"It was an overreaction on Coach Rupp's part," said Hall, "but I don't blame him, either. It was something Rupp thought he had to react to. There's a line you have to draw sometimes, but I couldn't understand Coach Rupp taking that path. [Bobby] was very intelligent, the kind of kid you would be proud to have play for you. The penalty in that case was way too great. If he had known Bobby Tallent like I knew him, he wouldn't have taken that drastic step."

Rupp knew his players on the basketball court, but not personally. "I don't think he ever called me by my first name," said Larry Conley. "I don't think he knew my first name."

Hall tells the story of his own experience as a player on Rupp's 1949 national championship team when Hall's parents came to Lexington for a game. "We were standing in front of the hotel and Coach Rupp was coming down the sidewalk, and I wanted my parents to visit with him.

So when the coach got up close, I said, 'Coach, you know my mother and dad.' He didn't even look at them. He just kept walking."

"The tradition and the program and all of that *was* the relationship," said Thad. "He was not the kind of person you would knock on his door and go in and ask him for advice. He just didn't do that. That just wasn't his thing. I probably liked him as much as most. He was really good to me. He gave me a lot of opportunity. But I wouldn't want to hang out with him . . . I mean, I just wouldn't."

There had been other verbal confrontations between Rupp and players, including several with All-American Cotton Nash, the star of his pre-Runts team. "He and Cotton would scream at each other," said Larry Conley. "There was something about him just staying after your ass all the time. You just finally reached the point where that's enough."

Bobby had the misfortune of having his defiance witnessed by reporters. Both Billies, Billy Thompson of the *Lexington Harold* and Billy Reed of the *Louisville Courier-Journal*, were sitting right behind the Kentucky bench eyewitnessing the altercation. Finally, Rupp's pride simply wouldn't allow him to back down, no matter who thought he should.

Tallent got two phone calls, one from the governor, one from the college president, each with the same question. "What's going on down there? Can't you straighten this out with Coach Rupp?" Bob told them both that he had apologized, that he would do anything to get back on the team, adding, "Maybe you could talk to him." The governor's response: "Oh, no, I can't do anything." The president said, "Well, maybe I will."

"[Coach Rupp] was just a strict guy," said Thad Jaracz. "Discipline was important to him. He believed that it was an honor to play basketball at Kentucky, that you should be as proud as you've ever been in your life. 'Something like this, against the system, the establishment, why would a kid do that? What's wrong with this kid?' That was the thought process."

Bob Tallent moved on with his life, transferring to George Washington University, where he set a single-season scoring record, met his future wife, and began his career as a college basketball coach using drills he learned from Rupp. "They were great teaching tools," said Tallent, adding, "I respected the guy."

37

He Changed Basketball

The phrase *He changed basketball* can be applied to both Don Haskins and Adolph Rupp. The Haskins change is distilled into one dramatic game. The Rupp change happened over decades. When reviewing Rupp's career it is easy to get caught up in the numbers, and his numbers alone are impressive. When interviewed for the head coaching job at Kentucky in 1930, the twenty-nine-year-old was asked why he should be hired. "Because I'm the best damn coach in the nation," said Rupp, who immediately set out to prove it. In his first two years he turned a moribund basketball program into a veritable juggernaut, posting a 30-5 record. By the end of his forty-two years at Kentucky he had won twenty-seven SEC Championships and four NCAA Championships, was a four-time coach of the year, and amassed an 876-190 win-loss record.

Although Dean Smith, Bobby Knight, and then Mike Krzyzewski later surpassed him in the wins column (Coach K ended the 2015–16 season with an impressive 1,043-321 record), their teams played ten more games a season than Rupp's. For an apples-to-apples comparison, add ten games a season to Rupp's "Games Played" column and assume his winning percentage of 82 percent. That adds some 344 additional wins for a grand total of 1,200. Assuming Krzyzewski coaches five more seasons (until his seventy-third birthday—Rupp retired at seventy) and wins thirty games a season, he falls seven games short, apples to apples. Right, he has five national championships to Rupp's four, and may add more, but from a pure numbers standpoint, Rupp is the winner.

Setting the numbers aside, Adolph Rupp's importance to the evolution of basketball is beyond question. When he began his coaching career basketballs were stitched together out of brown leather and had laces that made for sometimes erratic bounces. There was a center jump after each made basket. There was no three-second rule in the foul lane, no ten-second requirement for crossing the center line. By comparison with what was to come, the game was a tortoise with no hare in sight until the center jump after made baskets was eliminated in 1936. Other coaches were slow to adapt, but Rupp introduced an up-tempo brand of basketball that revolutionized the game. His teams blocked out, got defensive rebounds, and beat opponents up the floor. The fast break was born. He also initiated advanced techniques of ball movement involving intricate patterns of screens and pick-and-rolls. In the half court he ran a motion offense based on some ten basic plays, each with variations to respond to differing situations. While he built his defense around a tight man-to-man, he was among the first coaches to harness the potential of a trapping one-three-one zone (in those early days they called it "two-timing"). And more than any coach in his era, Adolph Rupp ran precision, no-nonsense practices where repetition was a constant and pressure was applied with a drill sergeant's vocabulary.

"It takes six or eight years to get over playing for Coach Rupp," said Vernon Hatton, who starred for the Fiddlin' Five in 1958, Rupp's fourth and final national championship team. "Once you get over it, you get to like him."

"Coach operates from an extreme competitive desire and his strong dread of losing," said Joe B. Hall, the assistant who succeeded him. Given Rupp's intensity it is not surprising that he never liked a poem written by sports columnist Grantland Rice:

For when the one Great Scorer comes
To write against your name
He marks not that you won or lost,
But how you played the game

Rupp's response: "If winning isn't so important, why do they keep score?"

In March 1977, eleven years after the Texas Western game, Rupp shared the stage with some of the coaching greats of his time, Meyer,

Iba, Hickey, and Wooden. After a banquet room full of high school and college coaches had heard the others talk about the future of basketball, it was Rupp's turn. As Joseph Litsch described it in the *Atlanta Constitution*, Rupp, "leaning heavily on the lectern," had another message. "Let me tell you about criticism," he said. "If you worry about what people say about you, you'll never last in this game." He then quoted a Rudyard Kipling poem he'd memorized as a high schooler back in Kansas, a poem he described as a philosophy "I always tried to live by":

> When earth's last picture is painted
> And the tubes are twisted and dry
> When the oldest colors have faded,
> And the youngest critic has died
> And only the Master shall praise us
> And only the Master shall blame
> And no one shall work for money,
> And no one shall work for fame
> But each for the joy of working,
> And each in his own separate star,
> Shall draw a Thing as he sees it,
> For the God of things as they are.

"There was an air of benediction," wrote Litsch, "but the reverence was broken by thunderous applause. The crowd stood, applauding and wondering if this would be the last time they would listen to the man in the brown suit."

It was. Coach Rupp died the following December of cancer of the spine. He was seventy-six.

Litsch described the scene as "hundreds of coaches filed past [Coach Rupp], shaking his hand. One young coach said, 'Now that is what I call a real legend. He *is* college basketball.'"

In the immediate aftermath of the championship game, the headline story was that Texas Western, a small West Texas college most people had never heard of, beat the mighty University of Kentucky Wildcats, arguably the preeminent basketball program in the country. In news conferences that night, reporters asked not a single race-related question of either Don Haskins or Adolph Rupp. Even Frank Deford, who'd written the week before that "all seven Texas Western regulars are negroes," didn't include that fact in his postgame *Sports Illustrated* article. That his "contest for racial honors" had been fairly fought and won wasn't mentioned. In retrospect, history had been made, but it would be years before the game would be recognized as an important event in the struggle for civil rights in America. Like *Brown v. Board of Education*, the Civil Rights Act, and the Voting Rights Act, the Texas Western win was the Haskins change, setting in motion a process that would change the course of history.

Cazzie Russell, who played (and lost) in the past two NCAA Championship games, went into the tournament hoping a third time would be the charm for his Michigan Wolverines. Watching with friends back in Ann Arbor, he could feel the pain of the loss to Kentucky that ended his college basketball career. "Possibly God had a plan," he would say five decades later. "Sometimes we have to give up something to get something. If we beat Kentucky, we may not have seen the emancipation proclamation."

It was Pat Riley who first used that characterization when he jokingly told reporter Ray Sanchez, "We didn't know we'd be participating in the emancipation proclamation of 1966." For basketball, that's just what it was. The Texas Western win precipitated a very gradual change in the recruiting practices of previously segregated colleges. It was all too obvious that, if schools were to be competitive, the barriers that walled out African American athletes would have to be breached. In 1967 Vanderbilt was the first SEC school to recruit a black basketball player, Perry Wallace. Slowly, cautiously, other schools began to follow. Coaches whose total experience was coaching white players started calling Haskins for advice on how to coach black kids. Haskins's answer was straightforward: He coached black and white kids exactly the same: *He rode their asses like a borrowed mule.*

"[Haskins] wasn't trying to make a statement," said Nolan Richardson, who would follow his coach and friend into the Naismith Memorial Basketball Hall of Fame. "It was a basketball game. He wanted to win regardless of what the races were and he was going to play whoever the best five or six or seven were." In the process he "opened doors for young black kids who were sitting on the bench at other schools because of this thing about only so many could be on the floor at one time. To me he changed basketball. He said to those guys out there, 'Play your best players,' and that's what happened."

To Richardson it was like what happened with the election of Barack Obama. "In my lifetime I never dreamed of it being . . . nobody ever talked about [a black person] being president. That's what it's all about. To have somebody out there that's already done that." When Richardson talked to Haskins about his history-bending role, the coach demurred. "I'm glad that everybody feels that way, but I'm just an old country boy who wanted to be a coach, and it just so happened that things worked out for all of us."

Epilogue

Long before Texas Western's historic win over the University of Kentucky, Jackie Robinson, Larry Doby, Monte Irvin, Hank Thompson, and Willie Mays had become established, and accepted, professional baseball players, judged on the content of their character (or at least their talent on a baseball diamond), not the color of their skin. Professional basketball was the same story. African American players had been in the NBA since 1950, and the Boston Celtics not only started five blacks in 1963 but made one of them, Bill Russell, their player-coach in '66. And still college basketball, southern style, remained resolutely white. "When negroes and whites meet on the athletic fields on a basis of complete equality," said Georgia state senator Leon Butts in 1957, "it is only natural that this sense of equality carries into the daily living of these people." The logic was impeccable.

When integrated northern schools played in the South, there was a "gentleman's agreement" that African American players were excluded from the game. Louisiana made it a matter of law in 1956: integrated athletics were illegal. In 1960, the year before Haskins arrived in El Paso, Texas Western agreed to leave its star forward Nolan Richardson behind when it accepted an invitation to play in the Centenary Tournament in Shreveport. The NCAA Tournament, integrated since 1950, presented a special problem for segregated schools.

Mississippi State University won the SEC Championship three out of four years from 1959 through 1962, each time declining the NCAA invitation because of the state's policy against interracial competition. When MSU won the SEC again in 1963, the team sneaked out of town to avoid legal intervention. Die-hard segregationists were not happy.

Athletic competition was important and all, but "our southern way of life is infinitely more precious."

Legally, the southern way of life was changed by the Civil Rights Act of 1964 and the Voting Rights Act of '65, but resistance continued. A dozen years after *Brown vs. Board of Education*, most public schools in the South were still segregated, universities still resistant to change. On southern campuses (including the University of Kentucky), where athletics were a Whites Only activity, fraternities were regularly entertained by all-black musical groups. There was Doug Clark and the Hot Nuts and a group one reviewer described as "raunchy and wild, sort of the Harlem Globetrotters of the music scene." The group called itself Thirteen Screaming Niggers. Bull Connor's Birmingham, Bloody Sunday in Selma, and the murder of voting rights activists were behind us by the mid-1960s, but the KKK (morphing into White Citizens' Councils) was still a potent political force in the Deep South. Voters in Georgia, Alabama, Arkansas, Mississippi, and Louisiana—the backbone of the Southeastern Conference—were still electing segregationist governors.

Enter Perry Wallace.

Wallace, an African American, led Nashville's Pearl High School to Tennessee's first integrated high school championship on March 19, 1966. Later that evening he watched as Texas Western beat Kentucky for the NCAA Championship. He'd been recruited by Kentucky assistant coaches Harry Lancaster and Joe B. Hall. "I got in trouble with local reporters for comparing him to Tarzan," Hall recalled five decades later, "but I was thinking about the athleticism of Tarzan in the movies. Perry would have been an excellent recruit." John Wooden, whose string of national championships at UCLA was interrupted in 1966, thought so too. So did Dave Strack, whose Michigan team lost to Wooden in the championship game the year before.

Wallace liked Rupp's assistants and might have gone to Kentucky if Coach Rupp had shown enough interest to meet him personally. "It wasn't that I wanted special treatment," Wallace told his biographer, Andrew Maraniss. "It was that this was a special situation. Anybody that wouldn't lend that personal touch, I couldn't go there. . . . [T]o have the top guy say nary a word; that was a very important consideration."

In the end, out of nearly a hundred schools that tried to recruit him, Perry decided to attend Vanderbilt, something he'd never considered until Commodores coach Roy Skinner visited the Wallace home. "When Skinner talked to his parents," wrote Maraniss, "he addressed them not by their first names, as would have been convention of the day [in much of the South] for a white man addressing blacks, but rather as Mr. and Mrs. Wallace." "That was a very, very big deal," Wallace recalled. "At that point, along with the comparison to those other schools that were recruiting me, I began to take Vanderbilt seriously."

Because freshmen didn't play varsity ball in those days, Perry was dreading his first road game as a Commodore against the University of Mississippi his sophomore year. "The jeers and cursing started the moment Wallace emerged from the tunnel," wrote Maraniss. "The words themselves were ugly, but they were made far uglier by the blithe enthusiasm with which they were delivered." During warm-ups, "Every time Wallace missed a shot, bumbled a rebound, or made even the slightest misstep, the Ole Miss fans near the courtside exploded in delight. Every time Wallace made a shot, the crowd booed. And in between, it was, *Go home, nigger! We're going to kill you, nigger. We'll lynch you, boy.*"

Given the vitriol that accompanied his appearance (he described his experience as "a long, hellish trauma") on basketball courts throughout the conference, it is not surprising that only one other African American was playing in the SEC by the time Wallace graduated in 1970, but the door had been opened. Two years later Mississippi State signed its first black player, and in 1973 the University of Alabama, where Governor George Wallace stood in the schoolhouse door to block integration a decade earlier, became the first SEC school to start five blacks. Little by little and then lot by lot, conference schools were competing with colleges across the country to recruit the best players, black or white.

By the time *Sports Illustrated* published a twenty-fifth-anniversary story of the Texas Western–Kentucky game, black players outnumbered whites in the SEC. The article advanced a revisionist history that morphed into conventional wisdom that persists to this day.

It started with a question by an *SI* writer. "Wasn't Adolph Rupp a racist?" Researching the article, the writer called the players, a student manager, anyone connected with Rupp's Runts. Wasn't Rupp a racist?

The response he got from Rupp's Runts' student manager, Mike "Slim" Harreld, was *No, no way.* According to Mike, "You could have been a three-armed purple-people-eater from Mars. If you could score points and win for Adolph, that would have been just fine with him. Would he sell you and all the gold in Fort Knox for another win? He might do that. Did he care about the color of your skin? No way in the world."

In *SI*'s anniversary piece—"The Night They Drove Old Dixie Down"— Curry Kirkpatrick wrote that Rupp "supposedly" paced the locker room after his most disappointing loss, "spitting out the initials of Texas Western College: 'TWC. What's that stand for, two white coaches.'" "The story may be apocryphal," wrote Kirkpatrick. "Rupp's feelings, however, were always right there simmering for all the world to know."

Supposedly? Apocryphal? What kind of reporting is that?

In researching the anniversary piece Kirkpatrick interviewed Larry Conley four or five different times over a two-week period when Conley was doing color commentary for ESPN. "He came to every game that I did and wanted to sit down to talk," said Larry. "And every time he asked me about Coach Rupp and about him being a racist." Larry's answer was always the same:

> "There's nothing there, Curry. I never heard the man say a racist word in his life." He would keep coming back. He would ask the question in another way. After about the fifth time of him asking me, I was out with the crew after [a Louisiana State University] game in Baton Rouge, drinking beer and eating shrimp. And he asked me about Coach Rupp again about racism. I had a beer in my hand and slammed it down. "That's it! No more! Don't ask me about him being a racist again. I don't care how you phrase it, but it's done. I told you he's not a racist; that's the end of it. I've given you the same answer four times. You've asked it four different ways. Now you've asked it a fifth different way. I'm not going to say it again." He was looking for that hook. If I had heard [Rupp] say something, I would have said, "Well, maybe, I don't know," but he never said anything, ever, in his life.

None of that appeared in the article.

For *SI* the fact that Kentucky had no black players in 1966 was proof enough that Coach Rupp was a racist. And because *Sports Illustrated* was regarded as the gold standard of sports reporting, that single article was considered Holy Writ, a crimson thread woven inexorably into the fabric of Rupp's long and storied basketball career, a stain on the legacy of a coaching legend.

"*Sports Illustrated* had a case to make," wrote Dave Kindred, who covered Rupp's Runts for the *Lexington Herald-Leader*, "and make it they damn well did."

After that writers who never spent a minute in Coach Rupp's presence felt licensed to refer to his "long racist legacy," sighting as prima facie evidence the 1966 NCAA Championship game.

Frank Fitzpatrick, who experienced the game years later by watching a grainy black-and-white kinescope, captured the scene in a 2003 special to ESPN. "The crowd is white. So are the NCAA officials, the referees, the coaches, the cheerleaders, and almost all the sportswriters on press row." Fitzpatrick spotted "Kentucky fans" waving a Confederate flag as Rupp's Runts lined up for the opening tap. "Then (you can almost hear the crescendo)—history steps into the picture.

"Walking toward the red *M* at center court [of the University of Maryland's Cole Field House] in their orange uniforms and white Converse All-Stars are the five starters for Texas Western. They are all black." Fitzpatrick wrote that "[Rupp's] foot-dragging on integration lent the game much of its significance," adding, in a rhetorical flourish worthy of a Dan Brown novel, "It was as if history demanded that for change to finally occur, a great hero and a great villain must meet. Rupp and [Texas Western coach Don] Haskins fit those roles perfectly."

Actually, what history demands is truth, and viewing that game and time from the perspective of today is like rewriting the story of David and Goliath. A kinescope of that biblical confrontation might reveal some previously unnoticed racial element, but adding it, ex post facto, is a distortion of reality. The writer of 1st Samuel gave us a simple story of David the giant killer, not a treatise on race relations circa 1000 BCE.

Adolph Rupp was a man of his times who never posed as anything but a basketball coach with an insatiable appetite for winning. Yet the beat goes on despite two rather significant facts. First, racial aspects of the game *were* widely ignored at the time. The subject of race didn't come up in postgame news conferences or in stories about the game. In a three-thousand-word article that appeared in *Sports Illustrated* the week after the game, Frank Deford made no mention of race. Deford wrote about Haskins "standing brazenly in the way of Kentucky and Adolph Rupp," who was "a remarkable old man hungry for his fifth national championship." He wrote about Conley's flu and Pat Riley's sore toe. He said the game "pitted Kentucky's offense against Texas Western's defense, and it was the defense that held." He wrote about Bobby Joe Hill's steals and the Miners' incredible free-throw shooting ("26 of 27 during one thirty-seven minute stretch"). He even wrote that "the manager, Mike Harreld, carried an extra suit with him, complete with shirt and tie," because he expected to be thrown into the shower after Kentucky won. He did not mention the single aspect of the game that is the focus of attention today.

Second, and perhaps more important, not a single person who spent any time around Rupp during his forty-two-year coaching career believes the racist charge. What about the *foot-dragging*? There was some of that, no doubt, but here context is essential. Writers who didn't experience the Deep South in the days of segregation glibly point out that the 1966 game was two years after the passing of the Civil Rights Act, as though that was the demarcation line between racism writ large and the promised land of tolerance, brotherly love, and kumbaya. People who lived it knew a reality that was very different.

"You go down there, Russ," Rupp told Lexington reporter Russ Rice, who would become his biographer. "You see the black and white water fountains. . . . We can't even put them up anywhere when we go down south." Rupp was referring to road trips to SEC schools in Georgia, Mississippi, and Alabama where blacks were barred from most hotels and restaurants. The more immediate obstacle to his recruitment of black players was a gentleman's agreement that had to be overcome.

In 1961 a proposal by University of Kentucky president Frank Dickey that Southeastern Conference schools recruit black athletes was soundly defeated. According to Dickey, his fellow presidents were emphatic, saying, "If you move in that direction, we're going to have to drop you from our schedule." The Dickey interview was part of a 2005 documentary titled *Adolph Rupp: Myth, Legend and Fact*, which included examples of a virulent backlash:

"Dear Mr. Dickey: Your willingness to integrate athletic teams in the SEC is repugnant and sickening ... a crime against the white race and a disgrace to decency. Presley J. Snow, Philadelphia, Mississippi."

"I cannot refrain from pleading that you do all within your power to enforce racial segregation ... prevent the awful catastrophe that will befall us if a halt is not called. Let each race live among themselves, according to God's plan. Sincerely yours, A Distressed Mother."

Despite the conference rebuff, Rupp began to prepare for the change that seemed inevitable. The documentary includes an interview with Neil Reed, a high school coach from inner-city Cincinnati who had done some scouting for Rupp. *"He* asked me a question," said Reed. "Who did I think was better, Oscar Robertson or Jerry West?" When Reed said Oscar, Rupp got a big grin on his face. "Would you be interested in coming to Lexington and helping me because we're going to be recruiting black youngsters and ... I want somebody who feels comfortable in their homes?" Reed became a Rupp assistant in 1962.

To prepare for the day when recruitment would be possible, Rupp sought advice from Branch Rickey, the Brooklyn Dodgers' general manager who broke Major League Baseball's gentleman's agreement by bringing Jackie Robinson to the Dodgers. While Reed took notes, Rickey laid out the necessary ingredients. Rupp's first black player needed to be: a Kentuckian, an excellent student, a player nobody is going to keep on the bench, a player who is going to be something, especially something you need.

A year later, in 1964, Rupp tried to convince Wes Unseld to become his Jackie Robinson. A six-foot-seven center from Louisville's Seneca High School, Unseld could have been the ideal player to break the SEC color barrier. He fit the Branch Rickey paradigm to perfection. From Kentucky: check. A good student: check. Nobody was going to keep him on the bench: check. Something Kentucky needed: double check.

According to Reed, word of Rupp's recruitment efforts brought numerous death threats and a visitation by a dozen UK boosters—including a former Kentucky All-American—trying to dissuade Rupp from signing Unseld or any other blacks. "They started in, and I could see [Rupp] was getting angry," Reed recalled. "He looked around the room and pointed that finger of his and he said, 'I want all you sonofabitchin' bastard racists out of my office, and don't ever come back.'" It was during that time when Rupp had a saying Reed recalled years later: "Right is right and wrong is wrong."

Larry Conley got involved in Rupp's recruiting effort, driving to Louisville for a little one-on-one persuasion. He told Unseld, "If you come, I think we have a chance to win the national championship." How good would Kentucky have been? Larry's answer: "Two games better." But what might have been ran up against a harsh reality. After receiving threats in the mail, including a dead chicken, Unseld told Larry, "I don't want to be the first one."

Unseld doesn't remember saying that, but he does recall that Rupp didn't really seem that interested. "Rupp was a stern older guy," recalled assistant coach Joe B. Hall. It was the Perry Wallace syndrome. "It was very difficult for him to get on the level of a high school athlete, black or white. For the black players that appeared, 'He doesn't really want me' or 'He's a little standoffish."

Under Rupp Hall says his mandate was to recruit the best, regardless of skin color, but when it came to closing the deal, "Rupp wouldn't get down from being the head coach to say, 'I want you. I need you.' . . . It was, 'You ought to want to come and play for me. I'm giving you that opportunity.' The black kids, I think they were a little afraid of him, to tell you the truth."

Maintaining distance from his players worked for Coach Rupp for most of his forty-two years at the University of Kentucky, until it didn't. His inability to relate to players on a personal level played an important, sometimes decisive, role when it came to recruiting a black player to become his Jackie Robinson.

The year before Hall became Rupp's assistant, Butch Beard was the one who got away. The six-foot-three Beard had led his Hardinsburg, Kentucky, team to the state championship game as a junior in 1964 only to be frustrated at the hands of Seneca High School and Unseld. With Wes now safely in college, Butch had another great season, this time winning the '65 state championship and Kentucky's Mr. Basketball honors in the process. An intelligent young man and a gifted athlete who would go on to a nine-year career in the NBA, Beard seemed the perfect candidate to break the SEC's color barrier. And, just as important, he seemed interested.

Beard was seen touring the campus with Kentucky Democratic governor Edward "Ned" Breathitt. When you have the governor showing you around, you're obviously a VIR, "very important recruit." Coach Rupp wanted him. The governor was obviously the clincher, except for one thing. Butch was also being recruited by Louisville, and Louisville had two things going for it. As an independent they weren't playing schools where the color of your skin made you an automatic target. And they already had a black player in the person of Unseld. Wes, whose older brother had played his college basketball for the Kansas Jayhawks, elected to remain in Louisville, where his parents could watch him play. His transition to college basketball had been a smooth one. Another factor that may have been decisive: Beard decided he'd rather play *with* Unseld than against him.

Years later, in his book *Adolph Rupp as I Knew Him*, Harry Lancaster wrote about Rupp's reaction to a meeting with John Oswald, who replaced Dickey as Kentucky's president in 1963: "Harry, that sonofabitch is ordering me to get some niggers in here. What am I going to do?"

"I can't believe that one ever came out of his mouth," said Thad Jaracz, the six-foot-five center on the Rupp's Runts team. "Not once," said Joe B. Hall, who was with Rupp for seven years. "I don't think he saw color. He saw basketball players. If there were any innuendoes that he was a racist, I never saw them."

While Hall doesn't believe Rupp used the *N* word, he knew the conflict between the coach and the college president firsthand. It was simple. Oswald wanted an integrated basketball team and didn't care whether the first black recruit was an outstanding athlete. Rupp wanted his Jackie Robinson. There were a number of gifted black basketball players coming out of Kentucky high schools that Hall might have recruited, but only a few who passed the Jackie Robinson test.

It wasn't until 1969 that Rupp signed his first African American, Tom Payne, a *Parade* High School All-American who was being touted as another Lew Alcindor. A seven-footer from Louisville's Shawnee High School, Payne was the big man Rupp so obviously needed, but hardly the Jackie Robinson he was looking for. While leading the Wildcats to the conference championship his sophomore year, he fell behind in his classes and left to play for the Atlanta Hawks. A year later, convicted as a serial rapist, Kentucky's first African American basketball player began to serve prison sentences that have kept him behind bars for most of the past five decades. When Rupp retired in 1972, Vanderbilt, Auburn, and even Mississippi had black players. Kentucky was once again all white.

In his book about the 1965-66 season—*And the Walls Came Tumbling Down*—Frank Fitzpatrick wrote, "The Kentucky coach possessed the power to push for change and he didn't use it." Maybe so, but the same might be said of all presidents before Lincoln and all Baptist ministers before Martin Luther King.

"I get a little irritated," wrote Frank Deford in his 2012 book, *Over Time*, "when people today look back on generations past and judge those people unsympathetically, by current standards, without context."

"We're all a product of the times in which we live," says Thad Jaracz.

It takes a real visionary to step out of those times and be somebody totally different. There are people like that, some of the civil rights leaders. Some of them were like that. You look at great scientists, great military guys. There are always people who can step outside. Adolph wasn't one of those guys. Adolph was a basketball coach, and he wanted above all else to beat people. And so to think that he would not want to get the best people to beat people with is just ludicrous. He was living within the confines of the situation he was in, the SEC. It's always been interesting to me. All of a sudden he becomes this pariah for the segregation of college sports. I just never saw that.

"I think he took a hit for the whole South," says Mike Lewis, the Montana recruit Rupp lost to Duke. "Unfortunately, he was out front: he was the guy that was easy to target because of his success and everything. I hated to see him painted with that broad brush of racism. I don't think it was fair."

Yet as Dave Kindred wrote in the *Atlanta Journal-Constitution*: "Rupp-as-racist stories now have been so embellished that the average basketball fan can be forgiven for imagining Rupp burning a cross in the yard of any black player who dared think of playing at Kentucky. That image is a lie."

Long before Rupp was vilified as a racist, Coach Don Haskins underwent his own time in cultural purgatory for the alleged sin of "exploitation." While he was still receiving hate mail for daring to defile the white man's game with his all-black starting lineup, Haskins was blindsided by charges that appeared first in a 1968 *Sports Illustrated* article and then in a James Michener book, *Sports in America*.

Texas Western (by then the University of Texas at El Paso, or UTEP) had gained "a national reputation from the muscles and skills of negroes," wrote *SI*'s Jack Olsen. "The black athlete is there to perform, not to get an education, and when he has used up his eligibility he is out."

The Olsen article brought in a different kind of hate mail. "No longer was it ignorant whites calling me a 'nigger lover,'" wrote Haskins. "It was black ministers calling me an exploiter." The negative press was bad enough, but the article largely negated the recruiting advantage of the national championship. "After the fallout, recruiting was virtually impossible," Haskins wrote. Opposing coaches would "go to a home visit with someone we were recruiting and pull it out." Often, that was that.

Some of the wounds had started to heal by the time the Michener book was published ten years after the championship season, but the scabs remained. To Michener, a Pulitzer Prize winner whose novels from *Tales of the South Pacific* to *Bridges of Toko-Ri* to *Hawaii* became major motion pictures, "The El Paso story is one of the most wretched in the history of American sports." Michener, whose research seemed to consist entirely of reading the Olsen article, wrote that black athletes at UTEP were "treated as poorly-paid gladiators," that they took "Mickey Mouse courses" to keep them eligible, that none of the seven who played in the championship game graduated. "When their utility was ended, they were thrown aside to make place for a new batch."

"If that were the case, Willie Cager wouldn't have gotten a degree," says Harry Flournoy. "If that's the case, Nevil Shed wouldn't have gotten a degree. If that's the case, I wouldn't have gotten a degree." As for being "thrown aside," Flournoy is one of many Haskins players, black and white, who know that wasn't so. "[Haskins] got me back into school after my eligibility was over," said Flournoy as the anniversary season approached. "When I couldn't find a part-time job, he dug into his own pocket to help me with my rent. I will always love that man. He was a very special person. . . . I was blessed to go to that school, championship or not."

That feeling among Haskins's players was close to universal. At the coach's memorial service some four decades after the championship season, Jimbo Bowden, an El Paso orthodontist who played guard for Haskins in the late 1970s, asked, "How many of you guys played for Coach Haskins? If you did, stand up." Fifty or sixty former players stood. "Now, here's the next question. How many of you liked Haskins when you played for him?" Everybody sat down. "Last question. How many of you loved him after you quit playing for him?" Every former player stood back up.

One of those standing was Steve Tredennick, the frightened freshman who learned of Haskins's three-a-day Thanksgiving practice schedule by daring to ask. He had survived the Bear's "ride them like a borrowed mule" coaching to become his lawyer and then a friend. Steve recalled how Haskins objected to a story about him beating professional pool player Willie Mosconi. "Hell, I never beat Mosconi," he groused after his cowriter included it in a draft of the Haskins autobiography Steve was reviewing. "Make him take it out." "But Coach," said Steve, "your good buddy says he was there and saw it happen." "He's lying," said Haskins, with characteristic gruffness, adding, grudgingly, "It wasn't Mosconi. It was Minnesota Fats." It was typical Haskins. A country boy, more comfortable in his pickup truck or calling coyotes down from the hills than with moments in the limelight.

Another aspect of the Haskins personality was his numerous acts of Good Samaritan kindness, like the time he came across a young family whose car had broken down on a country road ninety miles from nowhere. Haskins had the car towed to town, paid for the repairs, put them up at a local motel, and sent them on their way the following morning with a hundred dollars in their pockets. Typical Haskins, he wasn't happy when the story got out.

Haskins, says Eddie Mullens, "was one of the biggest-hearted individuals I ever met in my life." About the 1966 championship game, Mullens wrote, "That one win did more to change college basketball than the jump shot, the three-pointer or, maybe, those short skirts on today's cheerleaders."

The changes in college basketball didn't come overnight, but the Georgia state senator was right. When blacks and whites met as equals in athletics, it *did* carry into daily lives. "The role of sports in changing attitudes is huge," says political scientist Peter Dreier, who studies the intersection of sports, politics, and society. Dreier says Jackie Robinson and the integration of baseball played a crucial role in paving the way for the civil rights movement by forcing the issue of racism onto the national agenda. As with all cultural movements, that led to a polarization of attitudes and then "gradual changes in laws and practices." It is almost axiomatic. "The radical ideas of one generation are often the common sense of the next."

By the time Kentucky and Texas Western met for the NCAA Championship, the Civil Rights and Voting Rights Acts had been signed into law, but there were also the beginnings of a backlash. "The Watts riots of 1965 caused some to think things had gone beyond equality, beyond fairness," says Dreier. Polls taken the following March, two years after Martin Luther King won the Nobel Peace Prize, showed most white Americans saw him as a polarizing figure, a radical troublemaker, and, just possibly, a communist.

Dreier says the game with all-white Kentucky losing to a Texas Western team that played only African Americans "did something to a national atmosphere, polarizing and transforming at the same time. It forced people to confront their own stereotypes. It became part of an ongoing transformation of our culture and political atmosphere that made people think twice about maybe black people are equal to white people and maybe it's not just on athletic fields but maybe in the classroom and the office and the military and lots of other things."

President Obama, in his tribute to the team celebrating the fiftieth anniversary of their historic win, said:

> Fifty years ago, long before the Hollywood movie or Hall of Fame inductions, a group of basketball players in El Paso—black, white, Hispanic—just wanted to win some games. They did a lot of that, because, in basketball, it doesn't matter what you look like, just that you can play.
>
> Now the path to success wasn't usually so clear in America of the 1960s. So by becoming the first team to win an NCAA title with five black starters, the Miners weren't just champs on the court: they helped change the rules of the game off it. They didn't know it at the time, but their contribution to civil rights was as important as any other.

The Texas Western win showcased the Miners' quickness and athleticism (about which there had been little doubt), but it also put the spotlight on a basketball IQ that defied conventional wisdom. Instead of playing the kind of helter-skelter street ball presumed to be in their DNA, seven black athletes played a controlled, disciplined game despite the absence of the requisite white leader on the floor.

Harry Flournoy encapsulated the thinking when, in 2007, the Texas Western champions became the only collegiate basketball team in the history of the game to be enshrined in the Naismith Memorial Basketball Hall of Fame. Before March 19, 1966, said Flournoy, "People would tell you you can't put five black players out on the floor at the same time. Why? Because they're black. You can't have five black players out there and think that one of them is going to lead the team. Why? Because they're black. If you put five black players out there, when it gets tight they're going to quit on you. Why? Because they're black. We had to break that. We proved that a farce, a fallacy."

"By winning the game as we did, that sped things up," said David Lattin. "Dr. King was making things happen, but after that game all schools in the South started recruiting black athletes. It proved we were equal. Everybody's the same. We all got two eyes, got a brain, mouth, nose.

In fact, your blood, if you've got B-positive, it would fit in my body. It doesn't matter the color of your skin; either you can play or you can't."

"There was nothing racial about that game for the players," said Larry Conley, "but it was vastly important to the black population of this country. You tuned in to watch that game, and you see five black players beating five white players. To them it has never gone away."

Pat Riley, who would go on to coach five NBA Championship teams, called the loss to Texas Western "one of the worst nights of my life." Years later he told a reporter for the *Bergen (NJ) Record*, "I'm still proud to be part of something that changed the lives of so many people. Maybe they were playing for something a hell of a lot more significant. And, if that were the case, then maybe the right team won."

Hanging high above the court at Rupp Arena in Lexington are blue-and-white banners symbolizing the University of Kentucky's eight national championships, four of them won by Rupp-coached teams in a single decade between 1948 and 1958. Next to the '58 banner is one that reads:

NCAA Runner Up 1966

In the rafters of the Don Haskins Special Events Center in El Paso, affectionately known as the Don, there is an orange banner with white letters. It reads:

Texas Western College
NCAA Champions 1966

Their history-bending win was more than a half century ago, but Miners fans continue to celebrate. At the start of every home game there is thunderous applause when the public address announcer says: "Welcome to the Don Haskins Center, the home of the only Division I team from Texas ever to win the NCAA National Championship in men's basketball."

Of the fourteen players on the Kentucky roster for the start of the fiftieth-anniversary season (2015–16), ten were African American. At UTEP it was eleven of seventeen.

Where Are They Now?

TEXAS WESTERN MINERS

Jerry Armstrong—After graduation Jerry taught and coached high school basketball in Missouri until his retirement in 1996. Since then he has spoken to high school audiences about drugs, alcohol, and bullying. Jerry and his wife, Mary, make their home in Mountain Grove, Missouri.

Orsten Artis—An Indiana native, Orsten returned to his home in Gary, Indiana, where he became a member of the Gary Police Department, working both patrol and undercover before being tapped to join the Detective Division, where he remained until his retirement in 1999. He now lives in Merrillville, Indiana

Louis "Flip" Baudoin—After graduation Louis became an educator with the Academy in Albuquerque, New Mexico. After thirty-three years as a teacher, administrator, and coach, he retired in 2000. Louis and his wife, Mary, live in Corrales, New Mexico.

Willie Cager—After graduation Cager entered the education field as a teacher, coach, and coordinator with the Ysleta Independent School District's Basketball Program in El Paso. Now retired, Willie lives in El Paso, where he is continuing to work with children in the community on a volunteer basis.

Harry Flournoy Jr.—After graduation Harry taught and coached briefly in the El Paso School District before going into business in Los Angeles. Now retired, Harry and his wife, Sukari, make their home in McDonough, Georgia.

Coach Donald Haskins (deceased September 7, 2008)—When he retired from coaching in 1999, Haskins was tied for fourth among the NCAA's winningest Division I coaches with a 719-353 win-loss record. He is in both the Naismith Memorial Basketball Hall of Fame and the National Collegiate Basketball Hall of Fame. On retirement he and wife, Mary, stayed in El Paso, where she still lives.

Tyrone "Bobby Joe" Hill (deceased December 8, 2002)—After his playing days Bobby Joe went to work for the El Paso Natural Gas Company, where he rose to the executive level before retiring in 1996. B.J. is survived by his wife, Tina, and daughter, Michelle, who live in El Paso.

Henry W. "Moe" Iba—After five years as an assistant coach at Texas Western, Iba coached at Memphis State University, the University of Nebraska, and finally at Texas Christian University. Moe spent eight years as a scout in the NBA before retiring from basketball in 2005. He now lives in Fort Worth, Texas.

David "Big Daddy" Lattin—David played professional basketball for the San Francisco Warriors, the Phoenix Suns of the NBA, the Pittsburgh Condors and the Memphis Tams of the ABA, plus a year with the Globetrotters. He returned to his hometown of Houston, where he is a successful entrepreneur. David's autobiography is titled *Slam Dunk to Glory*.

Eddie Mullens—After a career as sports information director at Texas Western (UTEP), Eddie retired to Richardson, Texas, with his wife, Reda.

Richard Myers—After graduation Dick became an accountant and business executive, working for Farah Manufacturing in El Paso before accepting a position as vice president with the worldwide luxury fashion company Coach, Inc. (formerly Coach Leatherwear). Now retired, Dick and his wife, Elsie, live in Palm Beach, Florida.

David Palacio—After graduation David went on to a business career in the California music and record industry with Univision, becoming executive vice president and chief financial officer before retiring with his wife, Terri, in Roseville, California.

Albert "Togo" Railey—After graduation Togo entered the teaching profession, serving for thirty years as a basketball coach and teacher before becoming assistant principal at Port Neches High School. After he retired Togo and his wife, Mary, moved back to El Paso.

Nevil Shed—Nevil played the next season for Haskins's Miners. After graduation he spent his career as a coach and administrator at the University of Texas at San Antonio. He now lives in San Antonio with his wife, Melba.

Willie Worsley—After graduation Willie played professional basketball in the newly formed American Basketball Association before becoming a teacher and coach in New York City. He was dean of students at the prestigious Harlem Boys Choir. He came out of retirement to coach at Spring Valley High School in New York. Willie and wife Claudia make their home in Pomona, New York.

KENTUCKY WILDCATS

Cliff Berger—After playing Wildcat basketball two more years, Cliff attended UK's Dental School and married 1969 homecoming queen Marsha Jackson before setting up practice as an oral surgeon in Savannah, Georgia. Cliff and Marsha have lived in Lexington since his retirement.

Brad Bounds—After graduation in 1967 Brad started his coaching career at Jessamine County Kentucky High School, where he was fired four months later for starting five blacks. He moved on to Frankfort, Illinois, High School, where he taught for thirty-eight years, coaching for twenty. Brad and his wife, Patricia, are retired in Frankfort.

Steve Clevenger—Graduating in 1968, Steve coached for eight years at Harrodsburg, Kentucky, High School. He then joined a highway construction company in Lexington, where he rose to become a superintendent and minority owner. Since his retirement at age sixty, Steve and his wife, Pattie, have continued to live in Lexington.

Larry Conley—After graduation Larry played one season for the Kentucky

Colonels of the ABA. He was a representative for Nike before beginning a career as a color commentator for the three major networks, ESPN, and Raycom Sports. Larry and his wife, Lori, live in Atlanta.

Louie Dampier—After the 1966–67 season, Louie was drafted by the Kentucky Colonels of the ABA. After a nine-year career (seven times an All-Star), he played three years for the San Antonio Spurs of the NBA. In 2015 he was inducted into Naismith Memorial Basketball Hall of Fame. Louie and his wife, Judy, live in Louisville.

Gary Gamble—After graduation from college Gary Gamble sold caps, gowns, and rings for a scholastic company in Ohio before going to work as a supervisor at the Island Creek Coal Company in Arlington, Kentucky. In retirement Gary and his wife, Jo Ann, live in Madisonville, Kentucky.

Joe B. Hall—Hall was Adolph Rupp's replacement when he retired in 1972. He went on to coach the 1974–75 Wildcats to a Final Four finish and to a national championship in 1978, when he was named national coach of the year. In retirement Hall cohosted a daily radio program—*The Joe B and Denny Show*—for ten years with former Louisville coach Denny Crum. Coach Hall lives in Lexington.

Mike "Slim" Harreld—After graduation Mike got his master's degree in accounting from the University of Missouri. After two years in the army he began his business career with Arthur Andersen. He left Andersen to join the Georgia Power Company, where he ultimately became chief financial officer. In retirement Mike and his wife, Yvonne, make their home in Atlanta.

Thad Jaracz—Thad played two additional seasons for Kentucky. After graduation he enlisted in the army. He retired twenty-five years later as a lieutenant colonel. He and his wife, Sharon, live in Louisville.

Tommy Kron (deceased November 10, 2007)—After graduation Tommy was drafted by the St. Louis Hawks. Two years later he was taken in the expansion draft by the Seattle Supersonics. After five years in the NBA, Tommy and Dianne Kron moved to Louisville, where he began his career in wealth management. Dianne continues to be a courtside regular at University of Kentucky basketball games.

Harry Lancaster (deceased February 5, 1985)—After twenty-two years as Rupp's assistant and head baseball coach, Harry went on to become University of Kentucky athletic director from 1969 to 1975.

Jim LeMaster—Jim played for Rupp two additional years. He attended UK Law School, then practiced law in Lexington for twenty-five years, before becoming president of Anthem Blue Cross of Kentucky. He also served nineteen years in the Kentucky House of Representatives, including four years as Speaker. Jim lives in Lexington.

Larry Lentz—After graduation in 1966 Larry attended the UK School of Pharmacy before going to work in the Walgreen's drugstore in Lexington's Turfland Mall, where he remained for forty-three years. Larry and his wife, Diane, live in Lexington.

Tom Porter—After two more years as a Wildcat, Tom attended UK Dental School. He served two years in the air force before setting up practice in Hopkinsville, Kentucky, where he lives with his wife, Sandy.

Pat Riley—After playing another year for Kentucky, Pat had a nine-year NBA career before becoming a color commentator for broadcasts of LA Lakers games. He became assistant coach and then head coach in Los Angeles, New York, and Miami. Riley-coached teams won five NBA Championships, and he was named to the Basketball Hall of Fame. Pat and wife Chris make their home in Miami, where he is president of the Miami Heat.

Coach Adolph Rupp (deceased December 10, 1977)—In his forty-two years as Kentucky's coach, Rupp won twenty-seven SEC Championships and four NCAA Championships and was a four-time coach of the year. At the time of his death he had a win-loss record of 876-190, the best in history.

Bob Tallent—Cut from the team after a midseason dispute with Rupp the following season, Bob transferred to George Washington University, where he set a single-season scoring record of 28.9 points per game that still stands today. After college he coached at GW for ten seasons before beginning a thirty-four-year career in the health care industry, retiring in 2015. Bob and his wife, Eileen, live in Arlington, Virginia.

Bob Windsor—Drafted by San Francisco, Bob began a ten-year professional football career in the fall of 1966, playing five years with the '49ers and five with the New England Patriots. After retiring from football he opened a sporting goods company and established Bob Windsor's Football Camps throughout Maryland. Bob and his wife, Betty, live in Ellicott City, Maryland.

ACKNOWLEDGMENTS

When I first saw the pictures Rich Clarkson took of the 1966 NCAA Championship game, I knew they were essential illustrations of the story I was writing. How he came to take one photo in particular is a story in itself. Rich prepared for the Kentucky–Texas Western game the way he'd been preparing for NCAA Championship games since he covered his first one back in 1952. He did his homework. What he "knew," what virtually everybody "knew," was that the mighty Kentucky Wildcats would beat the lightly regarded Texas Western College Miners. "That's what we all thought was going to happen," said Clarkson, who would go on to cover a total of sixty NCAA Championship games and score thirty-five *Sports Illustrated* covers in his storied career. "Basically, I decided I wanted to sit on the end not for the game itself, but for the Kentucky bench." That would put him in the perfect position to photograph the celebration as Adolph Rupp's team won a fifth NCAA Championship for their legendary coach. The Kentucky championship didn't happen, but Clarkson's decision put him in just the right place to capture the game's most iconic moment, when Texas Western's Bobby Joe Hill snatched the ball away from Kentucky's Louie Dampier. It was the little guard's second steal in ten seconds, and it proved to be the turning point in the history-bending game. As Rich Clarkson would say five decades later, "We attend events on TV. We remember events with classic still photographs." My thanks to Rich Clarkson for his excellent pictures.

There are many other people to thank for helping me with this book, and chief among them are Steve Tredennick and Mike Harreld. Mike was student manager under Adolph Rupp for four years, including the Rupp's Runts season. A friend for more than thirty years, Mike shared with me his near-encyclopedic memory of that season. He also introduced me to some of the people who lived the extraordinary experience with him. Steve played a similar role in helping me capture the Texas Western side of the story. Although his playing career as a Miner ended with graduation the year before the championship season, Steve has a wealth of Haskins stories and a continuing relationship with the players and the Haskins family. He was also instrumental in helping the 1966 Miners become the first college team ever inducted into the Naismith Memorial Basketball Hall of Fame. My debt to Steve is beyond measure.

Both Steve and Mike have been readers of their respective sides of the story. Others who have read the manuscript at various stages along the way include Lawrence Bicy, Harry Flournoy, Joe B. Hall, Yvonne Harreld, Val and Jim Hill, Thad Jaracz, and Pat Riley as well as my son Christopher and brother, Dan, who provided valuable and detailed critique. Thanks to each of them and to my wife, Mary Lou, who has listened with a discerning ear, making thoughtful suggestions as I read each chapter (in its various iterations) aloud. Her love enriches my life, and her support has sustained me through the ups and downs of the process. I am also grateful for the continuing love and support of our sons and daughters-in-law—Erik and Austin, Christopher and Wendy—and our six amazing grandchildren.

Much of my narrative of the season came from interviews with players, coaches, and supporters of both teams. My thanks to Cliff Berger, Brad Bounds, Steve Clevenger, Larry Conley, Gary Gamble, Joe B. Hall, Thad Jaracz, Dianne Kron, Jim LeMaster, Larry Lentz, Terry Mobley, Tom Porter, Herky Rupp, Bob Tallent, and Bob Windsor of Kentucky. Texas Western Miners who have shared their stories include Jerry Armstrong, Louis Baudoin, Willie Cager, Harry Flournoy, Moe Iba, David Lattin, Eddie Mullens, Dick Myers, Togo Railey, Nolan Richardson, Fred Schwake, Nevil Shed, and Willie Worsley.

I also want to thank Cazzie Russell, who gave me his perspective on the two Michigan games that figure into the story, and former Duke player Mike Lewis, who told me his end of the Rupp recruitment story. I am grateful to Ron Sherman for being an excellent friend and for invaluable support with computer and photographic issues. I also want to thank

Robbin McGrath and Jessica Paletsky for their legal advice. Others who have helped along the way include Margie Anctil, Jeff Darby, Tim Donovan, Peter Dreier, Ron Garrison, Mimi Gladstein, Holly Henson, Bill Knight, Parker McCauley, Tanya Milton, Mike Myers, Bob Pezzano, Willie Quin, Ron Salley, Brain Sereno, Steve Yellen, and Clive Pyne, who provided the index for the book.

A special thanks to Mary Haskins, the coach's college sweetheart and wife of forty-eight years, who invited me into her home. Thanks, too, to her sons, Steve and Brent, who joined their mother for a trip down memory lane. Thanks to Dorothy and John Reiser and Linda and Lanny Golucke for their hospitality during my trips to Texas and to Joe Gomez, the Miners' biggest fan and supporter, for bringing to my attention important articles I might otherwise have overlooked.

Finally, I want to thank Rus Bradburd, a former Haskins assistant coach and author of the excellent Nolan Richardson biography *Forty Minutes of Hell*. Rus offered encouragement and advice at important junctures in the gestation of this book and made the suggestion that led me to the University of Nebraska Press and sports editor Rob Taylor. Rob and Courtney Ochsner provided thoughtful guidance that smoothed the road and helped bring *The Baron and the Bear* to publication.

APPENDIX

1965–66 Team Rosters and Season Results

KENTUCKY WILDCATS TEAM ROSTER

Cliff Berger*	6-8	C	So.	Centralia IL
Brad Bounds	6-5	F	Jr.	Bluffton IN
Steve Clevenger	6-0	G	So.	Anderson IN
Larry Conley*	6-3	F	Sr.	Ashland KY
Louie Dampier*	6-0	G	Jr.	Indianapolis IN
Gary Gamble*	6-4	F	So.	Earlington KY
Thad Jaracz*	6-5	C	So.	Lexington KY
Tom Kron*	6-5	G	Sr.	Tell City IN
Jim LeMaster*	6-2	G	So.	Paris KY
Larry Lentz	6-8	C	Sr.	Lakeview OH
Tom Porter*	6-3	F	So.	Gracey KY
Pat Riley*	6-3	F	Jr.	Schenectady NY
Bob Tallent*	6-1	G	So.	Maytown KY
Bob Windsor	6-4	F	Jr.	Ellicott City MD

* Played in championship game.

TEXAS WESTERN MINERS TEAM ROSTER

Jerry Armstrong	6-4	F	Sr.	Eagleville MO
Orsten Artis*	6-1	G	Sr.	Gary IN
Louis Baudoin	6-7	F	Jr.	Albuquerque NM
Willie Cager*	6-5	F	So.	New York NY
Harry Flournoy*	6-6	F	Sr.	Gary IN
Bobby Joe Hill*	5-10	G	Jr.	Highland Park MI
David Lattin*	6-6	C	So.	Houston TX
Dick Myers	6-4	F	Jr.	Peabody KS
David Palacio	6-2	G	So.	El Paso TX
Togo Railey	6-2	G	So.	El Paso TX
Nevil Shed*	6-8	F	Jr.	Bronx NY
Willie Worsley*	5-6	G	So.	New York NY

* Played in championship game.

TEXAS WESTERN COLLEGE SEASON RESULTS

12/4	East New Mexico State	H	W	89–38
12/9	East Texas State	H	W	73–51
12/11	Texas–Pan American	H	W	67–47
12/14	Weber State	H	W	74–63
12/17	Fresno State	H	W	75–73
12/18	Fresno State	H	W	83–65
12/21	South Dakota State	A	W	88–42
12/22	Nevada	A	W	86–49
12/29	Loyola (NO)	H	W	93–56
12/30	Iowa	H	W	86–68
1/3	Tulsa	H	W	63–54
1/6	Seattle	H	W	76–64
1/27	Arizona State	A	W	84–67
1/29	West Texas State	H	W	69–50
2/1	New Mexico State	H	W	104–78
2/4	Colorado State	A	W	68–66
2/10	Arizona	A	W	81–72
2/12	New Mexico	A	W	69–64 OT
2/14	Arizona State	H	W	69–67
2/19	Texas Pan American	A	W	65–61
2/24	West Texas State	A	W	78–64
2/26	Colorado State	H	W	72–55
3/2	New Mexico State	A	W	73–56
3/5	Seattle	A	L	72–74
3/6	Oklahoma City	NCAA Play-In Game	W	89–74
3/11	Cincinnati	Midwest Regional	W	78–76 OT
3/12	Kansas	Midwest Regional	W	81–80 2-OT
3/18	Utah	NCAA Semifinal	W	85–78
3/19	Kentucky	NCAA Final	W	72–65

UNIVERSITY OF KENTUCKY SEASON RESULTS

12/1	Hardin-Simmons	H	W	83–55
12/4	Virginia	A	W	99–73
12/8	Illinois	A	W	86–68
12/11	Northwestern	H	W	86–75
12/17	Air Force	H	W	78–58
12/18	Indiana	H	W	91–56
12/22	Texas Tech	A	W	89–73
12/29	Notre Dame	N	W	103–69
1/3	St. Louis	H	W	80–70
1/8	Florida	A	W	78–64
1/10	Georgia	A	W	69–65 2-OT
1/15	Vanderbilt	H	W	96–83
1/24	Louisiana State	H	W	111–85
1/29	Auburn	H	W	115–78
1/31	Alabama	H	W	82–62
2/2	Vanderbilt	A	W	105–90
2/5	Georgia	H	W	74–50
2/7	Florida	H	W	85–75
2/12	Auburn	A	W	77–64
2/14	Alabama	A	W	90–67
2/19	Mississippi State	A	W	73–69
2/21	Mississippi	A	W	108–65
2/26	Tennessee	H	W	76–64
3/5	Tennessee	A	L	62–69
3/7	Tulane	H	W	103–74
3/11	Dayton	Mideast Regional	W	86–79
3/12	Michigan	Mideast Regional	W	84–77
3/18	Duke	NCAA Semi-Final	W	83–79
3/19	Texas Western	NCAA Final	L	65–72

INDEX

Abdul-Jabbar, Kareem, 163
Abilene TX, 88
Adams, John, 17, 41, 68, 87, 132, 140
Adolph Rupp as I Knew Him
  (Lancaster), 15, 53, 245
African American(s): barriers against,
  2–3, 4, 235, 237; on Boston Celtics,
  237; in championship games,
  34, 61, 98; coaches in college
  basketball, xii; epithets against,
  124; injustices against, 2; as
  ministers and community leaders,
  ix; players in NBA since 1950, 237;
  and segregated schools, 237; in
  Texas Western's lineup, ix, 1, 3,
  61, 114, 235, 249; treatment of, by
  University of Mississippi, 239; at
  University of Alabama, 239. *See
  also* blacks
Air Force Academy, 35, 94–95
Alabama-Auburn Vet School, 141–42
Alcindor, Lew. *See* Abdul-Jabbar,
  Kareem
Allen, Forrest Clare "Phog," 103
Alonzo, 69–70
Alpha Delta Pi, 68
And the Walls Came Tumbling Down
  (Fitzpatrick), 246
Ann Arbor MI, 167, 235

Armstrong, Jerry: black teammates
  of, 61; and Bobby Joe Hill, 154, 157;
  and championship game, 80, 190–
  91; and David Lattin, 123; game
  performance of, 190; height of,
  49, 65; high school senior year of,
  49; and Jerry Chambers, 189–90,
  192; and Nevil Shed, 175, 179, 189;
  and Orsten Artis, 190; and Rich
  Tate, 189; shots of, 99; at team
  reunion, 190
Artis, Orsten: and Albert T. Railey,
  61; as cocaptain, 202; curfew
  violation of, 158; and Don Haskins,
  177, 217; and free throws, 217; at
  Froebel High School, 46; game
  performance of, 190, 216, 217; and
  Harry Flournoy, 202; height of, 46,
  209; and Jerry Armstrong, 190;
  shooting stroke of, 46; and Steve
  Tredennick, 35
Ashland High School, 51
Ashland KY, 227
Atlanta Constitution, 233
Atlanta Hawks, 246
Atlanta Journal-Constitution, 247
Atlantic Coast Conference, 72, 194
Auburn AL, 53, 141–42, 246
Auburn Shuffle, 141

Balanchine, George, 10

Baltimore Sun, 201–2, 214

Barnes, Jim "Bad News," 46–47, 173

the "Baron." *See* Rupp, Adolph "the
Baron"

Baron of the Bluegrass. *See* Rupp,
Adolph "the Baron"

Basketball Hall of Fame. *See* Naismith
Memorial Basketball Hall of Fame

Basketball Writers Association, 160

Baton Rouge LA, 240

Baudoin, Lou "Flip": at the Academy
in Albuquerque, 253; and Don
Haskins, 50, 82, 98, 123; and free
throws, 82; height of, 12, 99, 123;
and Jerry Armstrong, 61; and Nevil
Shed, 123; nickname of, 99–101;
on shooting properly, 123; on time-
outs, 98

Baylor, Elgin, 26

Bayne, Howard, 152

Beard, Ralph "Butch," 14, 244–45

Beck, Ed, 117–18

Benjamin TX, 84–85, 222

Berger, Cliff: and Adolph Rupp, 209;
and Blue-White scrimmages,
41, 93; and Claude Sullivan, 218;
dental career of, 255; as designated
screener, 139; and Double Five
drill, 119; free-throw percentage
of, 128; and Harry Lancaster, 218;
height of, 40, 87; and Larry Lentz,
40, 105; and Marsha Jackson, 255;
and Thad Jaracz, 40, 89, 93

Berger, Dianne. *See* Kron, Dianne

Big Blue Nation. *See* Kentucky Wildcats

Big Eight, 150, 176

Big Ten, 92–95, 114, 167, 169–70

Bing, Dave, 172

Bird, Darrell, 27

blacks: and all-white schools, 62;
barring of, from hotels and
restaurants, 242; on Boston Celtics,
237; and Don Haskins, 34, 98, 124,
190; and gentleman's agreement,
2, 237, 242–43; and Major League
Baseball, 3, 164; in Mississippi
State athletics, 239; recruitment
of, 242; in University of Alabama
athletics, 239. *See also* African
American(s)

Blue Grass Field, 68, 172, 183, 226

Bluffton IN, 40, 146

Boeck, Larry, 26

Boeheim, Jim, 172

Boston Celtics, 237

Bounds, Brad, 40, 146, 147, 151, 255

Bowden, Jimbo, 248

Bowie High School, 28, 36, 130

Bradshaw, Charlie, 205

Breathitt, Edward "Ned," Jr., 3, 133, 145

Bronx NY, 11, 46, 154, 224, 226

Brooklyn Dodgers, 3, 243

Brown, Irv, 86

Brown vs. Board of Education, 235, 238

Bryant, Bear, 52

Bubas, Vic, 180, 195

Burgess Hall, 63

Burlington Junior College, 48, 135

Butts, Leon, 237, 249

Cager, Willie: and Bobby Joe Hill,
154; and David Lattin, 123, 219; and
Don Haskins, 11, 20, 82, 177, 207,
226; and free throws, 82, 218; game
performance of, 217; and Harry
Flournoy, 213, 248; height of, 11,
207, 219; and Jo Jo White, 175, 177;
and Nevil Shed, 11, 154, 213, 224,
248; and Willie Worsley, 11, 224;
with Ysleta Independent School
District Basketball Program, 253

Cameron Junior College, 45

Carrico, John, 140

Carver High School, 167, 173

Centenary Tournament, 137

Centralia IL, 87

Chamberlain, Wilt, 48, 176

Chambers, Jerome Purcell "Jerry," 189–90, 192

Chapman, Wayne, 164–66

Charlottesville Daily Progress, 91

Chicago Bulls, 152, 173

Christopher, Jay, 62

Chuck Taylor Converse All-Stars Low-Cuts, 83

Cincinnati Royals, 173

Civil Rights Act (1964), 2–3, 235, 238, 242

civil rights bill, 133

Clarkson, Rich, 259

Clawson, John, 167, 170

Clay, Cassius, 173, 176

Clevenger, Steve, 138, 147, 205, 255, 260

Cole Field House, 2, 49, 171–72, 183, 184, 193, 205–6

College Park MD, 149, 179, 183, 184

Collins, Ben, 84

Colorado State, 134–35, 145

Combes, Harry, 92–93

Conley, George, 60, 88, 186

Conley, Larry: and Adolph Rupp, 15, 38–39, 58, 60, 95, 108, 198, 230, 240, 245; at Ashland High School, 51; and Billy Reed, 227; and Bobby Tallent, 105; career of, as color commentator, 256; and Cotton Nash, 231; and Curry Kirkpatrick, 240; and Don Donoher, 162; as facilitator, 92; and fast-break basketball, 41; with flu bug, 181, 194–95, 197–98, 242; and Frank Deford, 148, 242; game performance of, 216; and Harry Lancaster, 42–43, 195; as heart of Kentucky's defense, 204; height of, 7, 169, 207; with Kentucky Colonels, 256; and Louie Dampier, 14; and Mike Harreld, 125, 203; passing wizardry of, 120; and Pat Riley, 40, 92, 95, 111–13, 120, 126, 147, 149, 169; point-forward role of, 207; and practice sessions, 39, 55, 108; as senior cocaptain, 220, 227; as senior forward, 140–41; senior leadership of, 16–17; and team meeting, 15; and Thad Jaracz, 93, 120, 215; and Tommy Kron, 15–17, 56, 87, 92, 95, 111, 113, 125, 139, 147, 151, 169, 203–4, 220; and Willie Worsley, 215

Conner, Bull, 238

Cousy, Bob, 163

Cox, Johnny, 36

Crispus Attucks High School, 173

Cunningham, Steve, 164

Dallas TX, 36, 64, 82

Dampier, Louie: and Adolph Rupp, 75, 108, 142, 147, 150; as All-American, 212; and Bobby Tallent, 88, 104, 106, 163, 228; and Bob Verga, 196; and Claude Sullivan, 220; defense of, 96; on discipline, 150; on dissention, 38; and Don Haskins, 208; game performance of, 211; and Harry Flournoy Jr., 57; height of, 7; as Indiana all-stater, 51–52; with Kentucky Colonels, 256; knee injury of, 104; and Larry Conley, 14, 16–17; in Naismith Memorial Basketball Hall of Fame, 256; and Pat Riley, 16, 36, 67, 88–89, 92–93, 111, 113, 125–26, 132, 141, 147, 165, 195–96, 211, 215; and practice,

Dampier, Louie (*continued*)
112–13; as pure shooter, 180, 182; Rupp's Runts season of, 67–68; with San Antonio Spurs, 256; shooting percentage of, 88; and Thanksgiving weekend scrimmage, 16; and Tommy Kron, 110–11
Daniels, Mel, 48, 135–36
Darden, Oliver, 167, 169–71
Davis, Harold "Happy," 29–31
Davis, Miles, 66
Dayton, 103, 161–64, 169, 215
Dee, Johnny, 118, 120
Deford, Frank, 148, 188, 204–5, 210, 214, 216, 235; *Over Time*, 246
DeFore, Lee, 141–42
Detroit MI, 37, 135, 224
DeWitt Clinton High School, 47
Dibler, Bobby, 35, 78–79
Dickey, Bill, 114
Dickey, Frank, 242–43, 245
Dill, Craig, 167
Doby, Larry, 237
Don Haskins Special Events Center, 251
Donoher, Don, 162
Duke University, 105, 137, 172, 180–89, 193–201, 204–6
Dumas TX, 222

Eagleville MO, 49
Eastern New Mexico, 97
East Regional, 72
Egan, John, 98
Elliot, Carlton B. "Stretch," 124
El Paso Herald-Post, 217
El Paso Municipal Airport, 100, 179, 188
El Paso Technical High School, 46
El Paso Times, 225
El Paso Touchdown Club, 225
ESPN, 125, 240–41, 256

Fabulous Five, 14, 121
Fiddlin' Five, 25, 87, 121, 233
Finkel, Henry, 103, 161–63
Fisher, George, 187
Fitzpatrick, Frank, 214, 241; *And the Walls Came Tumbling Down*, 246
Florida Gymnasium, 126
Florida State, 67
Flournoy, Amy, 44–45, 63–64, 224
Flournoy, Harry, Jr.: academic deficiency of, 64; curfew violation of, 158; and Don Haskins, 20–21, 45, 63–65, 81, 98, 156, 202, 248; with El Paso School District, 253; game performance of, 100; height of, 18, 44, 209; on master and slave mentality, 98; and Nevil Shed, 156–57, 220; and Orsten Artis, 144, 202; and parental control, 63; and practice, 82; pregame routine of, 154–55; and racial taunts, 210–11; recruitment of, 44–45; and Willie Cager, 248; and Willie Worsley, 178, 207, 213
Fort Collins CO, 134–35
Fort Valley GA, 117
Freedom Hall, 25, 117, 119, 183
Freeman, Don, 94
Fresno State, 98–99
Friendship Field, 226
Froebel High School, 46

Gamble, Gary, 161, 256
Gardner, Jack, 187–88
Gary IN, 44, 46, 61
gentleman's agreement, 2, 237, 242–43
Georgia Tech, 72
Glory Road, x, 64, 202
Goodwin, Luster "Pony," 86
Green Bay Packers, 124, 152
Grunfeld, Ernie, 146

Hagan, Cliff, 25, 113

Hall, Joe B., 38, 53–56, 96, 132, 139–40

Hardinsburg KY, 244

Hardin-Simmons, 88–89, 199

Harreld, Mike "Slim," 24; as accounting student, 150; celebration of, 171; with Georgia Power Company, 256; and Harry Lancaster, 164–65, 171, 198–99; and Henry Finkel, 161–62; and Larry Conley, 125; and photographers, 91; as referee, 14, 16, 56–57, 108; and spying, 89; as student manager, 13, 27, 69, 72, 74, 77, 119, 126, 184, 203, 204, 240, 242; and Thad Jaracz, 151–52; and ticket selling, 70; at University of Missouri, 256

Harrodsburg KY, 181, 255

Haskins, Clem, 164, 167

Haskins, Don "the Bear": and African Americans, 3, 34, 61, 98, 124, 164, 202, 235; and black players, 34, 98, 124, 190; and Bobby Joe Hill, 12, 35–36, 48, 144, 177; and David Lattin, 9, 11, 47, 135–36, 144, 174, 203, 211, 214; drills of, 188; and Eddie Mullens, 197, 202; and Harry Flournoy Jr., 20–21, 45, 63–65, 81, 98, 156, 202, 248; and Henry Iba, 45, 48–49, 79, 214; and Jim Barnes, 45–46; and Lou Baudoin, 50, 82, 98, 123; and Louie Dampier, 208; and Moe Iba, 49, 79, 143, 157–58, 174; and Nevil Shed, 11, 19, 81–84, 99, 115, 123, 136, 157, 175–76; and Orsten Artis, 177; and Steve Tredennick, 10, 35, 78, 97, 248; and Thanksgiving practice, 9, 220, 248; and Willie Cager, 11, 20, 82, 177, 207, 226; and Willie Worsley, 19, 21, 83. *See also* Texas Western College Miners

Haskins, Mary, 79, 222, 261

Haskins, Steve, 225

Hatton, Vern, 26, 233

Hayes, Curley, 85

Hedley TX, 222

Heifetz, Jascha, 16

Hibner, Marty, 68

Highland Park High School, 12

Hill, Bobby Joe: and Abe Lemon, 223; and academics, 65; at Burlington Junior College, 48; competitive drive of, 20–21; curfew violation of, 158; and David Lattin, 66, 211; and Don Haskins, 12, 35–36, 48, 144; with El Paso Natural Gas Company, 254; and Frank Deford, 242; height of, 12, 209; injury of, 98, 100; and Jerry Armstrong, 154, 157; and Lou Baudoin, 12; photographic memory of, 65; and practice, 122, 144, 158; quickness of, 20, 36, 48, 200, 223; shooting streak of, 217; style of play of, 12; and Willie Cager, 154; at Worthing High School, 174

Hines, Paul, 32

Hobbs NM, 35–36

Hukel, George, 229

Hundley, "Hot Rod," 202

Hutchinson Junior College, 81

Hyder, Whack, 72

Iba, Henry "Hank": and Adolph Rupp, 233–34; and Bobby Joe Hill, 48–49; and Don Haskins, 45, 48–49, 79, 214; and Don Rolfes, 58; and Eddie Mullens, 197, 202; and Jerry Armstrong, 191

Iba, Moe: and Bobby Joe Hill, 157–58;

Iba, Moe (*continued*)
   and Don Haskins, 49, 79–80, 143, 157–58, 174; and Eddie Mullens, 157; at Memphis State, 254; as NBA scout, 254; at Texas Christian University, 254; as Texas Western assistant coach, 254; at University of Nebraska, 254; and white referees, 217
Ingram, Bob, 217
Iowa Field House, 161, 164–65, 171
Irvin, Monte, 237

Jackson, Doc, 119, 181, 184
Jaracz, Thad: and Adolph Rupp, 7–8, 14, 40–41, 142, 231, 245; as center, 87, 210; and Cliff Berger, 40, 53, 89, 93; game performance of, 94, 127, 128, 132, 163, 196, 181, 213, and Harry Lancaster, 52; height of, 7, 16–17, 132, 245; as high school senior, 125; and Joe B. Hall, 54; and Larry Conley, 93, 120, 215; and Larry Lentz, 40; and Lee DeFore, 141; as lieutenant colonel, 256; and Mike Harreld, 151–52; recruitment of, 41; and Tommy Kron, 130
John Paul Jones Arena, 90
Johnson, "Stand Tall for Paul," 3
Jordan, Michael, 20–21, 75

Kansas State, 24, 103
Katzenjammer Kids, 127
Kennedy, John F., 36
Kentuckian, 147
Kentucky Kernel, 229–30
Kentucky Wildcats, 17, 23, 24, 88, 259. *See also* University of Kentucky; *and specific players*
Kindred, Dave, 241, 247
King, Bernard, 146

King, Martin Luther, Jr., 2, 250
Kirkpatrick, Curry, 240
Knight, Bill, 262
Knight, Bobby, 232
Knodel, Don, 140
Knoxville Banner, 151, 152
Knoxville TN, 146, 151, 155
Krick, Ron, 174
Kron, Dianne, 67, 68, 109, 256, 260
Kron, Tommy "Wagon": and Adolph Rupp, 14, 147–48, 168, 196, 209; career of, in wealth management, 256–57; and Cazzie Russell, 169–70; game performance of, 128, 196, 212, 215; as guard, 40, 141, 182, 195; and Harry Lancaster, 57; height of, 7; and Jack Marin, 195; and Larry Conley, 15–17, 56, 87, 92, 95, 111, 113, 125, 139, 147, 151, 169, 203–4, 220; and Louie Dampier, 110–11, 215; and Mike Harreld, 203; nickname of, 14; and Pat Riley, 110, 149; and Ron Widby, 152; with Seattle Supersonics, 256; as senior cocaptain, 128, 220; with St. Louis Hawks, 256; and Thad Jaracz, 93, 119, 132; wingspan of, 58
Krzyzewski, Mike, 232
Ku Klux Klan (KKK), 3, 238

Lafayette High School, 52, 87–88
Lancaster, Harry: and Adolph Rupp, 14, 42, 51, 52–53, 57, 59, 68–69, 71–72, 91, 105, 151, 162, 167, 218, 257; *Adolph Rupp as I Knew Him*, 15, 53, 245; as assistant coach, 39, 218; and Billy Thompson, 102; and Bobby Tallent, 104–5, 152, 195, 218, 228; and Cazzie Russell, 167; and Cliff Berger, 218; focus of, 43; as head baseball coach, 257; and Jim

LeMaster, 104–5; and Joe B. Hall, 139, 238; and Katzenjammer Kids, 127; and Larry Conley, 42–43, 51–52, 106, 195; and Louie Dampier, 58; and Mike Harreld, 164–65, 171, 198–99; as offensive coach, 55; and preseason interactions, 53; and Thad Jaracz, 52, 108, 162; and Tommy Kron, 57, 126; as University of Kentucky athletic director, 257; and Wayne Chapman, 164–65

Las Cruces High School, 78

Lattin, David "Big Daddy": and Bill Russell, 48; and Bobby Joe Hill, 66, 83, 134, 144, 154, 211; and Dick Myers, 81, 101; and Don Haskins, 9, 11, 47, 82, 135–36, 144, 174, 211, 214; game performance of, 100, 213, 217, 218–19; with Globetrotters, 254; and Harry Flournoy Jr., 155, 207; height of, 9, 47, 66, 200, 209, 217; and Jerry Armstrong, 65, 123; and Jerry Chambers, 189; and Martin Luther King Jr., 250; and Mel Daniels, 135–36; with Memphis Tams, 254; motivation issue of, 144–45; and Nevil Shed, 66, 136; and Otto Moore, 145; as *Parade* High School All-American, 47, 211; and Pat Riley, 211; and Perry Wallace, 47; with Phoenix Suns, 254; with Pittsburgh Condors, 254; and Ron Krick, 175; with San Francisco Warriors, 254; *Slam Dunk to Glory*, 217, 254; and Thad Jaracz, 213, 215–17; and Tom Workman, 155; and Walt Wesley, 176–77; and Willie Cager, 11, 123, 155, 219; and Willie Worsley, 154; and Wilt Chamberlain, 48; at Worthing High School, 47, 174

Lattin, Elsie, 101, 221, 254

Lawton OK, 45

Ledford, Cawood, 23, 68

Lee, Clyde, 132

LeMaster, Jim, 102, 104–5, 147, 161, 228, 257

Lemon, Abe, 223

Lentz, Larry, 40, 105, 257, 260

Lesley, Bobby, 32

Lessons from the Big Guys (Wireman), 26

Lewis, Helen, 194

Lewis, Mike, 180–81, 193–94, 196–97, 246, 260

Lexington Herald-Leader, 120, 227, 241

Linton High School, 47, 52

Litsch, Joseph, 234, 324

Little Sisters of the Poor, 71

Loretto Academy, 61–62

Louisville Courier-Journal, 26, 231

Louisville KY, 25, 27, 41, 119, 244, 256

Lovellette, Clyde, 176

Loyola Field House, 181

Loyola of New Orleans, 97

Loyola University of Chicago, 98

Lubbock TX, 35, 102, 105, 158, 173, 198, 205, 209

Maddox, Lester, 3

Madison Square Garden, 113, 226

Major League Baseball, 3, 164, 243

Malaise, Dub, 36

Man in the Brown Suit. *See* Rupp, Adolph "the Baron"

Maraniss, Andrew, 238

Marich, Ruddy, 178

Marin, Jack, 180–81, 193, 195–96

Marshall, Thurgood, 2

Mason-Dixon line, 210

Mays, Willie, 237

McCarthy, Babe, 58–59, 72, 74, 151

McCarty, George, 34

McCracken, Branch, 93, 95
McGuire, Al, 126–27, 134
McIntosh, Dick, 128
McNamara, Robert, 133
Mears, Ray, 146–48, 151–52
Memorial Coliseum, 6, 23, 53, 90, 193, 227
Memphis Tams, 254
Meyers, James, 169–70
Miami of Ohio, 25
Mideast Regional, 25, 161, 171
Midwest Regional, 158, 173, 198
Miners. *See* Texas Western College Miners
Miners' Hall, 28, 32, 63, 84
Mississippi State, 58–59, 72–73, 131, 151, 160, 237
Mobley, Terry, 181, 260
Moore, Otto, 145
Moore, Ross, 21, 82, 85, 100, 143, 158
Morris High School, 46
Mostel, Zero, 204
Mullens, Eddie, 46, 134, 157, 175, 197, 208, 254
Municipal Coliseum, 104–5, 173
Myers, Dick, 81, 101, 115, 178, 220, 254

Naismith, James, 6, 103
Naismith Memorial Basketball Hall of Fame: about, 224, 235–36; Adolph Rupp in, 4; Al McGuire in, 126, 134; Don Haskins in, 33, 254, 260; Hank Iba in, 49; Louie Dampier in, 256; Nolan Richardson in, 4, 33; Oscar Robertson in, 173; Pat Riley in, 257; Texas Western champions in, 250
Naponick, John, 90
Nash, Charles Francis "Cotton," 118, 181, 231
Nashville TN, 47–48

National Basketball Association (NBA). *See specific players and teams*
National Collegiate Athletic Association (NCAA): approved practices of, 18; championships of, ix, 1–2, 14, 24, 27, 98, 118, 145, 149, 150, 151, 161, 216, 232, 241, 249; "death penalty" ruling of, 25; rules of, regarding practice time, 11, 50, 53, 70
National Collegiate Basketball Hall of Fame, 254
New Mexico Military Institute, 62
New Mexico State, 78, 125, 130, 143, 145, 187
New Orleans LA, 76, 97, 181
New Orleans Times-Picayune, 181
New York NY, 37, 46–47, 113, 255
New York Times, 224
Northwestern University, 94
Notre Dame University, 25, 117–20, 125, 183

Obama, Barack, 250
Oklahoma A&M, 9, 21, 79, 144
Oklahoma City Chiefs, 158, 173, 179
Oklahoma City University, 134, 157, 223
Olsen, Jack, 247
Oswald, John, 184, 227, 245
Over Time (Deford), 246
Owens, Ted, 178
Owensboro High School, 16, 165
Owensboro KY, 13, 24, 27, 52, 113, 204, 218

Palacio, David, 22, 101, 254
Parade, 119
Parade High School All-Americans, 47, 104, 211
Payne, Tom, 246
Payne, Vern, 96

Pearl High School, 238
Pearson, Preston, 94
Peeples, George, 114–15
Phoenix Suns, 254
Pillsbury Doughboy. *See* Hill, Bobby Joe
Pittsburgh Condors, 254
Porter, Tom, 257, 260
Presley, J. Snow, 243
public schools, segregated, 238
Purdue Airlines, 102, 183
Purdue IN, 102

Quad City airport, 100

Railey, Togo, 61
Raleigh NC, 172
Ray, Joseph, 34
Reed, Billy, 227, 231
Reed, Neil, 243–44
Regis College, 55, 96
Rice, Grantland, 233
Rice, Russell, 51, 120, 242
Richardson, Nolan, 235, 237, 260–61
Rickey, Branch, 3, 243
Riedy, Bob, 182
Riley, Pat: and Adolph Rupp, 14, 16, 52, 54, 71, 88, 94–95, 140, 147, 230; as All-American, 52, 211; and Bobby Tallent, 39, 88, 163; and Brad Bounds, 40; and Cazzie Russell, 170; as color commentator, 257; contact lenses of, 148; and David Lattin, 211; game performance of, 106, 142, 169; and Harry Flournoy, 213; and Harry Lancaster, 59; as head coach, 257; height of, 7, 169; and Joe B. Hall, 54; and Larry Conley, 40, 92, 95, 111–13, 120, 126, 147, 149, 169; at Linton High School, 52; and Louie Dampier, 16, 36, 67, 88–89, 92–93, 111, 113, 125–26,

132, 141, 147, 165, 195–96, 211, 215; as Miami Heat president, 257; in Naismith Memorial Basketball Hall of Fame, 257; NBA career of, 257; and Preston Pearson, 95; and Ray Sanchez, 235; recruitment of, 47, 52; and Thad Jaracz, 14, 113, 163, 195; and Tommy Kron, 110–11, 149, 198
Robertson, Oscar, 167, 173–74, 243
Robinson, Jackie, xi, 3, 164, 237, 243–46, 249
Rock Island IL, 100
Rolfes, Don, 58, 174–75
Rosemond, Ken, 127
Rouse, Willie, 15
Rupp, Adolph "the Baron": and Bobby Tallent, 69, 105, 147, 161, 195, 209, 229–31; and Butch Beard, 244–45; and Cazzie Russell, 103, 167–68; and Cliff Berger, 209; game-time frenzy of, 151; and Harry Lancaster, 14, 42, 52–53, 57, 59, 68–69, 71–72, 91, 105, 151, 162, 167, 218, 257; and Henry Iba, 233–34; and Jim LeMaster, 105, 161, 257; and Katzenjammer Kids, 127; and Larry Conley, 15, 38–39, 58, 60, 95, 108, 195, 198, 230, 240, 245; and Larry Lentz, 40; last-minute instructions of, 120; and Louie Dampier, 67–68, 70–71, 75, 108, 142, 147, 150; in Naismith Memorial Basketball Hall of Fame, 4; "No Girlfriends" rule of, 68; and Pat Riley, 14, 16, 52, 54, 71, 88, 94–95, 140, 147, 230; and practices, 8, 13–17, 38, 87, 110, 111, 112; and recruiting, 51; and Steve Clevenger, 147; and Thad Jaracz, 7–8, 14, 40–41, 142, 162, 231, 245; and Tommy Kron, 14, 147–48, 168, 196, 209. *See also* Kentucky Wildcats

Rupp, Herky, 15, 260

Rupp Arena, 251

Rupp's Runts, 3, 5, 17, 27, 61, 68, 73, 75, 90, 103, 109, 111. *See also* Kentucky Wildcats

Rusk, Dean, 133

Russell, Bill, 48, 237

Russell, Cazzie: and Adolph Rupp, 103, 167–68; at Carver High School, 167; and Greg Smith, 165; and Harry Lancaster, 167; height of, 164; and Jack Marin, 180; and Mike Lewis, 260; and Oliver Darden, 169; and Oscar Robertson, 173; and Pat Riley, 170; and Steve Cunningham, 164; and Tommy Kron, 168, 170; and Wayne Chapman, 164

Sanchez, Ray, 235

San Francisco Warriors, 254, 258

Sargeant, Phil, 32

Schenectady NY, 16, 47, 52, 70

Schwake, Fred, 10, 36, 260

Seattle University, 145

Seneca High School, 243, 245

Shadow. *See* Shed, Nevil

Shawnee High School, 246

Shed, Nevil: and Bobby Joe Hill, 65; and David Lattin, 66, 136, 177; and Don Haskins, 11, 19, 83–84, 99, 115, 123, 136, 157, 175–76; game performance of, 217; and George Peeples, 114–15; and Harry Flournoy Jr., 100, 156–57, 190, 220; height of, 123, 156; and Jerry Armstrong, 175, 179, 189–90; and Jerry Chambers, 189–90; and Jo Jo White, 178; and Lou Baudoin, 123; and Moe Iba, 11; at Morris High School, 46; parents of, 176, 221; and

Ross Moore, 82; scholarship of, 175; as the Shadow, 115, 175, 177, 189, 207, 224; at University of Texas at San Antonio, 255; and Willie Cager, 11, 154, 213, 224, 248; and Willie Worsley, 83, 188, 220

Shively, Bernie, 182–84, 230

Shockley, Ron, 84

Shreveport LA, 237

Silver Spring MD, 5, 183, 184, 205, 224

Skinner, Roy, 139, 142, 239

Slam Dunk to Glory (Lattin), 217, 254

Slim. *See* Harreld, Mike "Slim"

Smith, Dean, 232

Smith, Dwight, 164

Smith, Greg, 164–66

Smith, Pam, 67

Snow, Presley J., 243

South Dakota State, 97, 101

Southeastern Conference, xi, 3, 47, 58, 238, 242–43

Spivey, Bill, 25

The Sporting News, 56, 140

Sports Illustrated, ix, 114, 142, 147–48, 153, 154, 188, 191, 205, 210, 239, 241, 242, 247

Standiford Field, 102

Stegeman Coliseum, 127

Sterrett, Ted, 80–81

St. Louis Hawks, 256

Strack, Dave, 169–70, 238

Sullivan, Claude, 23, 218, 220

Syracuse University, 172, 180, 196

Tallent, Bobby: and Adolph Rupp, 69, 105, 147, 161, 195, 209, 229–31; and Blue-White scrimmages, 104; career of, in health care industry, 258; and Cliff Berger, 41; game performance of, 105, 106, 258; and George Hukel, 229; at George

Washington University, 257; and Harry Lancaster, 104–5, 152, 195, 218, 228; height of, 104; and Jim LeMaster, 105, 147, 228; and Joe B. Hall, 230; and Larry Conley, 105, 163; and Louie Dampier, 88, 104, 106, 139, 163, 228; and midseason dispute, 257; as *Parade* High School All-American, 104; and Pat Riley, 39, 88, 163; and Preston Pearson, 94; and scalpers, 70; and Steve Clevenger, 147; and Thad Jaracz, 106, 149; and Tommy Kron, 196

Tate, Rich, 189

Temple University, 25

Tennessee A&I, 47

Tennessee University, 146–53, 159, 205, 214

Texas–Pan American, 144–45

Texas Tech Red Raiders, 35–36, 102, 105, 107, 111, 173

Texas Western College Miners, ix, 1, 3, 61, 114, 235, 249. *See also specific players*

Thanksgiving break, 6, 8, 9, 13–17, 38, 87, 112, 220, 248

Thompson, Billy, 102, 231

Thompson, Hank, 237

Thompson, John, xii

Time, 133

Tredennick, Steve: and Bobby Dibler, 78; and Don Haskins, 10, 20, 35, 78, 97, 248; and Dub Malaise, 36; and Mike Harreld, 259; and Ron Shockley, 84; and Thanksgiving practice, 248

Tulane University, 150, 159–60

UK Basketball Facts Book, 87

University of Alabama, 52, 118, 239

University of Arkansas, x, x–xi, 33, 76

University of Cincinnati, 158

University of Georgia, 7, 75, 127–28, 141, 197, 214

University of Illinois, 92–93, 151

University of Indiana, 46, 52, 94–96

University of Iowa, 114–16, 122

University of Kansas, 100–101, 103, 157, 175–76, 178, 187, 198, 200–201, 245

University of Kentucky: All-Americans of, 26; all-white team of, ix, 1, 3; alums of, 138, 141; conditioning program of, 55; fans of, 119, 125, 159; fight song of, 23; in preseason polls, 96; students of, 141. *See also* Kentucky Wildcats

University of Louisville, 119, 245

University of Maryland, 2, 49, 172, 183, 241

University of Michigan, 163, 167, 169–70, 180, 194, 235

University of New Mexico, 48, 85

University of North Carolina, 127

University of St. Louis, 125, 256

University of Utah, 187–88, 192, 198–99, 201, 203

University of Virginia, 89, 91, 111, 124

Unseld, Wes, 118–19, 143–45, 245

Vacendak, Steve, 182

Van Arsdale, Dick, 95

Van Arsdale, Tom, 95

Vanderbilt University, 7, 42–43, 56, 132, 137, 140, 235

Vaughn, Danny, 32

Verga, Bob, 180, 182, 196, 198

Voting Rights Act (1965), 2, 235, 238

Wake Forest, 182

Wallace, George, 3

Wallace, Perry, 47–48, 137, 235, 238–39, 244

Wall Street Journal, 133

Washington Daily News, 201

Washington Post, 198, 201

Watson, Bobby, 25–26

Watson, Lou, 95

Wesley, Walt, 176–78

West, Jerry, 243

Western Athletic Conference, 134, 187

Western Kentucky, 125, 161, 163–67, 239

White, Jo Jo, 175–78, 200

White Citizens' Councils, 3, 238

Widby, Ron, 152

Wildcats. *See* Kentucky Wildcats

Wilson, Meredith, 114

Windsor, Bob, 140, 222, 258, 260

Wireman, Billy: *Lessons from the Big Guys*, 26

Wooden, John, 174, 180, 234, 238

Workman, Tom, 155–56

Worsley, Willie: in American Basketball Association, 255; and Bobby Joe Hill, 21, 216; at DeWitt Clinton High School, 47; and Don Haskins, 19–21, 83; and Frank Fitzpatrick, 214; game performance of, 99, 213, 217, 218; at Harlem Boys Choir, 255; and Harry Flournoy, 178, 207, 213; height of, 11, 154, 207; and Nevil Shed, 83, 188; at Spring Valley High School, 255

Worthing High School, 47, 174

Wright, Lonnie, 124